REFLECTIONS OF A PASSERBY

Jesus, Jung, and the Power of Choice

Eleanor L. Norris PhD

CHIRON PUBLICATIONS • ASHEVILLE, NORTH CAROLINA

www.ChironPublications.com

Cover photo of entry gate to Four Springs Retreat Center, Middletown, California, by Margaret Burdge.
Interior and cover design by Danijela Mijailovic
Printed primarily in the United States of America.

ISBN 978-1-68503-001-8 paperback
ISBN 978-1-68503-002-5 hardcover
ISBN 978-1-68503-003-2 electronic
ISBN 978-1-68503-004-9 limited edition paperback

Library of Congress Cataloging-in-Publication Data Pending

Dedication

To the late John Petroni, Guild leader par excellence, therapist, mentor, and friend, sometimes trickster, always supporter, I express my great love and gratitude. You were my spiritual guide into the great depths of psyche—and out again. Rest in peace.

Reflections of a Passerby

In the Gospel of Thomas, Jesus says to his listeners, "Be ye passersby."[1] It speaks of being a part of this life we have been given, not standing back to observe it as we pass by—but to *live it out fully*, as does the Jesus we come to know in the Synoptic Gospels.

Jesus, Jung, and the Power of Choice

In *The Choicemaker*, Elizabeth Boyden Howes and Sheila Moon write, "Man was created for the sake of choice!"[2] The choice was to discern and do the will of God. It's a choice for consciousness, in which the ego-personality lives in service to the something greater that Howes variously called the self, God, Great Patterner, Mystery, the Cry. Her concern was for life as it is lived by the individual, and for the "ongoingness of the planet."[3]

Contents

Foreword

Eleanor Norris is a brave woman. She willingly entered a realm where the deep penetrating and provocative questions beckon one out over the abyss, with no safety net below. There one must grapple with the meaning of life, because one's life depends on it. The questions themselves are psychopomps, leading us into the world of soul, the wilderness where there are no roads or fences, abandoning us to ourselves, where, even in the midst of companions and guides, ultimately, we wrestle alone. This is her profound gift to us as readers, for with her direct and personal writing she shows us how it is done and invites us into our own grappling for the sake of life.

It is often thought the Jesus story is an answer to life's most important questions, but what happens when that story is no longer an answer, but itself becomes a question? For modern consciousness that is exactly what has happened, and the traditional version of the ancient story about Jesus has become meaningless and confounding for many. This is what makes Eleanor Norris brave, for while the Christian Jesus story had ceased to hold her, there was something about it that still called. She chose to enter the realm of questions without knowing ahead of time what would emerge. The place where those questions were asked was the Guild for Psychological Studies' seminar exploring the life and teachings of Jesus through a critical and imaginative immersion in biblical texts along with powerful soul-evoking techniques. For many decades, the Guild has facilitated seminars exploring the psychological meaning of biblical stories and other mythologies, seminars that engage the whole person in the complex weaving of thinking, feeling, and imagination, provoked by the ultimate questions: What is the meaning of my life? Why am I here? Who am I? What do I serve? What is truth? Is there a "God"? What was Jesus all about?

Eleanor's explication of the theoretical ground of the Guild's seminar is clear and direct, as she leads us to a new psychological vision of both the Christian story and the life and teachings of the man Jesus. We see how both Jung's understanding of the self at the heart of the individuation process and the quest for consciousness, along with Elizabeth Howes' conviction that a historical Jesus can be found in the Synoptic Gospels, opens a new, fresh, and vivifying encounter with ancient teachings that have become irrelevant and incomprehensible for many. But the living, beating heart of this book is her memoir, bringing together her experiences of the many seminars she has attended over more than thirty years. Her extensive personal reflections bring us as close to an actual seminar without being able to attend one.

Each day of the seminar unfolds through the questions brought to the biblical texts and lively group sharing. Eleanor bares her soul as she struggles with old assumptions fading away and new insights challenging her to a larger sense of herself. She courageously allows the creative depths of the unconscious to move her, through unexpected insights, expressive art work, spontaneous body movement, and the spacious silence within which the work takes place. Over more than four decades of my own work with the Guild, I have had the pleasure of knowing Eleanor over thirty of those years, attending Guild seminars with her. I can attest to the genuineness of her spiritual and psychological struggle, the integrity she brings to the work, the suffering she has embraced, and the spontaneous delight and joy erupting at discovery and new realizations.

If you are a seeker and a questioner, if you are hungry for a new way to approach the Gospels that does not take anything for granted, that does not dismiss them out of hand, nor accept them unthinkingly, then Eleanor's journey through the Synoptic Gospels and into her own depths, engaging the hard questions, will feed your soul.

Hal Childs PhD, MFT
Vallejo, California
August 2021

Dr. Childs is a seminar leader with the Guild for Psychological Studies and the author of *The Myth of the Historical Jesus and the Evolution of Consciousness* and *God's Autopsy and the Living Truth of Soul: A History of Western Consciousness.*

Introduction

Am I a Christian?

In religious matters it is a well-known fact that we cannot understand a thing until we have experienced it inwardly.[4] — C. G. Jung

I'm in a quandary. How can I call myself a Christian when the dogma and the creeds, even the magnificent rituals of the Catholic and Anglican high churches no longer open the doors to the mystery of creation for me; no longer spark the presence of the *numinous,* the divine in my soul; no longer, to be truthful, match the sense of the reality I've come to hold?

Then again, how can I not call myself a Christian when the mythic themes of birth, death, and rebirth as told through the life and teachings of Jesus play themselves out in inescapable patterns in my life? The themes of trial and sacrifice in the service of something greater than myself and whose deity, the one Jesus called "God, Father, *Abba,*" are deeply present in my own experience.

Do I not call myself American even though that name masks the diversity of this vast and complex nation? Do I become "not American" when I oppose the direction our leaders take? I *am* an American through and through, by birth and by having lived in this country all my life. In the same sense, I was born into Christianity in my family and the particular Christian culture in which I grew up. I was born into this story with its central character, Jesus, teaching me about mercy and justice, the narrow gate, and doing the will of God even when it demands "selling all." Most of all, I was born into this core belief of the "kingdom" that is *within me*, or as Luke tells it, "is in the midst of you."[5] Just because these messages have been reduced to creeds and dogma, must I say I am not a Christian when the man and his teachings are still vibrantly alive for me?

The Heroine's Journey

Themes of birth, death, and resurrection—the hero's, or heroine's, journey—predate Christianity by thousands of years. There's the Egyptian myth of the dying and rising god Osiris, the Sumerian goddess Inanna's descent into hell where she was sorely tried and then returned to the upper world, and the Greek goddess Persephone's story of descent into Hades and return for a part of each year. These and the heroic journey of Jesus himself enact recurring themes of *winter and spring, trials and tribulations, death and resurrection*, and they resonate deeply within me.

Do I need to call myself a Christian to acknowledge and be guided by them? Jesus himself was not a Christian. Although I'm not gripped by Christianity as interpreted by today's church, I am gripped by the archetypal patterns of life, death, and rebirth from which it comes. Of all the world's myths, the one that grabbed me young and has not let go is the one carried by the Christian church, although I understand it very differently today from what I was taught as a child.

I wrote this book to examine these beliefs and perspectives, and explore the "inward expressions" that have brought me to a renewed understanding of the Christian myth. I've sought answers from intellectual study, and doing that has brought information and insights. But it's at the times my whole being has been engaged with confusion, rage, joy, and despair that I've been able to reach a deeper understanding. I believe this is what Jung means in the epigraph above, "In religious matters it is a well-known fact that we cannot understand a thing until we have experienced it inwardly."[6] My search for myself and my identity has undoubtedly been a "religious matter."

Jung also wrote:
Religion, as the Latin word denotes, is a careful and
scrupulous observation of what Rudolph Otto aptly termed
the *numinosum*, that is, a dynamic agency or effect not caused
by an arbitrary act of will. On the contrary, it seizes and
controls the human subject, who is always rather its victim
than its creator. The *numinosum* whatever its cause may be
is an experience of the subject independent of his will.[7]

The journey I'm on requires scrupulous observation of the
numinosum, which is at the same time (1) greater than myself, (2) a
part of myself, and (3) something of which I am a part. I've been seized
by this mystery, and I cannot step off the path—a journey that has led
me from the vaguely defined Protestantism of my childhood to years
of agnosticism after the God I prayed to did not save my sister from
dying of cancer. It led me back to the beauty of mystical Roman
Catholicism, on to an Eastern guru, and back to the social activism of
United Methodism. But none of these stopping points offered answers
to the deeper questions I held, so I set out again, not away from Jesus
or his story, but to find a way to free the story from the creeds, rituals,
and dogma of formalized religion.

Joseph Campbell described myth as "the secret opening through
which the inexhaustible energies of the cosmos pour into human
cultural manifestation," adding, "Religions, philosophies, arts, the
social forms of primitive and historic man, prime discoveries in science
and technology, the very dreams that blister sleep, boil up from the
basic, magic ring of myth."[8] Jung spoke of symbolic messages that come
to us from the psyche, the collective unconscious, the realm of the
archetypal patterns through dreams, fairy tales, and myth. Aniela Jaffé,
Jung's colleague and coauthor of his autobiography, *Memories, Dreams,
Reflections*, used the generative phrase *myth of meaning*.[9] I use the term
myth in the way Sheila Moon, a cofounder of the Guild for
Psychological Studies, does: *"Myths are interpreters of the depths of the*

human, carriers of life values, dynamic movements from timelessness and spacelessness into human time and space."[10]

When understood this way, *the Bible itself is a myth*, a story that comes from the depths of psyche. Jung wrote, "We must read the Bible or we shall not understand psychology. Our psychology, whole lives, our language and imagery are built upon the Bible."[11] From this perspective, the Christian myth as told in the Synoptic Gospels of Matthew, Mark, and Luke is the story of our own journeys of awakening.

Carl Gustav Jung (1875-1961) and Elizabeth Boyden Howes (1907-2002) each had a unique understanding of Christianity. Jung, the founder of analytical psychology, regarded the Christ as one of the central *symbols* of the self in the Western psyche. Howes, a Jungian analyst who'd had the opportunity to discuss her work with Jung during a 1955 visit to Switzerland, agreed that Christ symbolizes the self, but she focused her life's work on discovering the historical Jesus, the *hero* of the Christian myth.

Jung hypothesized that the Christ of the Christian myth was a great, albeit one-sided symbol of the center of the psyche which he called the *self*. "I have chosen the term 'self,'" he wrote, "to designate the totality of man, the sum total of his conscious and unconscious contents," adding "an ineffable totality which can only be formulated symbolically."[12] Jung theorized the human journey as the search of each individual ego personality to know more of this self. In keeping with Jung's style in his *Collected Works*, I spell *self* with a small "s" except when I am quoting authors who capitalize it. What Jung calls the self, others have called *God*, the godhead, the divine.

Jung called this journey to reclaim our wholeness *individuation*: "Individuation means becoming an 'in-dividual,' and, insofar as 'individuality' embraces our innermost, last, and incomparable uniqueness, it also implies becoming one's own self. We could therefore translate individuation as 'coming to selfhood' or 'self-realization.'"[13] He considered individuation to be essential for the evolution of human consciousness toward the *self*, and he saw Jesus's life as a journey toward individuation.

This is not the way the Gospel writers, most Christians, or New Testament scholars understand the Christian story, and it was not the language Jesus used when he talked about his relationship with God. For us today, however, I believe the depth-psychology perspective offers us a new window into Jesus's life and teachings.

The Lost Treasure

Like Jung, Campbell, and Moon, by *myth* I mean the stories that emerge from the *collective unconscious* into human consciousness and appear to us in symbolic images through dreams and imagination. From the beginning of time, humans have woven stories out of archetypal images and continue to do so in novels, films, TV, art, and creative works of all kinds. This perspective sees myths, dreams, and all artistic creations as expressions of the collective unconscious and, I daresay, messages from the divine as they are lived out in human form. Mythic stories include the hero's journey, the dying and rising god, the virgin birth, the father, the mother, and a multitude of other larger-than-life patterns. Studying the Christian story as myth allows us to do what archetypal psychologist James Hillman calls *seeing through* the surface of a narrative to the depths that gave rise to it— and want to be known through it.

In *Re-Visioning Psychology*, Hillman describes this as a process of critical thinking and intuition that can help us *see through* myth, art, film, dreams, or a client's representation of reality to the archetypal patterns hidden yet revealed within the symbolic language. "The psyche ... loves to be enlightened by *seeing through itself*."[14]

In 1984, I attended my first of a series of seminars on the Christian myth informed by Jung's depth psychological understanding, conducted by the Guild for Psychological Studies, and continued attending these gatherings over the next twenty-five years. The Guild method provided tools and processes to help me *see through* the

Christian story to the archetypal depths from which it emerged. Like Jung, I believe that when we see through the Christian myth, we find a human living out the journey of individuation, which, I believe, is the myth of meaning described by Jaffé. A psychological understanding of the life and teachings of Jesus leads to a man living out just such a meaningful life. My process was reflected well in Sheila Moon's description of her own:

> I am far more than my consciousness. I am my darkness, also. I am a being with a magnitude of unconscious dimensions and levels forever at work in me. Where I build masks and walls to conceal myself from myself, just there is the pain of the pressures of unfulfillment. Where I try bravely and poignantly to be what I am not, to disregard my deepest desires, just there is neurosis and emptiness. What I most need are the unconscious "others" in myself. What I *do* is to dismiss them as nonsense, or at best to spend guilty moments with them moments snatched from the much more important business of getting ahead.
>
> Psychological or religious redemption is the act of recovering for myself out of the small dark beginnings an essential value or values which I know to be my own and also recognize as having been lost. A genuine longing for this lost treasure is in no sense "escapism."[15]

Through the anguishing and arduous confrontations life presented me, then holding my images of Jesus and God and my images of myself in the sealed container of Guild seminars, I began to glimpse the *lost treasure* that has animated my life's journey, and I've come to a vision far greater than I could have imagined. In Jung's words, each of us *is* that "individual human being that infinitesimal unit on whom the fate of the world depends."[16] And we each have the choices and the responsibilities that come with it.

Note to the Reader

This book was recast from my PhD dissertation in mythological studies at Pacifica Graduate Institute. The book is divided into two parts, interweaving a theoretical overview of the subject with my personal journey grappling with it all. In Part One, I explain Jung's psychology, in particular the concepts of *psyche, self, archetypes of the collective unconscious,* and *individuation,* and Elizabeth Boyden Howes's focus on both the historical Jesus and her contention that the Christian story, when Christ is understood as a symbol of the self, can be a guide for each of our journeys of individuation.

In Part Two, I present the Guild for Psychological Studies' signature program: an annual sixteen-day seminar in nearly cloistered surroundings during which participants studied the Synoptic Gospels and searched for their own understanding of Jesus and his teachings. The text we used was *Records of the Life of Jesus,*[17] which presents in parallel form Jesus's story as told by Matthew, Mark, and Luke. During the seminar we compared and contrasted these three versions of the Jesus story. Some stories of the life of Jesus appear in one or two but not all three of these Gospels, and the same stories are sometimes told in different ways or in a different sequence. The seminar itself also came to be called *Records,* so throughout the book I'll use the word *Records* to refer to both the text and the seminar. It should be clear in context which one I mean.

I wrote Part Two as a memoir, sharing the daily activities of the seminars along with my struggles and aha moments while attending. Writing this part, I drew on my seminar notes, journal entries, conversations with the other participants as I remember them, and some of the stories told by the Guild's cofounders, Elizabeth Howes, Sheila Moon, and Luella Sibbald. The seminar includes the historical-critical method of study, along with journaling, art, music, drama, dance, ritual, silence, and the Jungian practice of active imagination. We worked with the Gospels beginning with Jesus's baptism up to his death on the cross, and then at the end struggled with the crucial questions: "*What do I think happened next?*" and "*Who do I think Jesus was?*"

The tones of Parts One and Two are different. Part One is an exposition of the theoretical foundations of the Records seminars and the life and teachings of Jesus. In Part Two I share my personal struggles with the Synoptic materials presented at the seminars.

I attended Guild *Records'* seminars in 1984, 1995, 2004, and 2012, and each was filled with not-knowing *and* breakthrough moments. I attended other Guild Seminars as well, some focused on mythic themes in the Synoptic Gospels and some on other myths. I took part in a yearlong study and several shorter Guild courses preparing to lead *Records* seminars, and was a participant-observer at a fifth *Records* seminar. In Part Two of the book, I share the study and participants' responses of these seminars without always specifying which year this teaching or that response took place. For the reader who would like that detail, my dissertation is available online.[18]

Everything we studied at Guild seminars was linked to everything else, weaving a tapestry with absolutely no predetermined outcome. Each day, seminar leaders introduced new Gospel passages and themes, and we responded from our experiences and beliefs, engaging body, mind, imagination, and emotions. As a result, each of us left the seminar with a unique "cloth." The tapestry I wove over the years expressed a yearning for meaning, purpose, and God whoever and whatever that might be. Though I attended seminars for twenty-five years and continue to reflect upon these issues, I still find myself wondering whether I'm doing the weaving or if something is weaving me.

Part One

The Christian Myth

C.G. Jung and Elizabeth Boyden Howes

Chapter 1

Jung's Vision of Christianity

[Christ] is the still living myth of our culture. He is our culture hero, who, regardless of his historical existence, embodies the myth of the divine Primordial Man, the mystic Adam .... These few, familiar references should be sufficient to make our psychological position of the Christ symbol quite clear: Christ exemplifies the archetype of the self.[19]
— Carl Gustav Jung

    I was introduced to Jung's vision of the Christian myth at a time I was struggling to understand my own relationship to Christianity. My childhood love of Jesus and his teachings gripped me, yet I no longer accepted the creeds and dogma of the church. The notion of a supernatural God "out there" who intervenes in this reality, its associated notion of a God who sent his son to die for our sins, was no longer tenable or life-giving for me. In studying both Jung and Howes, I began to find answers to my questions: I was able to explore the power of this ancient story and why it still gripped me even when I was unsure whether to call myself a Christian. Many who remain in the church while they question its creeds and dogma also find themselves gripped by the power of this myth. And many who have left the church continue to yearn for something that won't let them go. Is God an archetypal pattern within the human psyche? Is God "out there"? Are they mutually exclusive?

Questions like these set me on a search, which led to new ways of understanding the Christian myth. I encountered the work of New Testament scholar Bart Ehrman, who enumerated some of these contending beliefs in "the battles for scriptures and faiths we never knew," including some that were discovered in recent decades like the Gospel of Thomas.[20] Historian Jaroslav Pelikan astutely observed that each age depicts Jesus "in accordance with its own character,"[21] which had been Albert Schweitzer's sense when he wrote: "Each successive epoch found its own thoughts in Jesus, which was, indeed, the only way in which it could make him live."[22] Pelikan identifies a host of images of Jesus that have appeared through the centuries, including the rabbi, the light of the Gentiles, the Son of man, and the Prince of Peace. New Testament scholar Marcus Borg brought forward others' portraits of Jesus, including Burton Mack's sage wandering like a Greco-Roman Cynic; Elisabeth Schüssler Fiorenza's Wisdom prophet; Richard Horsley's prophet of social change; Borg's own spirit person; and John Dominic Crossan's Mediterranean Jewish peasant.[23] Millions more derive their images of Jesus from cinema and popular culture, such as Mel Gibson's film *The Passion of the Christ*, a literal Son of God who died for our sins. A depth-psychological understanding of Jesus of Nazareth brings a new lens to this old and respected tradition and asks, "What does this man have to say to us today?"

Was Jung a Christian?

C. G. Jung was born into a family of ministers and after his death in 1961, was memorialized in a service at the Swiss Reformed Church of Küsnacht and interred in the family plot. Did Jung consider himself Christian? Citing a 1944 letter penned to a Catholic critic, Aniela Jaffé says yes. In the letter, Jung concludes, "The Church having suffered a schism, I must be satisfied with being a Christian who is in the same conflict Christianity is in. I cannot disavow my brother who, in good faith and for reasons I cannot invalidate with a good conscience is of a different opinion."[24] A decade later, Jung wrote to Father Victor White that the Christian aeon was passing away but was not yet gone.

As he approached the end of his life, Jung came to an understanding of Christianity different from the institutional creeds and dogma. What the Christian myth sees as the intervention of the divine into one human being—the messiah it calls Jesus Christ—Jung saw as an intervention from the collective unconscious of *the archetypal self,* which, he hypothesized, all humanity shares. Human consciousness was awakening to its own unconscious. But in the view of both Howes and Jung, this vision was too vast for humans to bear, so it was *projected* onto just one God-human, Jesus Christ.

This is a psychological, not a theological understanding of the Christian myth. For Jung, the Christian story's account of the baptism of Jesus, when he heard a voice say, "You are my Beloved Son," is a story for all of humanity. The incarnation happens, in his view, for all humans, not just for one. Each individual has the potential to live out his or her own incarnation (as challenging a task as that may be) in the process Jung called *individuation.*

Jung called his idea of self a *hypothesis*; and his entire understanding of psyche, from a scientific perspective, outlined a *theory* that spawned decades of depth-psychological research, books, essays, and critiques. And the theory also created a *story* of humanity's journey that Jung regarded as a *myth*. In *Memories, Dreams, Reflections,* he referred to each person's contribution to the evolution of consciousness through living their own journey of individuation: "That is the goal, or one goal, which fits man meaningfully into the scheme of creation, and at the same time confers meaning upon it. It is an explanatory myth which has slowly taken shape within me in the course of the decades. It is a goal I can acknowledge and esteem, and which therefore satisfies me."[25]

We live by myths, and doing so gives life meaning. *Records* study, as it was conducted for more than fifty years by the Guild for Psychological Studies, brought students to question much—for some, all that they thought they knew about Jesus's life and teachings and even about themselves—and at the same time encouraged them to find the myth of meaning that exists when we "see through" the Christian story to its archetypal roots.

Christ as a Symbol of the Self

Jung's belief in the reality of psyche with its archetypes of the collective unconscious, central to which is the archetype of the self, led him to see Christ as one of the central *symbols* of the self in the Western psyche and to understand the Christian story as humanity's own story—ego's ineluctable, never-ending emergence from the collective unconscious through the journey of individuation. This story, in Jung's vision, happens within the psyche, not "out there" in some physical or metaphysical reality.

Jung chronicled his own encounter with psyche's depths in a journal he called *The Red Book*,[26] and later he wrote about it in *Memories, Dreams, Reflections*: "I hit upon this stream of lava, and the heat of its fires reshaped my life. That was the primal stuff which compelled me to work upon it, and my works are a more or less successful endeavor to incorporate this incandescent matter into the contemporary picture of the world." This molten lava, he says, became "the *prima materia* for a lifetime's work."[27]

In "Psychology and Religion," a collection of lectures given at Yale in 1937, Jung argued for the existence of "an authentic religious function in the unconscious"[28] and described his theory of archetypes, which led to a discussion of the power of the Christian myth residing not in a historical figure but in the archetypal reality that Christ symbolizes. In *Aion: Researches into the Phenomenology of the Self*, Jung discussed "the relations between the traditional Christ-figure and the natural symbols of wholeness, or the self."[29] "I add," he wrote, "to the many symbolical amplifications of the Christ-figure yet another, the psychological one,"[30] and he presented his concepts of ego and the archetypes of the collective unconscious. In 1950, he wrote that the

Christ-figure was "the still living myth of our culture ... [who] exemplifies the archetype of the self."[31]

In 1952, Jung wrote "Answer to Job" to try to clear up questions raised by his discussions in *Aion*, "especially the problems of Christ as a symbolic figure and of the antagonism Christ-Antichrist."[32] "Answer to Job" was one of Jung's most criticized works because of his argument for the all-inclusive God who was not only all-good *but also all-evil*. He argued that in the great cosmic battle between God, Satan, and Job—conducted in the arena of history and in the human psyche—it was Job, the human, who came out the better: "Anyone can see how [God] unwittingly raises Job by humiliating him in the dust. By so doing he pronounces judgment on himself and gives man the moral satisfaction whose absence we found so painful in the Book of Job."[33]

In *Memories, Dreams, Reflections* and in his *Collected Letters*, Jung's more spontaneous expressions reveal a passionate commitment to his ideas, even while acknowledging them as theories and hypotheses. Writing to a Protestant minister about churchgoers who want Christ to bear their cross, Jung wrote, "But we only want to talk of Christ's cross, and how splendidly his crucifixion has smoothed the way for us and solved our conflicts." In the next sentence, he wrote of "Christ's life [as] a prototype of individuation and hence [it] cannot be imitated: one can only live one's own life totally in the same way with all the consequences this entails."[34]

Psychological Interpretation of the Christian Myth

Christ would never have made the impression he did on his followers if he had not expressed something that was alive and at work in their unconscious. Christianity itself would never have spread through the pagan world with such astonishing rapidity had its ideas not found an analogous psychic readiness to receive them.[35] — C. G. Jung

Something in the human psyche was ready, Jung said, for whatever it was that Christ symbolized. For some, this *psychological* interpretation re-enlivens the Christian myth, while for many others it is anathema to what they believe is the *theological* reality.

That *something*, for Jung, was the self. At times he used the word *self* to refer to the ineffable *totality* of the human—conscious and unconscious. At other times the word *self* signifies an archetype within the psyche. In both cases, the self is numinous, inspiring awe and wonder so huge that it feels totally "other" and through the ages has been called *God*. For Jung, a central symbol for this totality is the Christ: "Christ exemplifies the archetype of the self. He represents a totality of a divine or heavenly kind, a glorified man, a son of God *sine macula peccati*, unspotted by sin."[36] This is a psychological under-standing of the story that Christianity wove around Jesus, and *from this perspective* what came alive in Jesus was the *self*, which remains present for all of humanity. In other words, something numinous that is present for and in all humans is *projected* onto Jesus, and believing that the object holding the projection was itself the self, Jesus's followers' stories were about *one* God-man rather than about all of us. Theology speaks of God incarnated in Jesus Christ. Jung speaks of the self incarnated *in each human*, a view that continues to bring him criticism.

Jung stressed that his view was psychological, and he did not deny the possibility of a supernatural God. He said he could not speak of anything outside psychic experience, so when he spoke of "God," he meant God-image *(Imago Dei)*, the *representation* of God that individuals have in their thoughts and experience. Jung made this clear in his letter to Pastor Walter Bernet: "I speak of the *God-image and not of God* because it is quite beyond me to say anything about God at all. ... I have in all conscience never supposed that in discussing the psychic structure of the God-image I have taken God himself in hand."[37]

He made a similar case in a letter to Martin Buber, the Jewish philosopher: "So if I hold the view that all statements about God have their origin in the psyche and must therefore be distinguished from

God as a metaphysical being, this is neither to deny God nor to put man in God's place."[38]

Jung's *Collected Letters* and many of his writings in the *Collected Works* affirm the vast interest and pointed criticism generated by his understanding of the Christian myth. His ideas have been explored by scholars of theology, biblical studies, and psychology; and yet the implications of his vision—that the human capacity is as immense as psyche itself, whose boundaries are unknown, that the human's destiny is to work toward ever-greater consciousness through the process of individuation, and that in this sense the human is co-creator with God—seem to have been appreciated by only a few. Jung's belief in the crucial place of the human in the evolution of consciousness is the centerpiece of what became for him the ground of a meaningful myth suitable for modern humankind.

Jung reminds us that he is an empiricist (one who studies knowledge based on experience derived through the senses) and a phenomenologist (one who studies the phenomena of consciousness, the experience of the mind), and that his concepts are hypotheses based on his own experience, that of his patients, and voluminous research. Yet the phenomena of which he speaks cannot be weighed or measured.

Wendy Doniger O'Flaherty, a scholar of Indian culture, tells us, "The empathetic scholar is the sage who acknowledges his need to live both in the head and in the heart."[39] I'd call Jung a sage who goes even further; he enters the undiscovered world of the psyche, the archetypal realm, where he encounters firsthand the gods and demons that influence our lives. Jung reminds us that he is speaking *metaphorically* (not literally) of this vast, mysterious realm that visits us in our dreams. Jungian author Robert A. Johnson asked, "On what level is it true?"[40] It's our challenge to discern what "reality" Jung speaks of as he attempts to express that which is known to him through messages from the unconscious. Johnson's dear friend and a Jungian as well as an Episcopal priest, John A. Sanford, called dreams "God's forgotten language."[41] Dreams, he wrote, are God speaking to us in the language of symbols, which we've forgotten.

Jung came to his revolutionary vision of the human through direct experience of the psyche, which conveys messages to consciousness through waking and sleeping dreams, art, fairytales, and myth. Psyche speaks through symbols that appear unbidden, and myths are narratives we weave around the symbols. The Bible is one such story.

Evolution of Jung's Christianity

On May 18, 1895, when he was not yet twenty, Jung addressed fellow members of the student fraternity Zofingia at the University of Basel, expressing his outrage at Albrecht Ritschl and other biblical scholars who were in search of the historical Jesus. Jung saw Jesus as one of those figures "who essentially represent a new species of man. The world does not give birth to them, but rather they create a world, a new heaven and a new earth. Their values are different, their truths are new."[42] Such persons *know* they come with a mission into this world and choose to live it out.

> They identify with the idea they bring to the world, and they live out this idea feeling that it will endure forever and that it is beyond violation by the exegesis of men. They *are* their own idea, untrammeled and absolute among the minds of their age, and not susceptible to historical analysis. ... They have not evolved from any historical foundation, but know that in their inmost natures they are free of all contingency, and have come only in order to erect on the foundation of history the edifice of their own ideas. One such man was Jesus of Nazareth. He knew this and he did not hesitate to proclaim it to the world.[43]

The young Jung took aim at the questers of a historical Jesus, saying, "After [Jesus] has been distilled through all the artful and capricious mechanisms of the critics' laboratory, the figure of the historical Jesus emerges at the other end."[44] Jung sees not an ordinary man of history, rather, "We should and must interpret Christ as he himself taught us to interpret him. The image of Christ must be restored to the idea he had of himself, namely, as a prophet, a man sent by God."[45]

In this 1895 lecture, Jung revealed his own commitment to follow the mission of Christ as he understood it. And even though he seemed to be talking about a historical figure, he said, "But if our Christianity is to possess any substance whatever, we must once again accept unconditionally the whole of the metaphysical, conceptual universe of the first Christians."[46] His frequent references to the *mystery* that gets lost in the quest for the historical Jesus spoke of his own awareness and experience of such a mystery, but at this stage of his thinking, the mystery was associated not with the reality of psyche but with a metaphysical reality.

Sixty years later, Jung wrote to Upton Sinclair in reaction to Sinclair's novel *Our Lady*. In it Jung revealed his continued belief that it is not the historical Jesus who gives rise to the power of the Christian myth, but neither is it the Christ of metaphysics. Rather, it is the self of the human psyche of which Christ is a great symbol. This is now not a matter of theology, but of psychology.

Sinclair's *Our Lady*, set in ancient Nazareth and contemporary Los Angeles, depicted in fictional and science fiction terms the experience of a mother, Marya, searching for her son, Yeshu, who has gone away on a secret mission. After complimenting Lewis on the novel, Jung wrote about something that troubled him, "… your common sense and realism, reducing the Holy Legend to human proportions and to probable possibilities."[47] It is not this human person and his life that gives this story its power:

> The fact that the original situation has developed into one of the most extraordinary myths about a divine *heros*, a God-man and his cosmic fate, is not due to its underlying human

story, but to the powerful action of the pre-existing mythological motifs attributed to the biographically almost unknown Jesus, a wandering miracle Rabbi in the style of the ancient Hebrew prophets, or of the contemporary teacher John the Baptizer, or of the much later Zaddiks of the Chassidim.[48]

Jung then wrote about what he believed is the source of the Christ myth and how the myth came to center on Jesus:

> The immediate source and origin of the myth projected upon the teacher Jesus is to be found in the then popular Book of Enoch and its central figure of the "Son of man" and his messianic mission. ... Thus it is the spirit of his time, the collective hope and expectation, which caused this astounding transformation and not at all the more or less insignificant story of the man Jesus. The true *agens* is the archetypal image of the God-man, appearing in Ezekiel's vision for the first time in Jewish history, but in itself a considerably older figure in Egyptian theology, vis., Osiris and Horus.[49]

This is Jung speaking of the process of projection by which the man Jesus becomes the archetypal God-man.

> The transformation of Jesus, i.e., the integration of his human self into a super-or inhuman figure of a deity, accounts for the amazing "distortion" of his ordinary personal biography. In other words, the essence of Christian tradition is by no means the simple man Jesus whom we seek in vain in the Gospels, but the lore of the God-man and his cosmic drama.[50]

In the sixty years between his Zofingia lecture and this letter to Upton Sinclair, Jung formulated his theory of archetypes of the collective unconscious and the process of individuation.

The Reality of Psyche

In *Memories, Dreams, Reflections,* Jung tells us that his life's work was dedicated "to service of the psyche." Psyche was the *numinosum* to which he devoted his life. In his 1937 Terry Lectures, he explained:

> Religion as the Latin word denotes, is a careful and scrupulous observation of what Rudolf Otto aptly termed the *numinosum*, that is, a dynamic agency or effect not caused by an arbitrary act of will. On the contrary, it seizes and controls the human subject, who is always rather its victim than its creator. The *numinosum*—whatever its cause may be—is an experience of the subject independent of his will.[51]

Jung says he was seized by material from the unconscious, which he often refers to as *psyche*, in the years following his break from Freud, up to the end of World War I. Speaking of those years, he says:

> But then, I hit upon this stream of lava, and the heat of its fires reshaped my life. That was the primal stuff which compelled me to work upon it, and my works are a more or less successful endeavor to incorporate this incandescent matter into the contemporary picture of the world.
>
> The years when I was pursuing my inner images were the most important in my life—in them everything essential was decided. It all began then; the later details are only supplements and clarifications of the material that burst forth from the unconscious, and at first swamped me. It was the *prima materia* for a lifetime's work.[52]

Apparently there is one more sentence in the German original that was deleted from the English translation: "The first imaginations and dreams were like fiery liquid basalt; out of them crystallized the stone that I could work."[53]

Jung speaks of what crystallized out of the *prima materia* as "the reality of psyche," which Jungian Wolfgang Giegerich refers to as the "notion of soul" and quotes Karl Kerényi: "It is taking the soul for real. For no psychologist of our time, the psyche possessed such a concreteness and importance as for [Jung]."[54] Giegerich underlines Jung's belief with another quote from *Memories, Dreams, Reflections*: "It was then that I dedicated myself to service of the psyche. I loved it and hated it, but it was my greatest wealth."[55]

Just what does Jung mean by *psyche*? The first thing that strikes me about Jung's conception of psyche is the immensity of what he intends by it. In "The Transcendent Function," he wrote, "The psyche, as a reflection of the world and man, is a thing of such infinite complexity that it can be observed and studied from a great many sides."[56] And in "Psychology and Religion," he added, "Indeed it is quite impossible to define the ultimate character of psychic existence."[57] In other places, he refers to psyche as the totality of psychic experience, conscious and unconscious, a definition that can apply equally well to *self*. In the following quotation, Jung could be speaking of psyche or of self:

> Indeed, it is quite impossible to define the extent and the ultimate character of psychic existence. When we now speak of man we mean the indefinable whole of him, an ineffable totality, which can only be formulated symbolically. I have chosen the term "self" to designate the totality of man, the sum total of his conscious and unconscious contents.[58]

Note that he says that the totality of man "can only be formulated symbolically." A *symbol*, Jung explains, "is the best possible expression for an unconscious element, whose nature can only be guessed, because it is still unknown."[59] He expands on this in "On the Relation of Analytical Psychology to Poetry":

> The true symbol differs essentially from [the sign], and should be understood as an expression of an intuitive idea that cannot yet be formulated in any other or better way. ... When Plato, for instance puts the whole problem of the theory of knowledge in his parable of the cave, or when Christ expresses the idea of the Kingdom of Heaven in parables, these are genuine and true symbols, that is, attempts to express something for which no verbal concept yet exists.[60]

This reminds us of the challenge Jung faced as he sought for words to express what he had experienced as the *prima materia*, the collective unconscious and the archetypes that are a part of that collective unconscious.

The Collective Unconscious and Archetype of the Self

In the early twentieth century, Jung was flooded by images and fantasies which he struggled to understand. When World War I broke out, he related some of his fantasies and dreams to the events leading up to that catastrophic event, but now he needed to understand "what had happened and to what extent my own experience coincided with that of mankind in general. Therefore my first obligation was to probe the depths of my own psyche."[61] It was during this period of probing "the depths" that he met the inner figures he called Philemon, Elijah, Salome, and others. Philemon, Jung tells us, "taught me psychic objectivity, the reality of the psyche."[62] Jung kept a journal with hand-calligraphed entries and stunning watercolors of these dreamlike images; it was not published until 2012, as *The Red Book*.[63]

Within psyche, Jung hypothesized, are both conscious and unconscious contents, and he believed he found in his own experience and research that the unconscious is composed of both personal and collective (universal) contents. In "The Ego," he called the *collective unconscious* "an omnipresent, unchanging, and everywhere identical quality or substrate of the psyche per se." Although he said it was "no more than a hypothesis," he nevertheless posited the "high probability that the general similarity of psychic processes in all individuals must be based on an equally general and impersonal principle that conforms to law."[64]

Within that collective unconscious are "archetypes that were present from the beginning."[65] Jung discussed what he meant by archetypes in many of his writings. I take this quote from "Psychology and Religion." He had been using the dreams of his patients to illustrate his concepts and in this quote, he is discussing themes that occur over and over again:

> Even dreams are made of collective material to a very high degree, just as, in the mythology and folklore of different peoples, certain motifs repeat themselves in almost identical form. I have called these motifs "archetypes," and by this I mean forms or images of a collective nature which occur practically all over the earth as constituents of myths and at the same time as autochthonous, individual products of unconscious origin.[66]

Among these archetypes is the self, which Jung defined in several ways. For example, it is "the psychic totality of the individual."[67] In "Individual Dream Symbolism in Relation to Alchemy," he wrote, "The self is not only the centre but also the whole circumference which embraces both consciousness and unconscious; it is the centre of this totality, just as the ego is the centre of the conscious mind."[68] Again we are reminded that it's often difficult, if not impossible, to distinguish *self* from *psyche*, and in fact it would appear that there is no distinction, as the quote above illustrates ("I have chosen the term 'self' to designate the totality of man, the sum total of his conscious and unconscious contents").

This similarity, even identity, of the terms *psyche* and *self* is discussed by Roger Brooke, who concludes in his *Jung and Phenomenology* that "in terms of their defined scope psyche and self would seem to be identical."[69] He notes Jung's own definition given in *Psychological Types*: "As an empirical concept, the self designates the whole range of psychic phenomena in man. It expresses the unity of the personality as a whole."[70] Brooke also points out "that the definition here given of the self as 'the whole range of psychic phenomena in man' is almost identical with the definition of the psyche as 'the totality of all psychic processes conscious and unconscious.'"[71]

Individual and Psyche

The above quote speaks about the range of psychic phenomena "in man," suggesting that psyche itself is "within" man and is "his." Jung himself sometimes referred to "my" psyche. For example, speaking of the upheaval he experienced after his break with Freud, "My first obligation was to probe the depths of *my own psyche*."[72] But he was very clear elsewhere that the psyche was not *in* the individual, but *the individual was in the psyche*. In a letter to Josef Goldbrunner, author of *Individuation: A Study of the Depth Psychology of Carl Gustav Jung*, Jung wrote: "You rightly emphasize that man in my view is enclosed in *the* psyche (not in *his* psyche)."[73] Brooke expands upon this, saying, "The psyche is not to be confused with or limited to the boundaries of the individual person, whose personal psychology is organized around the 'ego.' Thus there is strictly speaking not his or her psyche but rather *the* psyche ... within which he and she have individual perspectives and play their parts."[74]

Jung made the same point in his "Commentary on *The Secret of the Golden Flower*," where he likened the ego to fishes in the sea: "As I see it, the psyche is a world in which the ego is contained. Maybe there are fishes who believe that they contain the sea,"[75] and we may complete this thought with: *and maybe there are individuals who believe they contain the psyche.* This brings us directly to Jung's understanding of the relationship of the individual to the metaphorical ocean of psyche in which we swim.

Although Jung aligns ego with fishes in the sea, in this instance ego, in his view, is essential, crucial, in the development of consciousness. It is "the centre of the conscious mind";[76] it is "a conscious factor par excellence."[77] It is what "knows" that it is itself. It is this ego that speaks of "my" psyche, "my" self, even when the individual may understand its subordinate relationship to something greater than itself. Addressing the danger of muddling ego and self and thereby deifying the individual, Brooke stresses that the center of the self is not in the individual, it "is that to which I am related most deeply, and to which I try to return in times of ethical questioning, of crisis, of silence. It is a centre that is most intimately mine, yet is not 'in me' unless I put it there for a time."[78]

In Jung's view, ego emerges out of the primordial ocean of psyche in which it swims. Jung's writings make clear that this ocean exists *before* consciousness. This excerpt from "Psychology and Religion" emphasizes not only the relationship of the individual to psyche, but also the pre-existence of psyche:

> In the same way that the State has caught the individual, the individual imagines that he has caught the psyche and holds her in the hollow of his hand. He is even making a science of her in the absurd supposition that the intellect, which is but a part and a function of the psyche, is sufficient to comprehend the much greater whole. *In reality the psyche is the mother and the maker, the subject and even the possibility of consciousness itself.* It reaches so far beyond the boundaries of consciousness that the latter could easily be compared to an island in the ocean. Whereas the island is small and narrow, the ocean is immensely wide and deep and contains a life infinitely surpassing, in kind and degree, anything known on the island.[79]

In "The Undiscovered Self," we find further elucidation of Jung's theory of the pre-existence of psyche and, equally significant, his understanding of the crucial role of the individual:

> Without consciousness there would, practically speaking, be no world, for the world exists for us only in so far as it is consciously reflected by a psyche. *Consciousness is a precondition of being.* Thus the psyche is endowed with the dignity of a cosmic principle, which philosophically and in fact gives it a position co-equal with the principle of physical being. The carrier of this consciousness is the individual, who does not produce the psyche of his own volition but is, on the contrary, preformed by it and nourished by the gradual awakening of consciousness during childhood. If therefore the psyche is of overriding empirical importance, so also is the individual, who is the only immediate manifestation of the psyche.[80]

Jung's view of the centrality of the individual in the emergence of consciousness from preexisting psychic reality comes clear in the following account and reflections which came to him during his 1925 trip to Africa, a transformative journey as he wrote in *Memories, Dreams, Reflections* many years later. I quote from it rather extensively because of the striking language in which he expresses his realization of the role of the human in the overall scheme of things.

At one point, while traveling by train, Jung awoke at dawn to see "on a jagged rock above us a slim, brownish-black figure [standing] motionless, leaning on a long spear, looking down at the train. Beside him towered a gigantic candelabrum cactus."[81] He experienced "a most intense *sentiment du déjà vu*," a feeling-tone that remained with him throughout the trip. A few days later, he arrived at a great game preserve and looked out over a "magnificent prospect," an expanse filled with "gigantic herds of animals: gazelle, antelope, gnu, zebra, warthog, and so on."[82]

There was scarcely any sound save the melancholy cry of a bird of prey. This was the stillness of the eternal beginning, the world as it had always been, in the state of non-being; for until then no one had been present to know that it was this world. ... There I was now, the first human being to recognize that this was the world, but who did not know that in this moment he had first really created it.

There the cosmic meaning of consciousness became overwhelmingly clear to me. "What nature leaves imperfect, the art perfects," say the alchemists. Man, I, in an invisible act of creation put the stamp of perfection on the world by giving it objective existence.[83]

Then the memory came to Jung of "my old Pueblo friend" whom he had envied "for the fullness of meaning" in his belief that his reason for being was to help the sun rise each morning.

I had envied him for the fullness of meaning in that belief, and had been looking about without hope for a myth of our own. Now I knew what it was, and knew even more: that man is indispensable for the completion of creation; that, in fact, he himself is the second creator of the world, who alone has given to the world its objective existence—without which, unheard, unseen, silently eating, giving birth, dying, heads nodding through hundreds of millions of years, it would have gone on in the profoundest night of non-being down to its unknown end. Human consciousness created objective existence and meaning, and man found his indispensable place in the great process of being.[84]

Here we find the roots of what Jaffé called Jung's myth of meaning, his belief in the human's indispensable role in the evolution of consciousness. This, in Jung's view, is the story we see lived out in the life of Christ.

A Circumambulation of the Self

"One of the most shining examples of the meaning of personality that history has preserved for us is the life of Christ,"[85] Jung proclaimed. To understand what he meant by this, let us examine Jung's view of Christ as *symbol of the self* and the process of *individuation*, which, he argues, leads to *personality*.

Jung said that he wrote the book *Aion* in response to requests "to discuss the relations between the traditional Christ-figure and the natural symbols of wholeness, or the self."[86] Acknowledging the difficulties of this task because of layers of meaning attributed to the figure of Christ, he explained, "I add to the many symbolical amplifications of the Christ-figure yet another, the psychological one. I am not making a confession of faith or writing a tendentious tract, but am simply considering how certain things could be understood from the standpoint of our modern consciousness."[87] He then discussed ego, shadow, animus, and anima, all building to his hypothesis of the self, the "ever-present archetype of wholeness."[88] It is an archetype, he argued, that "cannot in practice be distinguished from a God-image."[89] Of Christ, Jung wrote:

He is the still living myth of our culture. He is our culture hero, who, regardless of his historical existence, embodies the myth of the divine Primordial Man, the mystic Adam. It is he who occupies the centre of the Christian mandala. He is in us and we in him. His kingdom is the pearl of great price, the treasure buried in the field, the grain of mustard seed which will become a great tree, and the heavenly city. As Christ is in us, so also is his heavenly kingdom.

These few, familiar references should be sufficient to make our psychological position of the Christ symbol quite clear: *Christ exemplifies the archetype of the self.* He represents a totality of a divine or heavenly kind, a glorified man, a son of God *sine macula peccati*, unspotted by sin.[90]

It is because the Christ is a symbol of the self, that is, of psychic totality—the totality of what it is to be human—that Jung wrote in "Answer to Job": "Christ would never have made the impression he did on his followers if he had not expressed something that was alive and at work in their unconscious. Christianity itself would never have spread through the pagan world with such astonishing rapidity had its ideas not found an analogous psychic readiness to receive them."[91]

The "psychic readiness" is *the archetypal self*, present in psyche and thus in all humanity. The journey to the wholeness that the self carries is to be traveled *not only by Jesus Christ, but by each individual* in the process Jung called *individuation*: "Individuation means becoming an 'individual,' and, insofar as 'individuality' embraces our innermost, last, and incomparable uniqueness, it also implies becoming one's own self. We could therefore translate individuation as 'coming to selfhood' or 'self-realization.'"[92]

Individuation, he contended, is a force of nature within the human that cannot be denied, even though it can never be attained. He expresses this in relationship to the archetype of the child: "The urge and compulsion to self-realization is a law of nature, and thus of invincible power, even though its effect, at the start, is insignificant and improbable."[93] Elsewhere he wrote, "There is no linear evolution; there is only a circumambulation of the self. Uniform development exists, at most, only at the beginning; later, everything points toward the center."[94]

This is the challenge the ego must face if it is to "come to self-hood"—to become more and more related to the archetypes at work within the psyche. Jung wrote, "The more numerous and the more significant the unconscious contents which are assimilated to the ego, the closer the approximation of the ego to the self, even though this approximation must be a never-ending process."[95]

In a footnote to the quote above, in which he referred to "coming to self-hood," Jung stressed that "this does not mean that the self is created, so to speak, only during the course of life; it is rather a question of its becoming conscious. The self exists from the very beginning, but is latent, that is, unconscious."[96] Emphasizing here again that psyche exists before consciousness, as he often does, Jung uses the terms *psyche* and *self* synonymously. His belief, or rather, his hypothesis that the self exists "from the very beginning," and is not "created ... only during the course of life" gives some clue to the meaning of his enigmatic statement in "Transformation Symbolism in the Mass": "Just as a man still is what he always was, so he already is what he will become."[97] A little further along, he wrote, "The ego stands to the self as the moved to the mover. ... The self, like the unconscious, is an *a priori* existent out of which the ego evolves. It is, so to speak, an unconscious prefiguration of the ego. It is not I who create myself, rather I happen to myself."[98]

Jung here placed *self* and *unconscious* alongside one another, rather than discussing *self, unconscious,* and *psyche* as synonymous. His intent was clear: ego, that is, consciousness, is born from self, from the unconscious, which exists from the beginning. The dance between ego and self goes on during the course of a lifetime and leads to the evolution of consciousness.

Who undertakes the task of individuation? Who hears and responds to the inner voice? "Only the man who can consciously assent to the power of the inner voice becomes a personality."[99] To enter this quest is to face the opposites that exist within psyche and that we experience within ourselves. To recognize and hold the tension between them *is to be crucified.* Jung points to the reality of these opposites in his reference to Matthew 5:48 "Be you therefore perfect" and in his allusion to Paul's familiar plaint in Romans 7:21: "The individual may strive after perfection ('Be you therefore perfect . . . as also your heavenly Father is perfect.') but must suffer from the opposite of his intentions for the sake of his completeness. 'I find then a law, that, when I would do good, evil is present with me.'"[100]

Jung's belief in the crucial role of the individual in the process of individuation is apparent in these sobering words: "The psychological rule says that when an inner situation is not made conscious, it happens outside, as fate. That is to say, when the individual remains undivided and does not become conscious of his inner opposite, the world must perforce act out the conflict and be torn into opposing halves."[101]

For Jung, then, the path of individuation, of coming to "self-hood" is essential, its urge for humankind inescapable even though not all will heed the call. Jung calls the individual human being "that infinitesimal unit on whom the fate of the world depends, and in whom, if we read the meaning of the Christian message aright, even God seeks his goal."[102] The inescapable, ineluctable urge to wholeness, writes Jung in "The Development of Personality," is why Christ, the symbol of wholeness, gripped and still grips individual men and women:

> The example of Christianity is perhaps the best illustration of my previous abstract argument [about the development of personality]. This apparently unique life became a sacred symbol because it is the psychological prototype of the only meaningful life, that is, of a life that strives for the individual realization—absolute and unconditional—of its own particular law.[103]

The Other Side of Christ

Thus far, I have focused on Jung's view of Christ as a symbol of the self, of wholeness. Yet Jung makes an equally strong argument that the Christ symbol is *not whole*, that its dark side has been split off leaving only an all-good Christ. This is exemplified in the institutional church's development of the doctrine of the *privatio boni*: that is, evil is the absence of good, which leads to the idea, "Omne bonum a Deo, omne malum ab homini" ("All good from God, all evil from man"). Jung took passionate and lengthy issue with this in *Aion*[104] and again in "Answer to Job," arguing that this proposition fails to recognize the reality and the power of evil and of the dark side of God and of Christ and thus of the human. This split in the Christ symbol prevents—or protects—us from facing and assimilating our own evil, and leads instead to its projection onto the world. Jung speaks of the devastating consequences of this projection when he writes, "One could hardly call the things that have happened, and still happen, in the concentration camps of the dictator states an 'accidental lack of perfection'—it would sound like a mockery."[105]

Nevertheless, despite the one-sidedness of Christ, he "is our nearest analogy of the self and its meaning."[106] Jung continues his discussion of the one-sided Christ:

> If one inclines to regard the archetype of the self as the real agent and hence takes Christ as a symbol of the self, one must bear in mind that there is a considerable difference between *perfection* and *completeness*. The Christ-image is as good as perfect (at least it is meant to be so), while the archetype (so far as known) denotes completeness but is far from being perfect. It is a paradox, a statement about something indescribable and transcendental.[107]

This statement expresses two points of Jung's that I want to emphasize: (1) Despite its one-sidedness, "Christ" is the best symbol of the self in history. (2) The archetypal pattern lived out in Christ's life is present in every human life. The Incarnation, spirit become flesh, which in Christian dogma happens only in Christ, happens in humanity itself:

> Since the life of Christ is archetypal to a high degree, it represents to just that degree the life of the archetype. *But since the archetype is the unconscious precondition of every human life*, its life, when revealed, also reveals the hidden, unconscious ground-life of every individual. That is to say, *what happens in the life of Christ happens always and everywhere*. In the Christian archetype all lives of this kind are prefigured and are expressed over and over again or once and for all.[108]

Each person, then, lives out an archetypal life, although becoming conscious of this takes a lifetime. We cannot look to Jesus Christ to be our Savior; we must each carry our own cross. Jung expressed this harshly in his 1952 letter to clergywoman Dr. Dorothee Hoch. He wrote first of Christ living out his own life, proclaiming a dangerous message in his times. Then he turned to us:

> But we? We imitate Christ and hope he will deliver us from our own fate. Like little lambs we follow the shepherd, naturally to good pastures. No talk at all of uniting our Above and Below! On the contrary, Christ and his cross delivers us from our conflict, which we simply leave alone. ... Instead of bearing ourselves, i.e., our own cross ourselves, we load Christ with our unresolved conflicts. We "place ourselves under *his* cross," but by golly not under our own. ... The cross of Christ *was borne by himself* and was *his*.[109]

Still speaking of churchgoers who want Christ to bear their cross, he continues, "But we only want to talk of Christ's cross, and how splendidly his crucifixion has smoothed the way for us and solved our conflicts." In the next sentence he writes of "Christ's life [as] a prototype of individuation and hence cannot be imitated: one can only live one's own life totally in the same way with all the consequences this entails."[110]

In Jung's view, to take up one's own cross is to engage with God in the evolution of consciousness that God does and does not want.

God Needs Man to Show Him to Himself

In "Answer to Job,"[111] Jung continues to explicate his theories of Christ, individuation, and the evolution of consciousness, and in doing so made arguably his most criticized pronouncements about the nature of God and the human-God relationship. In a prefatory note written for the journal *Pastoral Psychology* in January 1956,[112] he explained that he wrote "Answer to Job" to try to clear up questions raised by his discussions in *Aion*, "especially the problems of Christ as a symbolic figure and of the antagonism Christ-Antichrist."[113] This referred to his argument against the Church's doctrine of *privatio boni*, which can be understood as "all good from God, all evil from man." It is essential, Jung believed, that we recognize the existence of evil that exists in the human and, psychologically, in the self and thus in the image of God.

Jung said he hesitated to respond to these questions "because I was quite conscious of the probable consequences, and knew what a storm would be raised."[114] Still, he felt gripped by the problem and forced to undertake the writing "… describing a personal experience. I deliberately chose this form because I wanted to avoid the impression that I had any idea of announcing an 'eternal truth.' The book does not pretend to be anything but the voice or question of a single individual who hopes or expects to meet with thoughtfulness in the public."[115]

Despite these caveats, it's difficult not to be startled by Jung's portrayal of an unconscious, unreflecting, *amoral* God.[116] The degree of shock measures the degree to which the dogma of the all-good God and his Savior son holds us. Jung portrays a God readily seduced by his son Satan to tempt Job, a good man, and then behaves cruelly and unjustly to reduce Job to the extremes of illness, his children dead, his riches taken away. His wife and friends berate him, for surely he must have done something to deserve such punishment.

But Jung saw God, not Job, as the culprit here, as the one "too unconscious to be moral. Morality presupposes consciousness."[117] Jung does not assert that Yahweh is completely evil. "He is *everything* in its totality; therefore, among other things, he is total justice, and also its total opposite."[118]

This is a God, Jung contends, who needs his creation, the human, to show him to himself. "Existence is only real when it is conscious to somebody. That is why the Creator needs conscious man even though, from sheer unconsciousness, [God] would like to prevent [man] from becoming conscious."[119]

It's no wonder that this work and Jung himself were criticized. On the one hand, he continued to argue that in Christ a new consciousness was born, a new step was taken in the evolution of consciousness, one in which all humans have the potential to participate. And he also drew an image of a God who is unconscious, amoral, cruel, unjust—*and* their opposites. For this is an all-inclusive God, in whom are good and evil, justice and injustice, a desire to become conscious and a desire to remain unconscious.

The story told in Job is the unequal match between human and divine, and in Jung's view, it is Job who comes out the better of the two: "Anyone can see how [God] unwittingly raises Job by humiliating him in the dust. By so doing he pronounces judgment on himself and gives man the moral satisfaction whose absence we found so painful in the Book of Job."[120]

As Jung saw it, this engagement between God and Job was a precursor to God's Incarnation in Christ. Why did God create the human? Jung asks. "All the world is God's, and God is in all the world from the very beginning. Why, then, the *tour de force* of the Incarnation? one asks oneself, astonished."[121] Was Christ—is the human—to take away the evil of the world? Why doesn't God do that himself? Surely God could do away with Satan, "get rid of his pernicious influence, and thus eliminate the root of all evil. … One should make clear to oneself what it means when God becomes man. It means nothing less than a world-shaking transformation of God. … At the time of the Creation he revealed himself in Nature; now he wants to be more specific and become man."[122]

Jung argued that intimations of this were present from the beginning in the Egyptian myths, but "it was only quite late that we realized (or are beginning to realize) that *God is Reality itself and therefore—last but not least—man.* This realization is a millennial process,"[123] and the encounter with Job was the essential step along the way to the Incarnation, for in it God's consciousness was raised.

Remember that when Jung speaks of "God," he is not speaking metaphysically of a supernatural God, but psychologically of the *image of God, that is, the self.* He addresses this in response to a critique by Martin Buber: "It should not be overlooked that what I am concerned with are psychic phenomena which can be proved empirically to be the bases of metaphysical concepts, and that when, for example, I speak of 'God' I am unable to refer to anything beyond these demonstrable psychic models."[124]

He makes the same point in a letter to Pastor Bernet:

> You write, apparently without any misgivings, that I equate God with the self. You seem not to have noticed that I speak of the *God-image and not of God* because it is quite beyond me to say anything about God at all. … I have in all conscience never supposed that in discussing the psychic structure of the God-image I have taken God himself in hand.[125]

He is emphasizing that the *image of God* derives from psyche and tells us nothing about a transcendental God, whether it is or is not.

"Answer to Job" is about a grand psychic struggle for consciousness through an encounter between the individual human ego and the self. In Jesus's baptism experience, when understood psychologically, the self was born in the human with tremendous consequences for both. In scripture it reads that the Spirit descended into Jesus "like a dove; and a voice came from heaven, 'Thou art my beloved Son; with thee I am well pleased.'"[126] This, according to Jung, happens to all of us. This is the meaning of "One should make clear to oneself what it means when God becomes man. It means nothing less than a world-shaking transformation of God."[127]

This is the human-divine dance. When one is transformed, so is the other. Christ's experience is the blueprint of what is possible for all humans. Jung thus says, "Christ, the son begotten by God, is the first-born who is succeeded by an ever-increasing number of younger brothers and sisters."[128] Jung addresses the puzzle of God and the image of God, the *imago Dei,* acknowledging the great mystery:

It is only through the psyche that we can establish that God acts upon us, but we are unable to distinguish whether these actions emanate from God or from the unconscious. We cannot tell whether God and the unconscious are two different entities. Both are border-line concepts for trans-cendental contents. But empirically it can be established, with a sufficient degree of probability, that there is in the unconscious an archetype of wholeness.[129]

And he ends "Answer to Job" by recalling the limitations of the human ego-self, who nonetheless contains the "One" who Jung calls self, image of God, and God. "Even the enlightened person remains what he is, and is never more than his own limited ego before the One who dwells within him, whose form has no knowable boundaries, who encompasses him on all sides, fathomless as the abysms of the earth and vast as the sky."[130] This is indeed a mighty self, and the task Jung sets before us is no less than:

> man's creative confrontation with the opposites and their synthesis in the self, the wholeness of his personality. ... In the experience of the self it is no longer the opposites "God" and "man" that are reconciled, as it was before, but rather the opposites within the God-image itself. ... That is the goal, or one goal, which fits man meaningfully into the scheme of creation, and at the same time confers meaning upon it. It is an explanatory myth which has slowly taken shape within me in the course of the decades. It is a goal I can acknowledge and esteem, and which therefore satisfies me.[131]

Jung states clearly in many places that the collective unconscious and the archetype of the self are hypotheses, yet here he acknowledges this also as "an explanatory myth which has taken shape within me in the course of the decades." It is a narrative that brings together an understanding of all he experienced, learned, and hypothesized, the myth he longed for when confronted with his Pueblo friend who *knew* that his myth was to assist the sun rise each day.

Chapter 2
Other Jungian Views on Christianity

Jung's ideas captured the attention of theologians, psychologists, and laypeople during his lifetime and up to the present day. In *Jung and Christianity in Dialogue,* therapists Robert Moore and Daniel Meckel note "the burgeoning interest in the dialogue between Christianity and Jungian thought,[132] and Jungian analyst Murray Stein remarks on the hundreds of writings to be found.[133] Stein argues that Jung's message was about transforming Christianity. Edward Edinger and John Dourley see Jung's vision as potentially leading us through and beyond Christianity to a new dispensation. Lionel Corbett takes it a step further and argues that for most people, Christianity has already lost its relevance. In my view, the Christian myth continues to live as one of the great stories of the human journey.

Murray Stein: Transforming Christianity

In the introduction to his selection of Jung's writings on Christianity, Murray Stein argues against what he calls misconceptions of what Jung was about. Jung is no Christian apologist, "defender of Christian truths within a contemporary setting using modern concepts and language."[134] Nor is he an "evangelist" of a saved Christianity. Stein's view is that while Jung expresses concern about "a perceived lack of vitality in contemporary Christianity," Jung's focus "lies not so much on the church as on modern people who are spiritually adrift and need living symbols to find meaning and direction in their lives."[135]

The second notion Stein sets out to rectify is "that Jung was anti-Christian and out to destroy Christianity or to supplant it with his own psychological theory, analytical psychology."[136] Far from it, Stein contends. Jung's theories "are not attacks upon Christian belief and practice, nor do they foresee their demise or suggest their replacement by analytical psychology."[137] Rather, Jung "advocated the transformation of Christianity."[138] Jung viewed Christianity, Stein says, as "an ailing patient in need of therapy"[139] and that "the Christian tradition must transform itself or enter into a long and painful dying process."[140]

My understanding of Jung's vision of Christianity is quite different from Stein's. Jung was born into a long line of Protestant ministers. He was baptized a Christian and never removed himself from Christianity, although he didn't associate himself with any particular denomination. He was buried in the Swiss Protestant cemetery in Küsnacht, outside of Zürich.[141]

Jung's extensive writings on Christianity attest to the centrality of this myth in his life and thought. I see the Christian story as a vehicle that conveys his theories about the collective unconscious, the archetype of the self, and Christ as one of the great symbols of the self. Therefore, in my view, if Jung intended to transform anything, it was not Christianity or any creed or dogma, but humanity's vision of itself and each individual's vision of their relationship to the self greater than their ego-self. Jung was well aware that the Christian aeon was nearing its end, although when he wrote sixty years ago, he did not indicate that its time had come.

Jung's fundamental concern was the reality of psyche and the individual's role in the evolution of consciousness, a process that pivots on the individual's relationship to the self, the God-image, which is what we humans experience as God.

Edward Edinger: The Birth of a New God-Image

Psychiatrist Edward Edinger trained his analytical lens on Jung's ideas of psyche and all its related concepts for nearly three decades, until his death in 1998. Edinger explored how the concepts of the archetypes of the collective unconscious, especially the archetype of the self and ego's relationship to it through the process of individuation, emerge from psyche, the collective unconscious, and at the same time become the great myths of human history that reveal psyche to us. In Edinger's view, the Bible and the Christian story are such myths.

In *Ego and Archetype*, his earliest published work, Edinger discussed the process of individuation through which ego finds meaning by coming into the service of self, and Christ as a "paradigm for the Individuating Ego."[142] Elsewhere, he added that "the underlying meaning of Christianity is the quest for individuation."[143] At the same time, Edinger recognized, "The great symbol system which is organized Christianity seems no longer able to command the full commitment of men or to fulfill their ultimate needs. ... Whether or not a new collective religious symbol will emerge remains to be seen."[144]

Over the years Edinger expanded upon his understanding of individuation as life seeking its own understanding—God becoming conscious through God's endless dance with humanity. In psychological language, consciousness is achieved through the ongoing dialogue between ego and self. Humanity becomes cocreator with what it has forever called God. In *The Bible and the Psyche*, Edinger presents the Bible as "a self-revelation of the objective psyche,"[145] and its stories as "pictures of the encounter between the ego and the Self."[146]

Within the Bible, Jung said, "the Book of Job is a landmark in the long historical development of a divine drama."[147] But Edinger argued that the correct translation of *Entwicklungswege* that Jung's translator Richard Francis Carrington Hull rendered as "historical" should be translated "evolutionary." The German word, Edinger wrote, "denotes nothing about history. The word means development, or alternatively, evolution, so that it is a term that has a biological connotation, as well as a more general connotation." Edinger thus translated Jung's statement as, "The Book of Job is a landmark in the long *evolutionary* pathway of a divine drama."[148]

> The remarkable idea in the sentence is the phrase *divine drama*, referring to a dynamic process. The God-image is not a static entity. … [Jung's statement] means that in the course of the evolution of the human species and in the historical-cultural development of the human species, the God-image is a living entity, a living process that moves, that unfolds, that develops and undergoes transformations.[149]

There is a biological impetus for the dynamic process leading to transformation.

The Bible and Christianity have been central in this evolutionary journey, but Edinger saw us "on the verge of another such evolutionary leap in the development of the God-image," and wrote, "We are right on the verge of witnessing the birth of a new God-image as a result of Jung's work."[150] And he affirmed Jung's sense that the birth of this new God-image demands the participation of the human in an increasingly conscious dance between ego and self, ego and God. As I understand Edinger, Jung's vision is then not about transforming Christianity— even though Christianity has provided, and for many still provides, the central myth of Western culture. It is about transforming the human-God relationship.

John Dourley: "Humanity" as the Trinity's Fourth Dimension

Jung wrote often of the Trinity's lack of the feminine, the dark, evil, and the body, and stated in various places the need for a "fourth" joining the Trinity to form a quaternity. Although he didn't use the word *humanity* or *man* in these discussions, the incarnation of the divine—by which he always meant the coming into consciousness of both ego and self—can take place only in humanity. John Dourley

(1936-2018), a Jungian analyst, Catholic priest, and teacher, carried Jung's thought to his own conclusion: "Humanity is the fourth dimension of divinity where alone the eternal conflict of Father and Son, and of all divine opposites, is resolved in the psyche."[151] Dourley expanded on this in his discussion of "Answer to Job." Speaking of a God beset with inner contradictions that he cannot resolve, Dourley wrote, "As Jung continues his meditation from this point of departure [God's inner contradictions] he cannot escape the conclusion that divine life creates human consciousness as the sole point of conscious discrimination in existence. This paradigm makes humanity the fourth element in the Trinity."[152]

Like Edinger, Dourley understood that Jung's foundational belief is that psyche is the source of religious experience, that symbol and myth are expressions of the collective unconscious in human consciousness. For the Western mind for two thousand years, the Christian myth has carried, contained, and in Jung's view, protected humanity from these messages from psyche, for better and now perhaps for worse.

Like Edinger, Dourley built on what Jung said, and he acknowledged Jung's belief that Christianity is not the final revelation of God, or psyche. Both Edinger and Dourley understood that to follow Jung's thought onward may well lead Christianity out of its institutionalized religion into a new revelation. In my view, although Edinger says that humanity is "on the verge" of a new God-image, he does not take the next step that Dourley does in arguing that we are *already* beyond Christianity.

Dourley bases his position on a careful reading of Jung's works, including his extensive correspondence with Father Victor White. One letter in particular illustrates Jung's view of the importance and necessity of the Christ symbol, even though what humanity—and God—need is something beyond. In a 1953 letter, Jung argued that on the one hand, Christ is still a valid symbol, that we are "still within the Christian aeon," and at the same time expressed that *what is needed for the evolution of consciousness is the integration of the all-good Christ with Christ's brother Satan.* Only through this integration, Jung wrote, can humanity move into a new era, but humanity is not yet prepared for this step: "Our society cannot afford the luxury of cutting itself loose from the *imitatio Christi,* even if it should know that the conflict with the shadow, i.e., Christ versus Satan, is only the first step on the way to the far-away goal of the unity of the self in God."[153]

This is so, he believed, because of the enormous and dangerous power of psyche and the threat from its archetypal energies to ego itself. The role of the institutional church has been and continues to be to protect the unprepared ego from a direct encounter with this immensity. In this regard, Jung wrote, "The vast majority of people are still in such an unconscious state that one should almost protect them from the full shock of the real *imitatio Christi.*"[154]

And yet such an encounter is required—demanded—of humanity for the *ongoing* incarnation of God through the process of individuation. What is to come, Jung maintained, is the surpassing of the Christian age with the coming of the Paraclete, the Holy Spirit:

> It is true, however, that the *imitatio Christi* leads you into your own very real and Christlike conflict with darkness, and the more you are engaged in this war and in these attempts at peacemaking helped by the anima, the more you begin to look forward beyond the Christian aeon to the Oneness of the Holy Spirit. ... The state of the Holy Spirit means a restitution of the original one-ness of the unconscious on the level of consciousness. That is alluded to, as I see it, by Christ's logion: "Ye are gods" (John 10:34). This state is not quite understandable yet. It is a mere anticipation.[155]

Jung brought this letter to a close with these words:

> Thus I am approaching the end of the Christian aeon and I am to take up Gioacchino's anticipation and Christ's prediction of the coming of the Paraclete. The archetypal

drama is at the same time exquisitely psychological and historical. We are actually living in the time of the splitting of the world and of the invalidation of Christ.

But an anticipation of a faraway future is no way out of this actual situation. It is a mere *consolamentum* for those despairing at the atrocious possibilities of the present time. Christ is still the valid symbol. Only God himself can "invalidate" him through the Paraclete.[156]

A note explained that Gioacchino (or Joachim) de Flora (ca. 1145-1201) was an "Italian mystic and theologian. He taught that there are three periods of world history: the Age of the Law, or of the Father; the Age of the Gospel, or of the Son; and the Age of the Holy Spirit, or of Contemplation. His teachings were condemned by the Fourth Lateran Council, 1215."[157]

Jung recognized the coming of a new age but argued that a new symbol uniting the opposites of Christ-Satan cannot be created by conscious ego but must emerge from the collective unconscious. His letter to Father White did not reference his many writings which state that such an evolutionary step can happen only when self and the conscious ego participate together.

I hear Jung speaking with two minds here. The Christian aeon is coming to an end; we live in a time of a tremendous psychic evolution (or revolution), which will "invalidate" the Christ as symbol, but the new symbol has not yet emerged. I can only wonder if Jung himself, writing in the last decade of his tremendously creative and productive life, was not yet ready, or able, to accept that his thought had already taken him beyond the Christian aeon into the new dispensation.

Dourley, in contrast, recognized that this new age is already upon us, revealed outwardly by the flight by many from institutional churches to agnosticism, atheism, or the plethora of alternative spiritual movements, including "spiritual but not religious." He underscored Jung's recognition that psyche is basically religious and has within it the power to heal or to destroy. The destruction comes in the form of fundamentalist literalizing and concretizing psyche's messages, the belief in "one God"—"our God"—and the splitting of good and evil so apparent in today's world. Dourley then raised the question, "How can humanity deal with its inescapable faith-engendering facility without being destroyed by it?"[158]

The answer, Dourley wrote, lies within the individual who will "stay in conscious dialogue with that inner power which is the source of the world's religions."[159] He believed that Jung's psychology "holds out to the Christian or devotee of any stripe not the possibility of the revitalization of the dead but rather a surpassing compensation which would function with the force of a new revelation or dispensation."[160]

Dourley's argument and Jung's reference to the Paraclete bring to mind a similar statement in *Memories, Dreams, Reflections*: "A further development of [the Christian] myth might well begin with the outpouring of the Holy Spirit upon the apostles, by which they were made into sons of God, and not only they, but all others who through them and after them received the filiatio—sonship of God."[161]

Lionel Corbett: The Uncharted Territory of Immediate Experience

Lionel Corbett finds the religious impulse alive and well in the individual psyche, quite apart from any institutionalized dogma, including of course Christianity. In his book *The Religious Function of the Psyche*, we see that Corbett recognizes Jung's belief that the human is, by nature, religious, but as Corbett learned from his clients, individuals' images of the divine today are often not contained within traditional institutional religions. He himself writes of having had a numinous experience in a motel lobby in Mobile, Alabama.

Traditional religions, he argues, fail to recognize the validity of such personal experiences and instead ask their adherents to accept certain symbols and dogma as relayed by the institution, rather than their own personal experience. Corbett provides a bridge from the archetypal levels of experience to the personal, between "archetype and everyday psychodynamics."[162]

Corbett seems to have stepped out from the Christian aeon of which Jung speaks, into the uncharted territory of immediate experience of the divine, the transpersonal, or what Jung calls the objective psyche or collective unconscious. To find validity in one's own experience is, of course, Jung's own devout belief and the basis for all his theories. Nevertheless, Jung felt, to the end of his life, that the Christ symbol is still needed by Western humanity to provide a defense against the shadow side of the unconscious which could overwhelm the individual and the collective. Yes, there is something beyond Christianity—the coming of the Holy Spirit (still speaking in the language of Christianity but of course referring to something behind that language). But the symbol that would integrate the dark and the light has not yet appeared, so Jung believed at the end of his life. Corbett and Elizabeth Boyden Howes believe differently.

Taking the position that his depth-psychological approach to the sacred will not speak to those still held within the Judeo-Christian tradition, Corbett says that Christianity "represents a perspective which may not do justice either to Jesus himself or to the real profundity of his story.[163] Edinger also held this possibility open with his emphasis (drawn from Jung) on Christ as the great exemplar of individuation and his view that Christianity's "underlying meaning is the quest for individuation."[164]

Wayne Rollins: The Bible as an Expression of Psyche

Biblical scholar Wayne Rollins was the first to define psychological biblical criticism as having the hermeneutical intent of examining "texts, their origination, authorship, modes of expression, their construction, transmission, translation, reading, interpretation, their transposition into kindred and alien forms, and the history of their personal and cultural effect, as expressions of the structure, processes, and habits of the human psyche, both in individual and collective manifestations, past and present."[165]

Like Jung, Rollins sees the Bible "as a psychic product, reality, symptom, and event, and as a source of commentary on the nature, life, habits, pathology, health and purpose of the psyche/soul."[166] All the stories of the Bible, Old and New Testaments, can be read this way, as mythic and therefore psychological. New Testament stories, then, become explanatory tales about the human-divine relationship, relevant for all of us rather than the account of a once-only incarnation of God.

It is apparent from this brief overview how Jung's insights have inspired other psychologists and biblical scholars to read the Bible anew and reinterpret the entire Judeo-Christian tradition. Thank goodness there is no uniform consensus stifling Jung's creative approach which continues to give birth to new ideas. The process of psyche's unfolding is never-ending. For my part, the Christian story of Jesus approached psychologically, stripped of the moralistic and dogmatic interpretations that have, I believe, burdened and deadened it, offers a creative way to life here and now. Next I turn to Elizabeth Howes' groundbreaking work with the historical Jesus and his teachings. It was her interweaving of New Testament critical theory with Jung's depth psychology that opened new and vital avenues for understanding Jesus's relevance for modern individuals dissatisfied with the traditional religious approach.

Chapter 3

Elizabeth Howes's Search
for the Historical Jesus

Jesus was pre-Christian and perhaps post-Christian.[167]
— Elizabeth Boyden Howes

Elizabeth Boyden Howes, a twentieth-century Jungian therapist, took Jung's approach to the Christian myth—Christ as a *symbol* of being fully human—a step further, focusing on the *experient* (the person undergoing the experience), Jesus of Nazareth. Howes began studying the Synoptic Gospels in the 1930s, with New Testament scholar Henry Burton Sharman, as an account of a historical figure, a person who lived on earth and followed his destiny to its end. Though she was influenced by Jung's ideas about the archetypal Christ, Howes maintained her focus on "Jesus the man." In her 1984 book, *Jesus' Answer to God*, she presented her core belief that it is possible—and essential—to extract the figure of the human being, Jesus of Nazareth, from the divine Christ figure.[168]

The Pre-Easter Jesus

New Testament scholar Marcus Borg distinguished between "the pre-Easter Jesus and the post-Easter Jesus."[169] The former is "the historical Jesus, Jesus as a figure of history before his death."[170] The latter is "the Jesus of Christian tradition and experience. ... Jesus as the living risen Christ of Christian experience and tradition."[171] Elizabeth Boyden Howes's method and interpretations made clear that she sought the "pre-Easter Jesus":

> [*Jesus' Answer to God*] describes the life and person of Jesus shorn of Christian accretions and disidentified from archetypal identifications—Jesus living his life and his personal myth prior to the later Christian myth. When the original figure can be uncovered from the Christian overlay, he can be seen as bringing in a whole new psychological and religious evolution which could be a vitally transforming power. Jesus was pre-Christian and perhaps post-Christian.[172]

Howes believed in a human Jesus whose relationship to his God was transformed in his baptism and wilderness experience and who, for the rest of his life, sought to teach others what he had learned. And what he taught, in Howes's view, was very different from what Christianity has conveyed for the past two thousand years. For Howes, Jesus was a man related to the self, symbolized by Christ, and because of this, *he was able to show us a life fully lived.* Howes saw a man connected with his deepest source, what he called God and what depth psychology knows of as the God-image or self. *Although Jesus knew his connection with his source, Howes believed that he never identified with it, nor did he see himself as "Son of God" or as Messiah.* It was this Jesus and his teachings—and their significance for each of us—who Howes sought.

For Howes, the significance of the historical Jesus is in how he related to God—by which she means the depth-psychological God-image, the self—and the consequences of this relationship for the evolution of consciousness. With this sense, she brings Jung's depth perspective to her study of the historical Jesus, and I believe this is one of her major contributions.

Paradoxically, it was in the Synoptic Gospels, a primary source for Christianity's story of the God-Man/Savior, where she found teachings that can lead us into a new era in which each of us recognizes that we must carry our own cross and not look to Jesus to carry it for us. Howes's view, shared by Jung, was that we experience many deaths on many crosses along the road of life, each one followed by new life. Jung called this journey *individuation*, a life lived with choice and contributing to the evolution of consciousness of both the individual and the self. Bringing the depth-psychological perspective to the historical critique of the Synoptic Gospels helps us see the journey of individuation lived out in the life of one human being and thus serves as a model for the journey each of us can live out in our own lives.

Howes's next contribution was in questioning the continued value of the Christian myth itself: "We must ... realize that what has been the Christian myth no longer holds the deep values of the symbols of death and rebirth it has carried for vast numbers of people during two thousand years of history. For many, the traditional is still the main expression and carrier of religious truth. But for countless others, it does not have vital meaning."[173]

Howes's Search for Meaning

Lionel Corbett wrote, "[Christianity] represents a perspective which may not do justice either to Jesus himself or to the real profundity of his story."[174] Howes agrees, and goes a step further, pointing to the profundity found when Jesus's life and teachings are examined psychologically. She carried Jung's theory of the Christ as symbol of the self even beyond Jung's formulation through the seminar method of study that she helped develop and through her focus on the life and teachings of the historical Jesus.

Howes appreciated Jung's view of archetypes, with Christ as a symbol of the self. But she and Jung had important differences regarding the historical Jesus. Jung's view, expressed in his letter to Upton Sinclair, is that "the essence of Christian tradition is by no means the simple man Jesus whom we seek in vain in the Gospels, but the lore of the God-man and his cosmic drama."[175] Howes's contrasting belief is that:

> Analytical Psychology ... has provided the most com- prehensive and satisfactory explanation of the meaning of Christian dogma, and the experiences behind it, through an understanding of the archetypes. It has given us the possibility of interpreting such dogma on a psychological- mythological basis. ... But Analytical Psychology, too, has neglected the experient Jesus of the Synoptic Gospels ... as a genuine human contributor to the development of religious consciousness.[176]

Elsewhere, she wrote, "When the original figure can be uncovered from the Christian overlay, he can be seen as bringing in a whole new psychological and religious evolution which could be a vitally transforming power."[177]

During a visit to Zürich in the 1950s, Howes had the opportunity to meet with Jung: "Once, in a personal conversation with Jung, when I was explaining my work with the Records, he pounded his fist on his chair and said, 'My God, I've never heard anyone treat Jesus as an individual. I've only been interested in the dogmatic Christ.' A wonderful few minutes of dialogue followed."[178]

How I wish she had recorded those "wonderful few minutes of dialogue." In the absence of such a report, we're left with two questions: Is there a real difference between Jung and Howes in their regard for the significance of the archetypal Christ and the historical Jesus? What is the impact on our understanding of the significance of the Christian myth for our lives today when the emphasis is placed on a historical Jesus, a "real human being," living out his conscious journey of individuation, as Howes believed?

Theory into Practice

Howes was introduced to the study that became her life's work when she attended a seminar in 1931 led by New Testament scholar Henry Burton Sharman. Sharman had developed a parallel presentation of the three Synoptic Gospels, which is published as *Records of the Life of Jesus*, and which was the text of study in his seminars, held for five or six weeks each summer in the Canadian woods to assist participants in finding their own answers to this search for Jesus and the meaning of his teachings.

Howes was "gripped" by the work, as she recounts in an oral history recorded years later,[179] continued to study with Sharman, and soon thereafter began leading the seminar informally known as *Records*. She continued doing so for fifty years, until she was in her seventies.

In 1956, she and two associates, Sheila Moon and Luella Sibbald, founded the Guild for Psychological Studies to continue the work she'd been doing at that point for two decades. The location for the seminars was moved from Southern California to a secluded retreat in Lake County, north of San Francisco, called Four Springs. In addition to *Records*' study, Howes, Moon, Sibbald, and their many associates added myths of other cultures, such as Greek and Native American, always in search of the depth-psychological significance for the lives of individuals today.

Depth psychology had not been a part of Sharman's perspective. It was Howes who introduced it into the seminars in the late 1930s, after studying the work of psychologist Fritz Künkel and then of C. G. Jung. She and her Guild cofounders attended the opening of the Jung Institute in Zürich in 1948, and continued to visit there in succeeding years.[180] Howes herself, after other professional study, became an analyst in the Jungian tradition. She received her PhD from the University of California at Berkeley in 1945.

Sharman's participants had the luxury of spending five or six weeks at Camp Minnesing, 150 miles north-northwest of Toronto, to work their way through the *Records* book from beginning to end. The Guild's seminars were later shortened, and when they were last offered in the early 2000s, they were sixteen or seventeen days, still a residential immersion from morn till night working with depth psychology and the Synoptic Gospels. Mornings were devoted to study of selected texts, guided by trained leaders in a way similar to what Sharman had done in the early twentieth century.

Throughout the morning, one of the group leaders put "into the circle" what Howes called the "creative question" to elicit a "creative response,"[181] to encourage each participant to "wrestle" with the day's topic. The purpose of the question was not to lead the group toward a particular way of understanding or even to consensus, but for each individual to come to their own understanding of the material. Questions offered different perspectives on the Gospel texts to help participants reexamine the Christian myth.

Henry Burton Sharman had received his PhD from the University of Chicago Department of Theology in 1906. The book he created in 1917, *Records of the Life of Jesus,* presented a three-columned parallel version of the Synoptic Gospels which allowed students to see similarities and differences among the stories. Studying in this way, participants were able to come to their own decisions about which Gospel might have been the earlier version, which stories rang the most true, and what were the meanings of the similarities and differences. The Guild for Psychological Studies revised the *Records* book in 1991 using the Revised Standard Version translation of the text and included references not only to Hebrew Scripture, which Sharman had included, but also to the non-canonical Gospel of Thomas.

To Sharman's historical-critical study, Howes and her associates added expressive art, mime of selected Gospel passages, movement to music, inner dialogues, ritual, imagination, and silence, all designed to open participants to the depths of the unconscious. The seminar method wove techniques that drew upon mind, body, and soul, conscious and unconscious, to encourage participants to hear and understand the old stories anew.

To explore the imaginal techniques that were central to the Guild method, I will also draw on a book Howes cowrote with Sheila Moon, *The Choicemaker*, in which they present their guiding philosophy, which was parallel to Jung's own. "Man was created for the sake of choice! ... The words imply that man's destiny (and his planet's destiny) is bound up with his ability to make wise choices."[182] *The Choicemaker* presents mythic themes found in the Bible and discusses methods of working with these themes symbolically that are relevant for people today.

As I present the learning processes of the Guild seminars, I draw on a multitude of sources. In *Jesus' Answer to God*, Elizabeth Boyden Howes presented and commented on the major texts and themes of each day of a typical sixteen-day seminar. One of the central techniques of the seminar method—the creative question—is discussed in "The Eternal Question: What is it? Who Asks it?" Another source on the method is Walter Wink's *The Bible in Human Transformation*. Another Guild leader, Elizabeth Petty, wrote about the contribution of play-dialogues to the seminar process in "Drama and Religious Dialogue." And I draw from my notes from a yearlong class, "Transformation, Truth, Transition, Training," led by John Petroni to prepare Guild people to lead the *Records* seminar.

To understand the Guild's biblical critical approach, I present a brief overview of this method as discussed in Robert Funk and Roy Hoover's *The Five Gospels*, and turn to psychotherapist and biblical scholar Hal Childs for discussion of this method specific to the Guild's work. Childs sees the value of historical critical work as far more than trying to find a historical figure and his teachings. Rather, he says, the "historical critical method is a process in the differentiation and evolution of consciousness," and he refers to it as "spiritual and psychological practice."[183]

The critical work is only one element of the Guild method. In 1973, Howes and Moon wrote *The Choicemaker* to present many of the psychological techniques engaged to support "Holy Intercourse" between conscious and unconscious. Of these techniques, biblical scholar and Guild associate and leader Walter Wink says, "To the critical insights and the questioning method of her New Testament mentor, Henry Burton Sharman, Howes has added symbolic analysis and psychological insights drawn from her training under Fritz Künkel and Carl G. Jung."[184]

Wink recognized the addition of exercises to engage the imagination as enhancing the seminar's transformative value. In these is "a recovery of the revelatory function of art," which he saw as a way to make the story in the text "our story—that is, when feeling and insight merge in the symbolic matrix of our being—then the insight furthers the self-formative process."[185]

A Depth Psychological "Hearing" of Jesus's Life and Teachings

Who is the Jesus Howes finds when she looks at his life and teachings as portrayed in the Synoptic Gospels through the lens of analytical psychology? She finds a man who underwent a life-changing psychological transformation in the baptism experience[186] and "was driven" (as Mark 1:12 tells it) into the wilderness to wrestle with the consequences of that experience. Howes regards the baptism and the wilderness as essentially one great experience by which the Holy Spirit, messenger of God, entered into the human Jesus. "A change in the God-image was coming into being. A new I-Thou Process was born."[187] Howes regards this baptism experience as "the pivotal moment which conditioned everything that came into his life."[188]

Behind the Christian story she sees a man whose mission was to preach and to teach—always out of his baptism/wilderness experience— "not out of a desire for *imitatio Christi*, but because of a genuine challenge to find one's own full consciousness."[189] He taught that the kingdom of God is within, among, and between us, and that it is available to all who choose "the narrow gate" that brings life.

The analytical-psychological lens shows a man who knew that he was indeed a child of God, as all women and men are, but did not identify himself with the Messiah/Savior/Christ. This lens shows a Jesus who spoke of a "Son of man" who was not an apocalyptic Savior, nor only himself, but represented a quality or potential within all humans that brought them into relationship with God. This is the Son of man who is "Lord even of the sabbath"[190] and "has authority on earth to forgive sins."[191] Reading the synoptics this way reveals a man who knew about and included good and evil, light and dark in all humans *and in God*.

Howes doesn't claim that Jesus was the first depth psychologist: "I think it questionable whether Jesus knew of individuation in the more specific definition of that term as given by Dr. Jung."[192] She also doesn't use theistic language to describe a supernatural God *out there* who intervenes in our physical reality, to whom we pray, who judges, rewards, and punishes us. Instead, she believed that Jesus taught "that there is an element in man to be trusted, a center to be achieved, a new man to be born through responsibility and transformation."[193]

Howes's View of the Transcendent

Throughout her writings, Elizabeth Boyden Howes uses the language of depth psychology—the words *self* and *image of God*—as well as *God*, as Jung did. She also speaks of the *transcendent* (as did Jung) when, for example, she says, "This book's approach is based on the facts that Jesus lived his own inner myth as the immanent expression of God transcendent and incorporated it into his personal history, and taught others how to live their history. ... The Holy Spirit which had resided in the transcendent God became imminent in the psyche of the man Jesus."[194] Discussing Jesus's baptism experience, she says:

What was happening on the side of God? What had been heretofore held within the Transcendent now moved. A mutational shift was occurring—perhaps on both sides of the God-human dialogue. What was the God-presence needing? What was the human bringing to God and human evolvement? … A new radical alteration of consciousness had occurred.[195]

Like Jung, Howes recognized the reality of something transcendent—greater than a human ego-personality—from which arises the human-divine dialogue. But the question remains whether she was speaking of this transcendent God psychologically or metaphysically. As I searched through her writings for an answer, I found frequent references that only gave clues. For example: "He lived in relationship to the very deepest forces within himself and in the Universe."[196] Again she wrote (referring to the "I"): "It is then creatively submissive to the Mystery, and the Mystery, by becoming manifest in the individual, is potentially manifest in the outer world and its history."[197]

And here is an example in which she was clearly drawing an analogy between God and God-image and self. Referring to the baptism experience, she wrote, "This immanent quality, the indwelling of God in the psyche, the *imago dei*, the Self as the holy Other within, marked the beginning of newness of Jesus."[198] Note that she says, "the Self *as* the holy Other within." Both still existed in her thinking—Self and holy Other, one "inner," the other "outer." Is this "Other" a metaphysical or psychological concept?

Howes was much clearer in distinguishing between "supernatural" and "supranatural" when she discussed Jesus's actions told in the healing and miracle stories. In her discussion of one of these, she wrote:

Super-natural, as distinguished from supra-natural, power is seen as a special power exhibited by a human (here it is Jesus) in performing acts against natural laws. Supranatural power is the power *within* nature, beyond most human knowledge but not including a special power. It allows for all the discoveries today in the fields of nuclear physics and depth psychology of heretofore unheard-of-things but things within natural law.[199]

Clearly Howes understood Jesus's actions as occurring within the laws of nature. But was there a supernatural God in her thinking? Perhaps the best answer to what she meant by God was this brief statement made at the end of a presentation in 1984: "It may not be inappropriate to end by saying that we each need to find our own answer to God, as Jesus found his. We have really tonight defined God, not in an abstract way, but as the ever-emergent mystery from deepest depth to the height of fulfillment."[200]

What is important for our understanding of Howes's work is that, however she defined God and the transcendent, she made a clear distinction between the human ego-personality and that something that is greater, which Jung variously called psyche, self, and the archetype of wholeness. For both Howes and Jung, the conscious ego-personality is always in service to that transcendent self, which both of them sometimes called the image of God and sometimes God.

Christianity's Gifts and Failings

In the early 1950s, Howes was confirmed into the Episcopal Church in San Francisco by Bishop Kilmer Myers. She told a gathering of several friends afterward, "If I'm going to deal with what I think Jesus is talking about, which is beyond and separate from the Christian myth, I've got to get deeper into the Christian myth in order to get out of it, and that's why I've joined the church. … I've joined it with great sincerity, [but] I won't be staying in it."[201]

She addressed the relevance of Christianity today in her writings and directly in her final book, *Jesus' Answer To God*. Discussing Jesus's final hours, his prayer in Gethsemane, and his anguished death on the cross, Howes wrote that although Jesus died, "the Spirit of God did not die but could move out into the world in a new way."[202] She was not saying that this "new way" is found in a resurrected Christ, but in the new relationship with the self that each person finds for themselves.

Here is Howes's greatest criticism of Christianity:

Christianity has historicized (or made literal) the inner mythic elements Jesus lived and taught, and therefore there has been a mythologizing of the history of the man. The deep interior truths leading to individual consciousness that Jesus manifested have been turned into seemingly historical events which became dogma that had to be believed.[203]

She described Jesus as a human being living in relationship with God, with self, wrestling with what this relationship called him to do and be in this life. The historical significance of his life—a human being living out his destiny as each of us is to do—became lost in the mythic story of a God-human Savior who would take away the sins of humankind.

What were mythic experiences have been made into history. His baptism and wilderness experiences are seen as historical events in which God did indeed intervene into the world and proclaim, "You are my beloved son"[204] or "This is my beloved son."[205] The mythic nature of the story is lost. A transformative, life-changing event—which happens to many human beings—becomes the exclusive experience of Jesus. His life experiences then became codified into creeds and dogma to be *believed*, not lived by each of us.

Yet despite this criticism of Christianity, Howes believed it has had great value by keeping alive the myths and symbols that were attached to Jesus, which otherwise might have been lost.

In spite of all inadequacies and failures, the power of the Christian message cannot be underestimated. At Sinai monotheism (one God—I AM) was a great spiritual mutation. With Jesus, this evolved God found a dwelling place within the individual Self as another spiritual mutation. ... If these values had not been carried [by the Christian myth and religion], we would not have available the truths within them. The consciousness of Jesus of Nazareth, however distorted, would not be available to be understood, as a journey possible for each of us.[206]

Although Howes doesn't clarify what she means by "this evolving God," she expresses in many writings the belief that God (self) itself is in an evolutionary process. Jung makes this point in his controversial "Answer to Job," in which he concludes that it is Job who emerges the better "man" in this encounter with a divided, unconscious God.

Her phrase "within the individual Self" reveals Howes's failure to address or perhaps recognize the question of whether self is "inside" the human, or the human is in self. As Roger Brooke underlines, Jung sometimes falls into this confusion himself, but then again states clearly that the human is in psyche (a word he often used as synonymous with self), not psyche in the human. Would Howes accept *psyche* and *self* as synonymous? Would she agree that "we are in psyche," rather than psyche in us? My guess is that these are not questions that would concern her. She was concerned with guiding individuals to recognize their own relationship to this self, this God, which we experience as "my" self. Her language is visionary, even evangelistic in the sense of a passionate advocate for the transformation of the individual ego's relationship to God, but it is not precise or scholarly. She says as much herself:

It is out of my passionate concern for persons wanting fulfillment and for the ongoingness of the planet ... that I have been searching for the root meaning in and of Jesus, and the value of that meaning for individuals and for society. ... Will there be enough consciousness in some of us to help the Yes overcome all the Nos in our world?[207]

My intent is to convey Howes's basic beliefs about the significance of Jesus's life and teachings for people today, which first and foremost means to understand them psychologically. Howes believed the problem was that Christian symbols and myths were projected onto Jesus rather than being recognized as something in each "projector" himself or herself. Howes gave as an example the phrase *only-begotten Son*, which makes Jesus's baptism experience *unique* to him. She believed that Jesus's true message was, "All persons could become sons or daughters through inner awareness and changes, but not through belief."[208] Another example is the sentence *He died for our sins*, in which Jesus was made scapegoat and human beings are thereby cut off from the "archetypal redemptive process"[209] that each of us must live out.

Howes discusses three other losses:

1. We've lost "an authentic Jesus, a full image of God, and finally the need for consciousness of each person in human relationships."[210] This has meant "the loss of Jesus' own human reality, his struggle for the achievement of consciousness through dialogue with his God. He is seen too often as *acted upon*, not himself acting and taking responsibility for helping God."[211]

2. We've lost the "dark opposite," Jesus's teachings about the reality of evil and the opposites in God, conveyed so clearly in Hebrew scripture. We've also lost the *direct experience of God* present in Hebrew scripture, now mediated by "belief in Jesus as Christ."[212]

3. The greatest loss, she wrote, "has been the challenge to individual consciousness. In Christianity, the greater collective images of the church have held people,"[213] but occasionally "the true essence of the Self incarnate in a person"[214] emerges, as in Gandhi; she contends that Christianity neglected "the experience of Jesus. … Christianity has been and is a religion about Jesus or Jesus Christ. It has centered on the individual's experience of Christ as Saviour rather than on the relationship of the man Jesus to God. … The human catalyst has been forgotten."[215]

Did Howes think the time had come to move beyond Christianity? At the beginning of her introduction to *Jesus' Answer to God*, she called Jesus a "forerunner" for a new age. In "Analytical Psychology and the Synoptic Gospels," she addressed those for whom Christian symbols "are dead or dying," those "to whom the symbol of Christ is sterile," and those "whose experience of life demands a more inclusive God than Christianity has offered."[216] For these people, "what originally was the container for spiritual meaning has ceased to be so, and the individual is driven to search for a new inner experience of the reconciliation of the opposites leading to wholeness and peace."[217]

In *Jesus' Answer to God*, Howes presented a way of seeing that, she believed, revealed a Jesus before Christianity: "Jesus living his life and his personal myth prior to the later Christian myth."[218] This is a Jesus who speaks to women and men of all times about how to live their own lives. In her other writings, Howes also presented a Jesus of Nazareth whose life was "centered on his relation to God, the kingdom of God, the world of history, and the inner world of the soul,"[219] contending, "When the original figure can be uncovered from the Christian overlay, he can be seen as bringing in a whole new psychological and religious evolution which could be a vitally transforming power."

A New Vision of Jesus

Elizabeth Boyden Howes believed that Christianity overlooked the experience of Jesus the human and that analytical psychology "neglected the experient Jesus of the Synoptic Gospels."[220]

Yet by this omission, is it not possible that Analytical Psychology has made somewhat the same mistake that Christianity made—that is, to equate the experience of Jesus and the experience about the projections *upon* Jesus as Savior. If the experiences are *not* the same—and I believe they are not—then many questions must be asked and answered.[221]

Through careful study of the Synoptic Gospels, Howes believed, we can find our way through the projections to the experience of Jesus the human being. The *Records* book facilitates historical-critical study by setting the Synoptic Gospels side-by-side in parallel form, so students can judge for themselves whether the stories told in one Gospel are the same or different from another, why that might be so, and what difference it makes. Walter Wink points out that bringing critical questions to the text relieves the Bible and the Synoptic Gospels from their unquestioned authority and "can release us from the dogmas of biblical inerrancy and verbal inspiration."[222]

Through this process, we begin to see a consistent personality emerge which, Howes argues, is that of Jesus before Christian dogma and creeds solidified him into a man-God, Savior, and thus shut the rest of us off from our own direct relationship with God. *Records* study, Howes believes, provides a remedy for this loss by focusing on the person. Thus, while Howes recognizes the contributions of analytical psychology to the study of the Synoptics, or *Records*, she also believes that *Records'* study makes a significant contribution to analytical psychology:

> My own conviction is that a historical-critical study of the three Synoptic gospels, by which one can get behind the Christian accretions and editorial comments to something authentic, is truly possible. ... If one does this, there is revealed an experient of religious reality, the man Jesus, confronted by the numinous and spending his brief life attempting to express it, to relate to it, but never to identify with it.[223]

I turn now to the hypotheses and conclusions that Howes came to out of her lifetime of study. Remember that the seminar method neither desires nor intends to lead or drive participants to particular conclusions, but to come to their own, and these may or may not agree with Howes's views. Those who participate in this method of study over many years find their own understanding changing about particular passages, even about the nature of Jesus and the meaning of his teachings. Howes herself often remarked during seminars, "I never thought of it that way before."

In presenting Howes's understanding, I focus on six major themes that emerge out of study of Jesus's life and teaching:

1. The experience and significance of the baptism and wilderness

2. Jesus's teachings about the kingdom of God and the way to the kingdom

3. Insights into Jesus's meaning of Son of man

4. Ways of answering Jesus's own question, "Who do you say I am?"

5. Jesus's final days, from his prayer at Gethsemane to his death on the cross

6. The empty tomb and what happened next

1. Beginnings: The Baptism/Wilderness Experience

All three Gospels tell about the baptism and wilderness, although there are differences among them. Here is a synopsis of these events with comments on some of the differences when they help us see whether these Gospels present different or similar images of Jesus.

The Gospel of Mark begins with Jesus's journey to the River Jordan. John the Baptist has been "preaching a baptism of repentance for the forgiveness of sins,"[224] and Jesus comes to John to be baptized. As Jesus rises up out of the water, "immediately he saw the heavens opened [torn open][225] and the Spirit descending upon him like [as] a dove."[226] And he heard a voice from heaven: "Thou art my beloved Son; with thee I am well pleased."[227] The story continues: "The Spirit immediately drove him out into the wilderness. And he was in the wilderness forty days, tempted by Satan.[228]

Howes sees Jesus coming to John to be baptized as "the conscious choice of a man facing his own myth."[229] She contrasts Jesus's experience with the traditional view of the human-God relationship: "In a tradition that has tended to see the experience of God as outward in history, it is significant to see that Jesus' experience here was inward, a sense of indwelling sonship. This descent is not to be equated with going into the unconscious, although possibly some of the same elements are operative."[230]

Elsewhere she says, "He had a fundamental experience of knowing God within as well as without, the Other, the numinous."[231] He was grasped by the spirit. "Today," Howes comments, "we would say that he found spirit in substance. A new aspect of the Self was born at that moment; the spirit found a new dwelling place."[232]

In the baptism experience, Jesus undergoes an enormous change and Howes imagines that he was faced with terrible questions about his new relationship with God. He might have thought he was the "special one sent for the redemption of his people, the anointed one, to serve either politically or in some other way."[233] But she asks, "Did Jesus here consider himself as being the Messiah or Christ; did he see himself in those terms? ... If he experienced salvation or rebirth and vocation, could he naturally entertain the idea of messiahship which many others also had at that time?[234]

Howes is referring to the messianic expectations of the Jewish people of the time—the hope for a new king (anointed one, Messiah) to be a political leader, a savior from Roman oppression, a provider of abundance to a hungry people. These are the kinds of questions Jesus might have been struggling with after his baptism experience.

"The Spirit immediately drove him out into the wilderness," where he is tempted.[235] Mark tells us nothing of these temptations. His only other words about this are, "He was with the wild beasts; and the angels ministered to him."[236] Howes says that in his wilderness experience, Jesus "goes to aloneness, to the inwardly and outwardly unexplored, to ponder on the meaning of the demands of his God on him."[237]

Matthew and Luke provide more details.[238] As Matthew tells the story, the tempter says, "If you are the Son of God, command these stones to become loaves of bread." Next, "the devil took him to the holy city, and set him on the pinnacle of the temple, and said to him, 'If you are the Son of God, throw yourself down; ... [and] angels ... will bear you up.'" And finally, "the devil took him to a very high mountain, and showed him all the kingdoms of the world and the glory of them," and he said Jesus could have all those things "if you will fall down and worship me." And in all cases, Jesus said no. "Man shall not live by bread alone, but by every word that proceeds from the mouth of God."[239] "Again it is written, 'You shall not tempt the Lord your God.'"[240] "Begone Satan! For it is written, 'You shall worship the Lord your God and him only shall you serve.'"[241]

Howes points out that the three "temptations" Jesus rejected were "central, sacred, deeply-cherished concepts of his people."[242] He declined to become a savior, whether political, supernatural, or economic, and in so doing, "Jesus is acting in a highly conscious way, struggling with deep archetypal images of his people. ... He is cutting through all orthodox religious expectations."[243]

Howes views Satan not as the evil tempter, but as "an inner aspect or facet of God pushing [Jesus] into great consciousness. Here is no duality, but a man confronted by possibilities within the nature of God. Jesus labels these elements Satanic after he has rejected them."[244] Each of the proposals, she reminds us, are "good images" held by the Jewish people, but Jesus chooses not for these collective desires, but for something greater—consciousness. What he rejects, in Howes's view, is the unconsciousness contained in the temptations offered by Satan. In her words, "God and Satan here are two aspects of a whole. ... The material hope for a Messiah is a lure from the dark side of God."[245] In his rejection, Jesus "is separating out and discriminating between elements within the archetype itself," a choice Howes sees as "bringing the Christ-image back within the psyche to its genesis or origin," an act which "fundamentally altered the archetype of the God-man relationship."[246]

Elsewhere, she says, "The Holy Spirit which had resided in the transcendent God became immanent in the psyche of the man Jesus. … Put in this depth, Jesus could say, 'The kingdom of God is within.' The spirit has come to a new home within human substance."[247] This is the experience Christianity made into a one-time event in the life of Jesus Christ, denying its significance for Jesus the man who lived out his historical life, and for all other men and women. In Howes's words, "The continuous incarnation was made into a one-time, one-person, one complete incarnation."[248]

The baptism/wilderness experience also makes apparent the two faces of God—the one who tempts and the one who comforts. As Mark says, "He was in the wilderness forty days tempted by Satan, and he was with the wild beasts; and the angels ministered to him."[249] Howes interprets:

> Wild beasts could be deep, instinctual, unconscious forces—powers not necessarily negative but overwhelming, dark realities that had been unleashed in the baptism experience as part of God's reality. At the same moment that he was with these "wild beasts," "angels" were also present as potential integrative forces, as presences and powers that need to be known. Both wild beasts and angels, then, may be manifestations of God.[250]

The consequences of these transformative events—the baptism and wilderness experiences—were, in Howes's view, that Jesus knew himself as human, not God. "He never doubted himself as a channel, but he always escaped inflation and arrogance which come from identification."[251] Howes believes that it is out of the life-changing experience of the baptism/wilderness that all of Jesus's teachings arose.

2. The Kingdom of God Is ...

In Howes's view, "Jesus's central religious message is contained in his concept of the actualization of the kingdom of God, the realm where God, He/She, reigns."[252] She discusses the many passages which appear throughout Jesus's teachings that describe what this kingdom is and how to reach or attain it.

Several passages from the Sermon on the Mount refer to gaining and losing life, and the kingdom of heaven. These are shown in Table 1. Howes discusses the first six and the last one, Matt. 7:21. Of the first passage, which speaks of the narrow and hard way, she says, "Perhaps no statement of Jesus' is more challenging, leaves gray so untouched, and stays with black and white."[253] As she notes, "There are ... two ways, two outcomes, and one choice,"[254] for life or destruction.

Then she asks, "What do the outcomes of life and destruction refer to?" and turns to the next five passages which suggest the answer: to go through the narrow gate to life is like good fruit, like the house built on rock; to choose the wide gate and destruction is like the evil fruit, the house that falls. She comments: "These are three vivid descriptions of outcomes. They can be characterized as a life of futility, boredom, sterility, hecticness, meaninglessness, versus a life of meaning, fulfillment, adventure, spontaneity."[255]

She comments further that the wide gate allows many people to enter. This represents the collective movement and contrasts with the narrow gate through which individuals can go only one at a time, with little "baggage or encumbrance."[256]

The final passage in Table 1 tells us that it is not the one who says, "Lord, Lord," who enters the kingdom of heaven, but the one "who does the will." One enters the kingdom—by doing, not just "calling Jesus 'Lord, Lord'—or perhaps calling anyone else 'Lord, Lord.'" Howes continues, "This in itself gives insight into where Jesus placed the emphasis, which was not on himself or any other religious figure, but on an attitude toward God."[257] I would add that the passage about building the house on rock also speaks about "doing," not merely "hearing," a point Howes doesn't make but which does not detract from her argument.

Table 1 **Teachings on Life and the Kingdom of God**
For the gate is narrow and the way is hard, that leads to life, and those who find it are few (Matt. 7:13-14; §38M).
You will know them by their fruits. Are grapes gathered from thorns, or figs from thistles? (Matt. 7:16; §38P).
So, every sound tree bears good fruit, but the bad tree bears evil fruit (Matt. 7:17; §38Q).
A sound tree cannot bear evil fruit, nor can a bad tree bear good fruit (Matt. 7:18; §38S).
Every tree that does not bear good fruit is cut down and thrown into the fire. Thus you will know them by their fruits (Matt. 7:19-20; §38T).
Every one then who hears these words of mine and does them will be like a wise man who built his house upon the rock; and the rain fell [. . .], but it did not fall [. . .]. And every one who hears these words of mine and does not do them will be like a foolish man who built his house upon the sand [. . .], and great was the fall of it (Matt. 7:24-27; §38W).
Not every one who says to me, 'Lord, Lord,' shall enter the kingdom of heaven, but he who does the will of my Father who is in heaven (Matt. 7:21; §38U).

Howes links the two outcomes: "It does not seem strange to assume that entrance into the way of Life and entrance into the kingdom of God would be describing the same thing. To be in the Kingdom is to have life."[258] The kingdom thus becomes not a place or a time, but an attitude and an action that is here and now. Choosing to do the will of God "can be done voluntarily." This was not a new concept; it was deeply embedded in Jewish tradition and belief. But, Howes continues, Jesus's teachings bring something new to the table: "The exhortation to do the will of God *assumes* that this will can be known, and can be acted upon if it is chosen."[259]

She then provocatively asks which comes first among interweaving factors of choosing, knowing, and doing the will of God: Does one specifically know what the will is before choosing to do it? Or does one make a commitment to do the will before specifically knowing what that will is? Howes suggests that if one looks to know the will before choosing to do it, "there is not necessarily any clarity of perception as to what the will of God is, because the choice to do it has not been made." And that "One's prejudiced, personal predilections will all color the choice."[260]

Howes references John Middleton Murry here: "The will of God known beforehand is not the will of God," suggesting an answer to the question whether we can know the will beforehand. In *Jesus' Answer to God,* she argues that to choose to do the will *before* one knows the will, even before the situation arises that demands action, "so alters the perception and so cleanses the personal desire that there is a much greater chance that the best and deepest value in the situation will be found."[261] "It is to affirm in all situations that no matter what the content is—pleasurable or painful, easy or difficult—we will act out of what we see as the Will of the highest and deepest value. ... It is to say that no matter where the Will leads, we will follow."[262]

The authority for making this discernment of what is the highest and deepest value and then choosing to do the Will, the choice for Life, lies within the individual, not in laws or creeds. Such discernment must include the possibility that our choice may turn out to be wrong, even when made as well as we can.

The choice to do the Will of God leads to Life, she continues, and leads to such a transformation of personality,

that it can be said one has entered the kingdom of God. …
Instead of the egocentric will that dominates and pushes us
into unfulfilled lives, it is possible now to see life lived in the
new kingdom of 'He/She.' Instead of constrained sterility,
futility, and unhappiness because we do not get our own
way, there is a new blossoming, a rebirth, and a new
purposiveness.[263]

The kingdom of God teachings are prominent in two other Gospel
accounts, several parables, and Jesus's statement, "The Kingdom is
within." I turn first to six of the parables that illustrate Howes's view
that Jesus is teaching not an apocalyptic message, but one of slow,
steady, and powerful growth both in society and in the individual. As
she turns her attention to the parables, Howes alludes to Jesus's
frequent adjuration, "He who has ears, let him hear," and she advises
her readers to come with "free eyes and ears" to ask of each parable,
"What is the central, dynamic new point about the Kingdom?"[264]

Table 2 presents these parables and asks, "Are the Kingdom
parables descriptions of a process pervading society or of a process
within one person?"[265] She considers the first four to be speaking of
the kingdom in society (parables of seeds and leaven), while the final
two address what the individual must do to attain the kingdom within.

What does Howes regard as the "new point" in each parable? The
first two are from Mark. The first tells of the man who sows a seed, and
it sprouts "he knows not how. The earth produces of itself." Then comes
the harvest, and the wheat is put to the sickle. Howes asks whether the
central point is "the slow growth of the Kingdom, or the cutting at
harvest time?"[266] The latter reminds us of John the Baptist's apocalyptic
preaching, while "the former describes the possibility of the kingdom
of God growing slowly in a natural, evolutionary way."[267] Such an
understanding is in direct contrast to the apocalyptic expectation of
the coming Messiah—an expectation widely held in Jesus's time. The
parable of the mustard seed tells not of a cataclysmic, apocalyptic event,
but of a small beginning that has the capacity to spread throughout the

Table 2 The Kingdom Is Like . . .
Mark's parables:
1. The kingdom of God is as if a man should scatter seed upon the ground, and should sleep and rise night and day, and the seed should sprout and grow, he knows not how. The earth produces of itself, first the blade, then the ear, then the full grain in the ear. But when the grain is ripe, at once he puts in the sickle, because the harvest has come (Mark 4:26-29; §48D-E).
2. With what can we compare the kingdom of God, or what parable shall we use for it? It is like a grain of mustard seed, which, when sown upon the ground, is the smallest of all the seeds on earth; yet when it is sown it grows up and becomes the greatest of all shrubs, and puts forth large branches, so that the birds of the air can make nests in its shade (Mark 4: 30-32; §48E).
Matthew's parables:
3. The kingdom of heaven may be compared to a man who sowed good seed in his field ... [I paraphrase here]: in the night the enemy sowed weeds among the wheat, which grew up with the wheat. The servants ask the master, "Didn't you sow good seeds?" And the master replies, "An enemy has done this." The servants said to him, "Then do you want us to go and gather them?" But he said, "No; lest in gathering the weeds you root up the wheat along with them. Let both grow together until the harvest; and at harvest time I will tell the reapers, Gather the weeds first and bind them in bundles to be burned, but gather the wheat into my barn" (Matt. 13:24-30; §48A-C).
4. The kingdom of heaven is like leaven which a woman took and hid in three measures of flour, till it was all leavened (Matt. 13:33; §48F).
5. The kingdom of heaven is like treasure hidden in a field, which a man found and covered up; then in his joy he goes and sells all that he has and buys that field (Matt. 13:44; §48N).
6. Again, the kingdom of heaven is like a merchant in search of fine pearls, who, on finding one pearl of great value, went and sold all that he had and bought it (Matt. 13:45-46; §48O).

land. Jesus is teaching that "The Kingdom will grow in a natural way from very small beginnings to an all-encompassing reality."[268] Jesus's preaching of a slow and natural growth of the kingdom, Howes concludes, is what is new.

She turns next to the four parables of Matthew. In the first, again there is the sower who sows good seed, but this parable tells us that "the enemy" came in the night and sowed the seeds of tares (weeds) so that the harvest included both wheat and weeds. The master lets both grow until the harvest, at which time the wheat and the weeds will be separated, the weeds to be burned. Howes notes that the emphasis of this parable may be "the fact that the wheat and the tares must grow together for a considerable time, or the fact that at the end they are divided and spread apart."[269] Again she points out that the latter is reminiscent of John the Baptist's apocalyptic preaching, whereas the first point, that the wheat and the weeds are permitted to grow together, is quite different.

Howes asks and answers, If there are enemies, wheat, and weeds within the kingdom, "What does this assume? That there is, along with the potential for growth or good, an enemy, a power *against* growth— the ambivalence—and … the distinction … is not always easy."[270] She raises the possibility that the words about separating wheat from weeds might be a later addition, splitting good from evil, leaving the kingdom to be only good, and she offers her understanding in contrast, "The Tree of the Knowledge of Good and Evil in the Garden of Eden reminds us of a Unity that contains opposites, but does not split them."[271]

Howes sees the parable about the leaven as speaking of "the potency and pervasiveness of the Kingdom, which is hidden and small to begin with, but which eventually infuses the whole."[272] It is her contention that these four parables speak not of cataclysmic, apocalyptic events but of slow growth from small but potent beginnings, a view that is in marked contrast to "dominant religious concepts of the time."[273]

Next she turns to the two parables in which, she believes, Jesus teaches how the kingdom grows in the individual as well as in society, and how one may attain the kingdom. Howes sees this kingdom as "inner," but that one must *take action* to enter it. "Surely we have arrived at Jesus' contribution, not as to how the Kingdom grows in society (as in the earlier parables) but how it comes to be born and grows in the individual."[274] While focusing on this *inner* kingdom, she asks, "What must the individual do to enter into the Kingdom?"[275] It must be "actualized in and by individuals."[276] Individuals must *act* to "enter" the kingdom. And what is that act? Thus far, Jesus has said it's to "do the Will," and now he adds, "*to sell all.*"

Jesus's hearers have heard him say the kingdom is here and now and it grows of its own accord (seeds that sprout; leaven). Now he explains what individuals need to do to enter. In one parable, a man finds a treasure planted in a field. In another, a merchant is actively seeking fine pearls. Both men instantly recognize the great value, and both are willing *to sell all* they have in order to attain it.

What does it mean "to sell all"? Howes describes it as "the most authentic action on which [Jesus] based his life and teaching, which is death-rebirth."[277] That is, "selling all" entails ego's choice to die to its own desires in order to live for the desires—the demands—of God, of the self. This is the journey and the choice we see lived to the end, when Jesus prays to his Abba, Father, at Gethsemane, "Remove this cup from me; yet not what I will, but what thou wilt."[278]

What does *all* mean? Material goods, success in the world? "Attitudes and egocentricities?"[279] Howes says that "negative self-will" has at its core "the determination to direct our own life the way we want to, the effort to personally control things as we want and to dictate them. ... Thus, the right to have things our own way seems to be the most precious possession one has, for it can and does determine everything else."[280] This, she says, is the "all" that we must sell:

To sell the "all," the one thing, means to renounce that right to choose specificity of one's own desire and to let oneself be molded by the Patterning of the moment. Through such conscious choice we give back to its true owner what we have been given. It is as if our life were on loan. We either take it and run away to shape it as we will, or we turn it back to its Source in a volitional act of choice which makes us co-creators with the process of God.[281]

Even though Howes includes Jung's theory about psyche and self in her study of the Synoptic Gospels, she does not use that language here and, I dare say, seems to confuse psychological and theological ideas. In so many places she speaks clearly in depth-psychological terms, so I would interpret the above statement as describing ego-personality's continuous interaction with the self, ego's choice *for self's goal*, not its own. The "Patterning" and the "Source" of which she speaks are that transcendent reality which she sees not as supernatural, but *supranatural—within nature—*even if beyond our comprehension at this time.

She asks, Does one sell all only once, or is it "a single and yet continuous act"? And she responds, "On the one hand it is a complete act as far as one's consciousness encompasses it, but on the other hand it must be renewed as new areas of the psyche are discovered."[282] She expands on this with her next question, "To whom do we sell?" to which she responds, "To God as Will, intentionality, desire to be discovered in all moments. Selling all to God requires a once-and-for-all affirmation that includes every known area of one's Self and that needs constantly to be repeated as new areas of Self are found to bring into the single act."[283]

This reminds us of Howes's belief that we make the choice to do the Will even before knowing what that will is and what will be demanded of us. It's a conscious choice to seek the higher value, whatever the situation. To make such a choice is to sell all of one's ego-desires in service to the self.

I turn now to a passage in Luke in which Jesus speaks about the kingdom, where it is, and when it will come. When the Pharisees ask when the kingdom is coming, Jesus answers, "The kingdom of God is not coming with signs to be observed; nor will they say, 'Lo, here it is!' or 'There!' for behold, the kingdom of God is in the midst of you."[284] Howes comments that the phrase "in the midst of you" can be translated either as "within you" or "between you." For Jesus to say, "The kingdom of God is within you," Howes believes, "is by far the most radical statement for his contemporaries."[285] It is, she adds, "a statement of the deepest truth Jesus knew out of the baptism-wilderness experience, for it was there that the God Jesus knew as a Jew—the transcendent process of the restless, wandering God—came into his being."[286] What had been projected outward onto the messianic hope is now turned inward. It is within the psyche. "An inner archetype was alive and experienced by Jesus, and history began to change."[287] This archetype, Howes believed, as did Jung, is the self.

While Howes makes much of the inner kingdom, the transcendent becoming immanent, she also stresses that the transcendent remains … transcendent. In an earlier discussion of this passage, she says, "Notice, he did not say 'only within you,' but 'within you,' leaving the presence of the kingdom of God as a Transcendent reality expressing itself in the social. This reality, he was saying, also has its counterpart inside the psyche."[288]

As she closes her discussion of the passages about the kingdom, Howes makes clear her position that Jesus did not say that *he* was the kingdom. It is not something, she contended, that will come in an apocalyptic way. It is here and now, among and within us, of tremendous value, and each individual is invited to enter "as he or she pays the price of entrance, which is to 'sell all' and 'do the will of God.'"[289]

Is Howes inconsistent in arguing that while the kingdom exists both within and without, we must take conscious action to enter it? On the surface, it may seem so, yet she is building on Jesus's own teachings that the kingdom is within, between, and among us; and yet we must "do the Will" and "sell all" to enter it. Using Jung's language, we may say that the process of individuation requires active engagement between the individual ego-personality and that self which is immanent and transcendent, a position that Howes also held. This exchange—the conscious choice to sell all and to do the will—"makes us co-creators with the process of God."[290] As Jung wrote, the individual is essential in the evolution of consciousness and, in Howes's words, in actualizing the Kingdom here and now. In Howes's view, "The birth of the Kingdom out of potentiality into a new reality, in the individual and in society, is the major thrust and dynamic of [Jesus'] message."[291] This is among the many original interpretations of Jesus's teachings and purpose that Howes made. Another was her hypothesis about the depth-psychological meaning of the words—and the concept they convey—*Son of man*.

3. The Son of man

The title of Howes's lecture, "Son of man—Expression of the Self?" conveys immediately her hypothesis, as she herself calls it, of a depth-psychological interpretation of an enigmatic phrase in both Hebrew Scripture and the New Testament. In this lecture, she said:

> I shall maintain that the term "Son of man" is related to but is not the same as the archetype of the Self, or to [sic] the God-Man archetype. It was used by Jesus to describe the main image which dominated his life and which can be found by others, as it describes in a rather rare way the Self as it operated through him. The "Son of man" phrase describes the Self *at work in concrete life*, a Self lived existentially, not as a hope or a vision; but it is not the same as the Self.[292]

She continued:

> My hypothesis is that Jesus himself historically did use the term "Son of man" about himself, and as a potential in others, but by it he referred to the ego-manifestation and

particularization of the Self archetype at his moment of history. It was his way to express the central archetype but not to identify with it or identify the Son of man and the Messiah-Christ image.[293]

Howes's hypothesis, seen as unorthodox, received much attention in *Records* study and is one of the central strands in Part Two of this book.

In *The Human Being: Jesus and the Enigma of the Son of the Man*, Walter Wink comments:

It was the seminal contribution of Elizabeth Boyden Howes, following the lead of her mentor Jung, to recognize that the "son of the man" was not a title or a nickname or a circumlocution or a myth, but an archetypal image. As an archetypal image it functions as a symbol of wholeness, less august and almighty than the Messiah or Christ, more mundane and daily than the heroes of myth, more a catalytic agent of transformation in the service of the Self than a symbol of the Self as such.[294]

In his introduction to the same book, Wink wrote:

In this book I explore the hypothesis that this opaque figure, the son of the man, is a catalyst for human transformation: unchanging and unchanged, yet changing those who dare to come in contact with it. It seems that within us, deeply buried or just below the surface, is something that knows better than we the contours of our true face, or that "new name that no one knows except the one who receives it," as Rev. 2:17 hints.[295]

Wink gives this "catalytic agent of transformation" several names: the Human Being, the Child of the Human One, Sophia's Child, the New Being, and the Sisterchild,[296] neither masculine nor feminine. Like

Howes, Wink believed that in the Son of man passages Jesus was referring not only to himself, but also to something within all persons: "The implication seems to be that Jesus intentionally avoided honorific titles, and preferred to be known simply as 'the man,' or 'the human being.' Apparently he saw his task as helping people become more truly human."[297]

"One is met by question-mark upon question-mark," writes Howes,[298] and Wink adds, "Scarcely any topic in New Testament studies has received more attention, and with less result."[299] Both work their way through what they consider the historical (as contrasted with the apocalyptic) passages in the Synoptic Gospels in which the phrase is used to come to their own understanding of what it might mean.

Howes notes that the phrase appears in the Gospel of John, in Acts, and in Revelation, as well as in Hebrew Scripture. But it is its use in the Synoptic Gospels that provides the grist for her study of what Jesus might have meant, for it is here that the *Son of man* phrase "comes to its fulfillment, as my thesis will be, in Jesus' own use of it."[300] Howes points out that in the Synoptic Gospels the phrase is used thirty-nine times—always from the lips of Jesus. No one else uses this phrase. Sometimes it's used in only one gospel, sometimes in two, sometimes in all three. She stressed that the phrase *Son of God*, on the other hand, was never said by Jesus, only by others.

Through the historical-critical method of New Testament scholarship, Howes identified twelve of the thirty-nine passages as "historical." Fourteen she identified as "apocalyptic," and thirteen as not clearly one or the other. The historical passages, she believed, "probably come from Jesus," whereas those she considers nonhistorical contain material with a "Christian" intent.

Here is an example of "an apocalyptic passage," drawn from Daniel 7:13.[301] The words are attributed to Jesus by all three Gospel writers, each in a slightly different way. I quote Mark: "And then they will see the Son of man coming in clouds with great power and glory. And then he will send out the angels, and gather his elect from the four winds, from the ends of the earth to the ends of heaven."[302]

In the twelve passages that she considers to be historical, Howes says, "There is no reference to a coming, to sending forth angels to gather together from the four corners of the earth, to clouds of heaven, or to an authority or a judgment."[303] These are the kinds of factors that distinguish apocalyptic from historical passages. In the former, the Son of man speaks of the future, not the present. He will come as judge from on high, "as divider, as cosmic authority with angels."[304] Jesus is *identified with* the Son of man, which Howes believes he did not do. It is in these passages that Howes sees what happened in the disciples after the death of their beloved leader: "The archetype of Christ as Son of man, having been consciously lived by Jesus, now falls into the unconscious through projection. And to study the non-historical passages is to study the Christ image in its archetypal, unlived, and projected form."[305]

I would restate it thus: The human face of the self, that is, the Son of man which Jesus lived consciously and which had come alive however briefly in his disciples, "now falls into the unconscious through projection."[306] It becomes the Christ most clearly represented in the Gospel of John. What was to be lived out "through personality"[307] has become something lived out only through Jesus Christ as the only Son of God, and was projected into the future when the Son of man would come in clouds of glory.

The twelve passages Howes considered to be historical are summarized in Table 3. As noted, when passages are studied in the course of a *Records* seminar, no conclusions are presented by the leaders, and no consensus on what Jesus might mean is sought or even desired. Questions are posed by the leaders to help participants question their own assumptions about what the passages may mean, but the leaders do not give their own interpretations or even the ones Howes presents in her writings. Her writings are available in the retreat library for any who wish to read them, but there is no encouragement or even desire by the leaders for participants to read them. The purpose of the seminar method is for participants to use their own critical faculties to arrive at their own interpretations, to speak with their own authority, and not rely on Howes, Jung, or the leaders to provide answers.

The questions asked in the seminar about Son of man passages include these: Is Jesus referring to humankind in general? to a quality in Jesus only? to Jesus as the Messiah? a quality available in each person as well as in Jesus? Questions like these help us clarify for ourselves how Jesus saw himself in relation to the *Son of man*, and help us reflect on who Jesus is for us.

Howes's conclusion was that the Son of man speaks "in terms of vocation, functioning, activity, and inner power. [Son of man] includes a sense of destiny and fulfillment. In this sense, these Synoptic passages may be opening for us a description of the Self-in-behaviour, existential-incarnation rather than projected potential."[308]

In Table 3, the first example tells about the healing of the "palsied man." Contrary to Christian understandings that Jesus healed the man, Howes points out that Jesus didn't say "I heal you," or "I forgive you." He said, "Your sins are forgiven," and then, "But that you may know that the Son of man has authority on earth to forgive sins [...]" he told the man to get up and walk. Howes wrote, "Forgiveness is redefined here as the affirmation of the margin of freedom, however tiny, whereby a man can move from his bed, from his neurotic determinism, into action."[309] She continued, "For Jesus, healing came from a personal relationship to a God whose essence is a freedom in the individual, a God who demands only that we use that freedom in a turning toward our deeper sources... Son of man is the expression of the Self making possible forgiveness of sins as an individual internal act.[310]

Questions often posed in a seminar to push people's thinking were, "Who did the healing? Was it Jesus? Was it the palsied man? Was it a relationship between them?"[311] The central question in Table 3, "Who do men say that I am?" is summarized in the ninth example.

Table 3
Summary of "Son of man" Passages Howes Considers Historical

1. Jesus is criticized by the scribes after a scene in which Jesus says to a paralyzed man, "My son, your sins are forgiven" and then, "Which is easier, to say to the paralytic, 'Your sins are forgiven,' or to say, 'Rise, take up your pallet and walk?'" And he continues: "But that you may know that the Son of man has authority on earth to forgive sins"—he said to the paralytic—'I say to you, rise, take up your pallet and go home'" (Mark 2:1-12; §29).

2. After picking grain on the sabbath, Jesus and his disciples are questioned by the Pharisees for doing "what is not lawful on the sabbath." Jesus replies: "And he said to them, 'The sabbath was made for man, not man for the sabbath; so the Son of man is lord even of the sabbath'" (Mark 2:23-28; §32).

3. In a lengthy account which differs in its particulars among the three Gospels but is essentially the same story, Jesus is portrayed as healing "a blind and dumb demoniac," and then is accused by Pharisees that he has acted "by Beelzebul, the prince of demons." Jesus then gives the well-known discourse "How can Satan cast out Satan?" and concludes: "Therefore I tell you, every sin and blasphemy will be forgiven men, but the blasphemy against the Spirit will not be forgiven. And whoever says a word against the Son of man will be forgiven; but whoever speaks against the Holy Spirit will not be forgiven" (Matt. 12:22-32; §45).

4. A man says to Jesus he will follow him wherever he goes, and Jesus replies: "Foxes have holes, and birds of the air have nests; but the Son of man has nowhere to lay his head" (Luke 9:58; §81A).

5. The imprisoned John the Baptist sends his disciples to ask Jesus, "Are you the one who is to come, or shall we look for another?" (Matt. 11:2; Luke 7:19). After a long discourse, first to the disciples and then to the crowds about him, Jesus reminds them that when John the Baptist comes eating no bread and drinking no wine, he is accused of having a demon. Yet, "The Son of man has come eating and drinking; and you say, 'Behold, a glutton and a drunkard, a friend of tax collectors and sinners!' Yet wisdom is justified by her deeds" (Matt. 11:2-19; Luke 7:18-35; §41A-J).

6. James and John ask that one of them sit at Jesus's right hand, the other at the left. Again Jesus comments on their request and concludes: "For the Son of man also came not to be served but to serve, and to give his life as a ransom for many" (Mark 10:45; §120K).

7. Speaking about a sign for the times, Jesus says "no sign shall be given to it except the sign of Jonah. For as Jonah became a sign to the men of Nineveh, so will the Son of man be to this generation" (Luke 11:29-30; §88 BC).

8. Jesus has invited himself to have dinner in the home of Zacchaeus, who because he is a tax-collector is considered to be a sinner even though he has done many good things. "And Jesus said to him, 'Today salvation has come to this house, since he also is a son of Abraham. For the Son of man came to seek and to save the lost'" (Luke 19:8-10; §122).

9. Jesus asks the disciples, "Who do men say that I am?", and then, "But who do you say that I am?" Peter responds, "You are the Christ," and Jesus charges them "to tell no one about him." Then "he began to teach them that the Son of man must suffer many things, ... and be killed, and after three days rise again." Then Peter "began to rebuke [Jesus]." But he rebuked Peter, and said, "Get behind me, Satan! For you are not on the side of God, but of men" (Mark 8:27-33; §71-72).

10. Jesus is teaching his disciples and says to them, "The Son of man will be delivered into the hands of men, and they will kill him; and when he is killed, after three days he will rise" (Mark 9:31b; §76).

11. As they were going to Jerusalem, Jesus says to "the twelve," "Behold, we are going up to Jerusalem; and the Son of man will be delivered to the chief priests and the scribes, and they will condemn him to death" (Mark 10:33b; §119).

12. Jesus has prayed for deliverance at Gethsemane but concluded, "yet not what I will, but what thou wilt." He has asked his disciples to keep watch with him but they fell asleep three times. On the third time he says, "Are you still sleeping and taking your rest? It is enough; the hour has come; the Son of man is betrayed into the hands of sinners" (Mark 14:32-42; §140).

Turning to the second example ("The Son of man is lord even of the sabbath"), Howes pointed out that Jesus did not say that it is "man" who is in charge of the sabbath, but the Son of man. In *Jesus' Answer to God* she asked, "Is Jesus here identifying the Son of man with himself and saying that only he can be lord of the sabbath?[312] She thought not.

If so, it would be highly inconsistent with what we have seen him say throughout the first part of his teaching.* It seems, rather, that the Son of man refers to an element of psychic reality inside the natural human being, an element which forms a basis for creative decision making. ... The Son of man becomes the bearer of choice.[313]

She then warned that such a conclusion—that there is a quality within the human which is the choice-maker—is "dangerous indeed, because the line between an egocentric, negative, self-oriented choice and some deeper source is very small."[314] Yet if it is so, "The implications of this are tremendous for the recreation of human beings, society, and social institutions. Ultimately it is the question Who or what is to be trusted?"[315] These questions augment her discussion about choosing to "do the Will" and to "sell all." It is the individual who makes this choice. Her hypothesis about the Son of man suggests that the agent for making that choice is the Son of man present or available to all women and men. In her words, "The Son of man, then, is that element within the individual which, if the individual finds it, enables him to make his own decisions."[316]

She expands on this when she refers to an alternate text from *Codex Bezae*, which scholars date to the fifth or sixth century: "Jesus, seeing a man working on the sabbath, says, 'Blessed art thou if thou knowest what thou doest.'"[317] Howes comments, "The value lies in consciousness."[318] Jung referred to this same passage in "Answer to Job" and said that the saying "betrays an ethical standard very different from what is expected. Here the moral criterion is consciousness, and not law or convention."[319]

---

* Howes does not specify the teachings she is referring to, but by the time Jesus makes this statement about Son of man as lord of the sabbath, he has experienced the baptism, rejected the messianic choices offered in the wilderness, and has not said "I forgive" to the palsied one (Example 1), but rather, "You are forgiven." Howes understands Jesus to be separating himself from identification with the Son of man, as she believes he separates himself from identification with the Holy Spirit.

One of the most significant statements that Howes sees as differentiating Jesus from the divine is in the passage that says all sins will be forgiven except one—blaspheming the Holy Spirit (example 3). The scribes accuse Jesus of performing healing acts out of the power of the "prince of demons." Jesus responds, Why would Satan cast out his own kind? Howes believes that the scribes knew that Jesus was acting out of the Holy Spirit, and yet "out of sheer self-defensiveness and jealous manipulation they perverted and corrupted it."[320]

Why does Jesus say this is a sin which "never has forgiveness?" Howes responds, "The terrible damage in this sin apparently resides in the fact that in committing it one is harming the central moral aspect of personality—the power to discriminate. This power is man's blessing and curse."[321] It is this very power of discrimination, to see differences in values and make conscious choices, which is "the condition *a priori* for forgiveness."[322] She says it even more strongly in *Jesus' Answer to God*: "The essence of the human being is the ability to know values, whatever their content. This is to eat of the Tree of the Knowledge of Good and Evil in the Garden of Eden. To cover over that knowledge by falsity is to do away with our humanness."[323]

Howes now turns her attention to Jesus's distinction between blaspheming the Son of man (which will be forgiven) and the Holy Spirit (which will not be forgiven), and says Jesus is making clear that the Son of man is not to be identified with the divine—the Holy Spirit. The Son of man can be criticized, blasphemed against. "But nothing can be said against the Holy Spirit, the center out of which the Son of man speaks or acts."[324] Howes believes that the distinction Jesus makes between Son of man and Holy Spirit reveals the Son of man as "an inner element which is separate from the Holy Spirit, and yet is akin to the Holy Spirit as it faces towards the human."[325]

She summarizes, "Son of man is in part the ego related to the divine, it is in part almost the interaction between the two. ... It is certainly not the ego, but it is also not only the divine. It is the dialogue between the two. ... Here one sees the two faces of the Self."[326] Does Howes mean here that the Holy Spirit is the other face of the self? Does she equate Holy Spirit with self, of which "the Christ" is a symbol? In my reading, despite the creativity of her hypothesis about the Son of man, these are not distinctions which Howes attempts to clarify, and perhaps wasn't even aware were needed.

4. Who Do Men Say I Am?

If Jesus did not identify himself with the Holy Spirit *or* with the Son of man, and did not (in Howes's view) identify himself with the Messiah image, how did he see himself? And who did his disciples believe he was? Four questions are posed at different stages of Jesus's life that speak to this puzzle. The first was asked by John the Baptist, early in Jesus's teaching life; the second was one Jesus himself asked of his disciples after he had been teaching and before he set his course to Jerusalem; the third was asked by the high priest during the first of Jesus's trials that led to his crucifixion; and the fourth was asked by Pilate in the second trial. What do the responses—his and his disciples—understood psychologically, tell us about this man?

The first time the question was asked was when John the Baptist, who had been imprisoned by Herod, sent his disciples to ask, "Are you he who is to come, or shall we look for another?"[327] This passage is example 5 in Table 3. Jesus replied that as great as John the Baptist was, "He who is least in the kingdom of heaven is greater than he."[328] Howes interprets that Jesus knew John was a great ethical teacher, "but after the experience of the baptism and wilderness, Jesus knew John's values were not enough for entrance into the Kingdom. Yet without John as catalyst there couldn't have been a Jesus."[329]

But what is Jesus's answer to the question, "Are you the one?" Neither yes nor no. He responds with a quote from Isaiah which speaks of things that are happening: "The blind receive their sight, the lame walk, lepers are cleansed, and the deaf hear."[330] Howes comments, "There was healing: blind, lame, deaf were being transformed and receiving new fruits. Jesus says, 'It is happening, but I am not doing it.' Implied also is that no one else is coming."[331]

Jesus continues his discourse and points out that John the ascetic was accused of having a demon, yet when the Son of man came eating and drinking he was called a glutton and drunkard. And the passage ends with a puzzling statement, "Yet wisdom is justified by her deeds."[332] Howes understands in this passage that something about the Son of man distinguishes him from John:

> Jesus contrasts John with himself as Son of man, the contrast being between John as an ascetic, 'neither eating nor drinking,' and he, having found the Son of man, who, 'came eating and drinking, and behold you call him a gluttonous man and wine-bibber.' Yet both have been criticized and rejected. So what one does is not important. What is important is the relation of the Son of man to Wisdom (Sophia) from whom actions come, "and Wisdom is justified by her work."[333]

Howes understands the sentence, "Yet wisdom is justified by her deeds,"[334] to be saying that what is important is not what one does but rather the relationship of the Son of man to Wisdom. Wink makes a clarifying comment that the *Human Being* (his term for Son of man) "here is virtually identical with Divine Wisdom in the Wisdom of Solomon 7:27"[335] and quotes:

> Although she is but one, she can do all things
> and while remaining in herself, she renews all things,
> in every generation she passes into holy souls
> and makes them friends of God and prophets.[336]

"Wisdom," says Wink, "is a catalytic agent, who changes things without herself being changed, and who inspires the prophets."[337] The inclusion of this phrase, "Yet wisdom is justified by her deeds,"[338] or "by all her children"[339] draws the link between Wisdom and Jesus. "Luke preserves the earlier tradition, in which Jesus and John are both Wisdom's children. Matthew identifies Jesus with Wisdom, thus replacing her with the male Jesus."[340] Howes in several of her writings stresses that Jesus is inclusive of the feminine, but isn't as clear as Wink in drawing this relationship between Jesus and feminine Wisdom/Sophia.

We come now to the second time a question about Jesus's identity is posed, and here it is Jesus himself who asks it. This is example 9 in Table 3. Jesus and his disciples are traveling "to the villages of Caesarea Philippi, and on the way he asked his disciples, 'Who do men say that I am?'"[341] The disciples say that people liken him to John the Baptist, to Elijah, to other prophets. Then Jesus asks, "But who do you say that I am?"[342] When Peter responds, "You are the Christ," Jesus "charged them to tell no one about him."[343] In the next passage, Jesus "began to teach them about the Son of man, that he must suffer many things."

This injunction is often understood to imply that Jesus was the Christ but wanted it to be kept secret. Howes understands it differently, especially in light of his teachings about the Son of man being rejected and killed:

> It is one of the strikingly few places where Jesus does not say a simple Yea or Nay. But he goes on immediately to speak the passage of the Son of man being rejected and killed. Implicitly, yet absolutely clearly, Jesus has renounced the current expectations. Cutting across all orthodoxies, he has almost re-defined the Christ in terms of the vocation of the Son of man being that of wholeness.[344]

Howes, I believe, sees Jesus distinguishing between "Son of man" and the messianic role ascribed to him, that the *Son of man* will be rejected and killed—not that Jesus himself will be.

Howes also comments upon this passage, in which Jesus speaks about his suffering and death, to two others (examples 10 and 11 in Table 3). She points out that all three came at the end of his life.

In these final statements, Son of man again refers to that in the person which takes the individual way, involving conflicts with the orthodox and with the collective, suffering rejection by the collective, and the final willingness to meet annihilation. We have here some exceptional clues as to the meaning of what the Self is, as to what it means to pursue the Son of man as expression of the Self.[345]

Relating this to our lives today, Howes says that although we might not have to endure an outer crucifixion, if we go *the individual way* "there must inevitably be terrific conflict, inner and outer. And if one follows it to its fulfillment, it is bound to lead to an even deeper death and rebirth."[346] This is Howes's understanding of the relationship between the Jesus and Son of man of the Synoptic Gospels, and our lives today. Jesus was acting out of his relationship with the divine, with the Holy Spirit—with the archetype of the self—and this relationship is available to be lived out by all of us.

Howes makes an indirect comment about the phrase that ends all three accounts, that if Jesus spoke of his future and said the Son of man would be rejected, killed, and then raised up, why did he ask, "Who do you say I am?" According to Howes, "We see a man deeply puzzled, burdened with new realities and messages, struggling to clarify for himself and others, and perhaps for God, concerns not in his head but in his heart and at the core of his being,"[347] adding, "It was an agonizing inner-outer time, and we can see the true stature of this human becoming ever clearer."[348]

When Peter said, "You are the Christ," why did Jesus tell him to tell no one? Peter responds by rebuking Jesus, to which Jesus says: "Get thee behind me Satan! For you are not on the side of God, but of men." Howes notes that Peter's responses—first, "You are the Christ," and then his rebuke of Jesus for speaking about Jesus predicting his rejection and death—must have come out of Peter's deep longing for a messiah to relieve the populace from oppression. He wasn't longing for apocalyptic change in the future, but for a change to happen now.

Peter must have seen something in Jesus, Howes surmises, that he thought could lead to great relief for the Jewish people, but whatever he saw, "Peter was certainly seeing it manifested only in Jesus. The meaning of the saving element behind savior, redeemer, was felt by Peter to belong only to Jesus as the Christ."[349] Howes believes it was this belief that drew Jesus's sharp rebuke. Howes believes that Jesus's own sense of himself was quite different: "Up to this point Jesus had in no sense affirmed or denied he was the Christ. ... He wanted his disciples and the people to know what he had known since the baptism-wilderness: that God functioned in the psyche as well as in history; that God could be experienced in the human soul as immanent Reality."[350]

But why did Jesus not reply, No, I am not or Yes, I am? Howes gives three possible answers: (1) Jesus himself was not yet clear about his role; (2) a simple yes or no answer would not suffice; or (3) it was clear to him, but he didn't want people to know. "To have said yes would have been to lie; to have said no would have been equally untrue because what lay behind the hope of the messiah was a Reality that he could not refute or refuse."[351] Howes continued, "He, Jesus, knew himself now to be a vessel, a container of newness of God, yet he hardly knew what to do with it. So to have said no would have denied this new archetypal Reality within, now in a birthing process."[352]

In her Son of man lecture, Howes raised the question, why did Jesus use the "Son of man" phrase instead of "Son of God" or simply "I"?

Essentially, I believe, he used Son of man because it described in the best available language what he felt about himself—his own self-consciousness. In Christian dogma, one does not have to be concerned with Jesus as a figure separate from the Christ. But *if* one is, one perceives how the use of the phrase "Son of man" represents Jesus' attitude toward himself and his own religious experience. ... He himself fulfilled the conditions he stated for Self-achievement: the losing of life, the selling all, the transformation from multiplicity to singleness.[353]

The third time the question was asked about his identity was by the high priest at Jesus's first trial in Jerusalem. There are four accounts (shown in Table 4) of how Jesus replies to the high priest. In Matthew, he says, "You have said so." In Mark, he says, "I am." Why would Matthew report Jesus's answer, "You have said so" rather than follow Mark's "I am"? Howes believes it's likely that Mark's original Gospel said, "You have said so," but was later changed.

Matthew's Gospel is used to show Jesus as Messiah and includes references to "church" which Jesus is not believed to have actually said. Matthew reports Jesus saying, "And I tell you, you are Peter, and on this rock I will build my church."[354] In another passage, Matthew tells us that Jesus is speaking about reconciling with your brother and if he listens, "You have gained a brother. … But If he refuses to listen to them [two or three witnesses], tell it to the church; and if he refuses to listen even to the church, let him be to you as a Gentile and a tax collector."[355]

Howes then turns to Luke's account, in which Jesus's answer to the first question is, "If I tell you, you will not believe," and his answer to the second question is, "You say that I am." This is the response the chief priests interpret as yes, leading to his second trial before Pilate, the political authority. In Howes's view, Jesus threw the question back to his questioners, an act which she regards as showing "the integrity of the man at that moment. It would have been futile and foolish to attempt to explain. … And to explain what?"[356]

Table 4 **"Are you the Christ?"*** **The Trial Before the Jewish Authorities**
And the high priest said to him "I adjure you by the living God, tell us if you are the Christ, the Son of God." Jesus said to him, "You have said so." (Matt. 26:63-64A; §142E)
Again the high priest asked him, "Are you the Christ, the Son of the Blessed?" And Jesus said, "I am…" (Mark 14:61b-62A; §142E)
And they [the chief priests and scribes and their council] said, "If you are the Christ, tell us." But he said to them, "If I tell you, you will not believe; and if I ask you, you will not answer … " And they all said, "Are you the Son of God, then?" And he said to them, "You say that I am." (Luke 22:67-70; §142N, O)

The Trial Before Pilate

And Pilate asked him, "Are you the King of the Jews?" And he answered him, "You have said so."[357]

Then comes the central question, "What was his real answer to himself and to God in these closing days of his life?"[358] What did he know at that moment? Howes gives a lengthy and impassioned response to her own question: "He knew that what was behind the Messianic longing for a savior to redeem the people had been manifested inside him, and knew that the same reality could happen to others. He knew it was a genuine longing, issuing from the heart

---

* All three passages continue with references to the Son of man which Howes regards as apocalyptic, thus not historical, and does not discuss: "you will see the Son of man seated at the right hand of Power, and coming on the clouds of heaven" (Mt 26:64; Mk 14:62; §142E) and "the Son of man shall be seated at the right hand of the power of God" (Lk 22:69; §142N).

and depths of humankind, but *not* to be fulfilled by any redeemer figure."[359]

Continuing, she says, "He knew that all the dynamic energy behind the Messianic image needed not to be projected into one person but to be unfolded into a process that was available to all. ... A new step of evolution was ready and he was a vehicle for it."[360]

She goes on to say that for him to have said yes or no would have cut off the "process at work in him."[361] Elsewhere she puts it this way, that Jesus did know his inward relationship to "the Christ image and knew it as a present numinous factor in the psyche of each man. He did not identify himself with it, as later Christianity did. He did not say he *was it*, but he could never deny it as real and alive because it was exactly what he had touched."[362]

There is a second trial, this one before the Roman governor, Pilate. The exchange between Pilate and Jesus is also shown in Table 4. Once more Jesus is asked who he is: "Are you the King of the Jews?" and once more he does not answer directly but says, "You say that I am." This is parallel to his response to the chief priest, "You have said so" in Matthew's account and, Howes believes, also in Mark's. So in all three Gospels, Jesus has deflected the question back to the questioner, never responding, "Yes, I am."

In many places using different words, Howes conveys her belief that Jesus's responses at the trials come out of his experiences, beginning with the baptism/wilderness, and his growing recognition of his relationship to self, to God. Earlier, she discussed Jesus's prayer at Gethsemane, "Abba, Father, all things are possible to thee; remove this cup from me; yet not what I will, but what thou wilt."[363] Howes hears in this exchange the great contribution of the human. Jesus doesn't simply say, whatever you want. He expresses his own will— remove this cup, let me live—but he remains open to the higher value, the will of God. Howes expresses her understanding in this way: "By voicing his yearning to live and having the courage to open the question of what was the Will, he saved himself from the death of a martyr or from a passive resignation to the will of God as his death has so often been interpreted. Rather, he expressed in fullest terms that in very truth it is a co-creation that God wants."[364]

In "Analytical Psychology and the Synoptic Gospels," Howes argues that Jesus's prayer in Gethsemane is "a supreme moment of human achievement,"[365] in which the human acknowledges his own limitations and desires, yet lives out his commitment "to the demands of God and eternity and the fulfillment of destiny."[366]

Whether or not his message continued after his death was not paramount to him, Howes argues, but rather, "his fulfillment as person."[367] "This constant interaction between God and Jesus is a quantum leap that had been brought about by his life and activity at this time of history. Out of this interaction, Jesus is giving his answer to God by saying, 'Howbeit [However] not what I will, but what thou wilt.'"[368]

Out of the relationship between himself and God, Jesus could answer—and had to answer—neither yes nor no, but "You have said it." Howes says of Jesus's experience of Gethsemane and the trials, "Weak or not weak, Pilate's actions were not the ultimate, decisive issue. Judas betrayed, Peter denied, Pilate was weak, and Jesus encompassed, by what he had seen in Gethsemane, his own answer to God."[369] I interpret her words "seen in Gethsemane" as "come to know." He could offer such a prayer only out of a new relationship between himself and the God he knew, the transcendent which was also immanent. In the words of analytical psychology, his prayer came out of his deep exchange with and in relationship to the self.

5. Death and Resurrection

I began this exposition of Howes's ideas about Jesus's life and teachings with the baptism/wilderness experience, which Howes saw as the transformative events out of which came Jesus's life of preaching and teaching. Now I come to the end of the story, his death on the cross and the empty tomb which, of course, is the beginning of a new story. Christianity has told this new story in one way. What is the story that can come out of a depth-psychological understanding of these events?

Howes sees Jesus as a man who "cut through all current collective standards,"[370] actions which led ineluctably to the cross. The cross for Jesus "was completion, finality, what he had earlier called being 'perfected.'* It represented the utmost loyalty to the principle of consciousness."[371] And by accepting the cross, Jesus took "full responsibility for the task of being human, thus changing the nature of God."[372] Jesus's prayer, "My God, my God, why hast thou forsaken me?"[373] shows us "a man who knows that, at this moment, God can do nothing because man has channeled His, God's power into consciousness and therefore reduced God's omnipotence."[374] Jesus's cry

> is the cry of this human who has always stayed related to the ultimate transcendent being of God and has now known this God incarnated within himself, immanent, powerful, almost overwhelming. ... Jesus cries out not because God is not present but because His/Her presence is a new manifestation in substance producing an agonizing suffering. The Spirit of God on which Jesus has always relied is not absent to him but is silent. God is more present than ever, is suffering incarnation in Jesus, but God in substance does not lend the same kind of support.[375]

Howes is convinced that omnipotence has been diminished by entering into substance. She continues this line of thought in *Jesus' Answer to God*: "The dominance of the spirit side was renounced for more totality. Entrance into the flesh always means diminution of

---

* Lk 13:32; §101A. It should be noted this word is found in the English Revised Version of the Records, published by Sharman in 1917, and will not be found in the 1991 Revised Standard Version used throughout this book. *(ed.)*

infinite power. Limitation of the Spirit by being held in the consciousness of a human fulfilled the longing of God but also deprived God of omnipotence."[376]

Both Howes and Jung are clear that God, or self, is changed by the human-divine encounter. However, in contrast to Howes, Jung argues that God is changed by the encounter with the steadfast Job, but he also suggests that the One he calls God, *imago dei,* and self is not diminished. "Even the enlightened person remains what he is, and is never more than his own limited ego before the One who dwells within him, whose form has no knowable boundaries, who encompasses him on all sides, fathomless as the abysms of the earth and vast as the sky."[377]

Howes's writings also reveal that she believes the transcendent remains transcendent, even when it has become immanent. Why, then, does she state that its power has been diminished? I don't know. I offer a different view which I believe accords better with a depth-psychological perspective. Is it possible that God—and I say again that "God" speaks only of the *image* of God, the self—*could* have done something, but wouldn't? The human, here Jesus, fully accepts his destiny, as Howes says, to reconcile the opposites in God represented by the cross itself. To accept that destiny means to play it out to the tragic and bitter end, without the intervention of God. In Jesus's cry of abandonment, we meet the human being *in extremis* who experiences the existential aloneness of being human.

Do we (does Howes?) want more of Jesus? Do we want him to hear God's words of comfort and presence in his greatest anguish? Do we want Jesus not to have cried out, "Why have you forsaken me?" Do we want to know that God is there for us, always? Perhaps that is why Luke's accounts of what Jesus says on the cross are so different and much more comforting: "Father, forgive them for they know not what they do"[378] and "Father, into thy hands I commit my spirit!"[379] This is a Jesus fully accepting his destiny, never doubting God's presence. Howes discusses Luke's account, in contrast to the Marcan story, and concludes that it "may have come in later as more consistent with the Christian attitude."[380] She doesn't expand on this statement, but I believe she is saying the Lukan responses are more fitting with an image of Jesus who accepts his destiny and his suffering without complaint, because he knows God is with him. While she acknowledges that Jesus's words in the Lukan account "feel similar to what he has been doing all his life, and this could be the final affirmation,"[381] she believes Mark's account to be more authentic: "It seems impossible to imagine the Mark account as being added [at some later time by an editor], though it would be possible to imagine it being said by Jesus."[382] Her interpretation of why she believes God was present but silent, and why Jesus said these words, however, remain puzzling to me. I can only speculate that Howes herself did not fully accept the existential aloneness of the human which Jesus's cry reveals, even though her writings show that she knew full well the terrible burden the human bears when he or she enters into the process of the evolution of consciousness.

Now Howes speaks of the events after Jesus's death—the rending of the veil of the temple, reminiscent, she reminds us, of "'the heavens rent asunder' at the baptism. The veil of the temple is over the Holy of Holies for the Jews, and now that is torn apart and God is revealed in a new way."[383] If Howes had stopped there, one might imagine that the "new way" is the Christianity that evolved after Jesus's death, but she doesn't. With Jesus's death, the opposites of God are brought together: "It is as if the two hands of God, the right and left, are united by a third element: a human who has taken on the burden of freedom."[384]

> The person in the physical body died. Yet the realities in him, the central archetypes on which his life was based, did not die. … The descent-ascent, life-death motif was the dominant one of his life. The ascent to the cross had led to the deepest descent and death, from which the Spirit—as the Substance aspect of God—emerged newly. This is a description of the resurrected life. Love became possible in a new way because of the way the "enemy," the dark, had been overcome.[385]

Howes sees the cross symbolizing "dialogue between God and Jesus," a dialogue in which God suffers and yet triumphs because the human being, Jesus, "had taken on the problem of freedom and met Evil with Love."[386] She refers to Job's encounter with God, in which "God became something new because of what a human did."[387] This is the message Jung conveys in his "Answer to Job," in which he argues that in that great struggle between human and God, the human, Job, came out the better by staying true to his own integrity in the face of an unconscious God, and thereby God was changed.

At this point in her argument, Howes pauses to clarify that it was not "the Jews" who killed Jesus. In response to the question, who did kill Jesus or contribute to his death, Howes concludes it would have been a combination of some of the Pharisees and scribes, some of the religious authorities, Judas, Pilate, the people who cried out to save Barabbas rather than Jesus, and "finally, Jesus himself, because of his choices, especially to eat so fully of the Tree of the Knowledge of Good and Evil, and because of his teaching."[388]

After that, she proceeds to discuss the significance of *the presence of the feminine*, both at the crucifixion and then at the empty tomb. She reminds us that at the crucifixion, the women are "watching from afar." And it is the women ("Mary Magdalene, and Mary the mother of James and Salome," according to Mark's account)[389] who come to anoint Jesus's body in the tomb and find it empty. Rather than accepting the traditional Christian understanding of the physical resurrection of Jesus, Howes presents a different interpretation, speculative as she acknowledges when she ponders, "Could it have been something like this?"[390] She begins by acknowledging some of the ways the story has been interpreted: the body had been stolen; the story is a "mythic telling of what was behind the resurrection experience";[391] the body was never put into the tomb; Jesus did not die at all.

Then she comes to her own speculation, "that the body had not been stolen and was there but was not seen as a corpse *because of a transformation in the women* who had a vision of a new figure."[392] All the beliefs and hopes they had placed on Jesus had been shattered by his death, yet out of this terrible emptiness came a spiritual transformation.

Howes doesn't use psychological language here, but I will, although my words are as speculative as hers. It was *the self* that came alive in Jesus at his baptism, came alive in the women during their experiences with him, and after his brutal death was projected onto a "risen Christ." In this speculative scenario, the Jesus the women "saw" in the garden was a projection of the self, the Christ, onto a man they met at the tomb who became ever after, the Risen Christ of Christianity.

What is perhaps most compelling about Howes's discussion is that it argues for the necessity of the feminine in the process of this new birthing that she believes came as a result of Jesus's death. "Symbolically, because the tomb was cared for and nurtured by the Feminine, a new birth could come from it. … The tomb became the 'manger' for this birth in the disciples."[393] The message of Jesus, all that he had been in touch with, still exists, so the potential for relationship for each of us with this God, this self, is still available. What happened, Jung and Howes both say, is that the human could not contain such enormity, and the potential was projected onto one person, Jesus, who became Jesus Christ, Savior.

According to Howes, what came from Jesus's life and death was "a new historical development, Christianity. Out of the loss of his life and the despair it must have caused, a new vitality and a message of the risen Christ erupted and changed the Mediterranean world."[394] Before Jesus became the center of the story as Jesus Christ, Howes speculates, the disciples themselves did feel this God, this self, alive in themselves, yet they identified their experience not as their own, but as Jesus alive in them—and thus arose the story of the resurrected Jesus. Howes recognizes the contribution Christianity made in keeping alive the archetypal shift that she believes Jesus's life and death express:

If these values [of the Church] had not been carried, we would not have available the truths within them. The consciousness of Jesus of Nazareth, however distorted, would not be available to be understood, as a journey possible for each of us. With Christianity, the within-ness became identified with Jesus as Christ. This has kept the archetype alive culturally.[395]

And she continues, "Now another step is necessary, where each individual carries his or her own religious meaning."[396]

Whither Christianity

In "Son of man—Expression of the Self" and *Jesus' Answer to God*, Howes presented her clearest statements about the implications of the Christian story that depth psychology tells: that the one-sided, all-good image of Christ does not allow for the integration of opposites—good and evil, light and dark—in the personality. In the Son of man literature from Hebrew scripture to the Synoptic Gospels, Howes suggests, we have a "prevision for our age, a symbol of mediation that is inclusive and having to do with concrete experience and its fulfillment."[397] Jesus lived this out, "not identifying himself with the new self-aspect of God within, as the Gospel of John makes him do, but was using the term 'Son of man' to describe the human expression of this archetype. ... We find in Jesus' Son of man image there is an inclusiveness that is much needed today."[398]

In *Jesus' Answer to God*, she wrote that with Jesus's death, "the Spirit of God did not die but could move out into the world in a new way."[399] This statement came as she pondered what was happening to the Holy Spirit that had "descended from God into new manifestation" in the baptism, as Jesus was dying on the cross. I assume that this Holy Spirit was, to Howes, the other face (along with the Son of man) of the self. I believe she was saying that whatever motivated Jesus's own "seeing and knowing" did not die with Jesus on the cross. The Christian message of a physical resurrection of a Savior who has taken away our sins is no longer tenable; what is needed is baptism and wilderness— a rebirth—*in each human being*. Jung wrote, "A further development of [the Christian] myth might well begin with the outpouring of the Holy Spirit upon the apostles, by which they were made into sons of God, and not only they, but all others who through them and after them received the *filiatio*—sonship of God."[400]

Howes, the little-known scholar working and writing in her own little corner of the universe, saw something that Jung and no doubt many others saw, too—that the Christian myth as it has been understood has been shattered. The "something new" that was incarnated in Jesus the human being and then projected onto Jesus Christ can no longer be contained within Christianity. It has to be lived out in each individual's relationship to the self in the process that Jung called *individuation*.

Howes thought the time for humanity to move beyond Christianity is now, and failure to take this step "may tip the balance not only for our own lives but for the ongoing of the planet."[401] She ends her book *Jesus' Answer to God* with an impassioned argument for the necessity of "larger dimensions and horizons" in which each of us takes our own authority, rather than placing it in Jesus as Christ: "The issue today is no longer Christianity or the church or Jesus, but the God-human process of dying and rebirth carried into every phase of personal and social living."[402]

> Somehow, the new age must and can be one where the reality behind the symbol of the Christ, the deep Self, *imago dei*, can be experienced as the expression of the transcendent God of Judaism with all its *tremendum*. And what must be added is Jesus' emphasis on the Son of man as the expression of the Self (reflecting God) in action, but not the ego. It is this Son of man in each of us which may truly live the resurrected life in us.[403]

By *resurrected life*, she means one in which we live out our relationship with the reality behind the symbols, recognizing and healing the opposites within the human and God, living out the death and rebirth process that occurs in every life. I liken Howes's *resurrected life* to Jung's *individuation*, which Jung, no less than Howes, believes is crucial for the individual and for the world. Howes moved beyond Jung in believing a new age beyond Christianity must be lived out *now*. She remained passionate in believing that Jesus's life and teachings, discerned through study of the Synoptic Gospels, "with the help of depth psychology [offer] a source for living through dying—the life of relatedness and fullness."[404] She did not leave Jesus or his teachings behind, or the Jewish God he knew, but in her view the story is no longer the one Christianity tells about Jesus Christ, but a story of Jesus the human being who teaches us all how to live.

Howes's Contributions to the Study of Jesus

Elizabeth Boyden Howes's greatest contribution, I believe, was to free the Christian story from its boundaries by bringing the insights of Jung's analytical psychology to the study of Jesus of Nazareth. In doing so, she added to Jung's hypothesis of Christ as a great symbol of the self by placing at the center of the story the *human*, not a God-man, not the Christ which is the center of Jung's understanding. She found in her understanding of the Christian story a man who lived out his own destiny in relation to that self, never identifying with it, never claiming to be that self, that God. Through the method of study that she and her associates in the Guild developed and evolved over the years, an avenue opened for students to see beyond Jesus to the story of humanity itself.

What Howes called *the resurrected life* is lived by each individual who consciously carries his and her own cross and recognizes the death-rebirth process that such a choice requires. Howes's language was still familiarly Christian, but her vision went beyond the Christian myth to the reality from which it arose. She believed passionately in the words from the Jewish Kabbala that she and Sheila Moon used as the title of their book *The Choicemaker*: "Man was created for the sake of choice!"[405] The choice, she made clear in many of her writings, was to discern and do the will of God, to "sell all" in order to enter the Kingdom. It's a choice for consciousness in which the ego-personality, the "I," lives in service to the something greater that Howes variously called the self, God, Great Patterner, Mystery, the Cry. Her concern was for life as it is lived by the individual, and for the "ongoingness of the planet."[406]

Specific contributions Elizabeth Boyden Howes made to the study of the life and teachings of Jesus include the following:

1. Her view of Jesus's baptism and wilderness events as the transformative experiences of his life, out of which all his preaching came—in the baptism, he had the "inward experience" of sonship to God; in the wilderness, he faced the messianic implications of that relationship and said no to each one.

2. Her insights into Jesus's teachings about the Kingdom of God—Jesus knew through the baptism experience, she believed, that this Kingdom was within as well as without. In Howes's words, "The birth of the Kingdom out of potentiality into a new reality, in the individual and in society, is the major thrust and dynamic of [Jesus's] message."[407] But it is not a Kingdom to be lived without effort. It is what we enter (or attain—she uses both images) when we choose to do the Will, to sell all, and in so doing, become "co-creators with the process of God."[408]

3. Her hypothesis that the Son of man was not a phrase Jesus used to refer to himself, and that far from applying only to him or to an apocalyptic being who will come on clouds of glory, *the Son of man is a quality within all human beings*—The title of her lecture, "Son of man—Expression of the Self" signals this hypothesis. Jesus taught "that there is an element in man to be trusted, a center to be achieved, a new man to be born through responsibility and transformation."[409]

4. Howes's interpretation of Jesus's life and teachings such as are seen in his responses to the questions, "Are you the Christ?" and "Are you the King of the Jews?" show him never to identify himself as either. His refusal to reply either Yes or No (as she interprets the passages) left

the "new man," the new human, free to be born in each person, not carried solely in Jesus.

5. Her belief that Jesus knew that he had to go to his death on the cross and that he chose to do so, to live out his destiny of doing the will of God, of selling all for the Kingdom. This is revealed, for example, in his prayer at Gethsemane when he expressed his will to live, yet turned his will over to God's will. Accepting the cross "represented the utmost loyalty to the principle of consciousness."[410] In his death on the cross, Jesus has reconciled the opposites in God, brought together God's right and left hands.

6. Her speculation that the so-called appearances after Jesus's death came out of projections, first of the women at the empty tomb and later by the men, of what had come alive in themselves projected outward onto the Christ figure. This is not different from Jung's own hypothesis, but Howes gives more emphasis to the necessary role of the feminine expressed in the women who were present at the crucifixion and at the empty tomb. "The tomb became the 'manger' for this [new] birth in the disciples."[411]

Howes's stated purpose in writing her final book, *Jesus' Answer to God*, was to separate myth from history in order to recognize the value of each. *Myths convey the archetypal patterns lived out in human life; Jesus as a historical figure shows us a man living out his own destiny as each human being needs to do.* Her vision and method of study presuppose the existence of a historical Jesus.

Howes believed that the historical figure of Jesus, the "experient" of the story studied in *Records* seminars, has been lost both in Christian creed and dogma and in analytical psychology. The archetypal self, of which the Christ is a symbol, is the essential background of the story, the reality that Jesus knew, but Howes saw it as a reality that became fully expressed through Jesus's life and teachings. Jung, on the other hand, saw the historical Jesus as of little consequence. For him, "the essence of Christianity is by no means the simple man Jesus whom we seek in vain in the Gospels, but the lore of the God-man and his cosmic drama."[412] Jung argued that this great myth arose because of the powerful action of the pre-existing mythological motifs attributed to the biographically almost unknown Jesus, a wandering miracle Rabbi in the style of the ancient Hebrew prophets, or of the contemporary teacher John the Baptizer, or of the much later Zaddiks of the Chassidim. ... The true *agens* is the archetypal image of the God-man, appearing in Ezekiel's vision for the first time in Jewish history, but in itself a considerably older figure in Egyptian theology, vis., Osiris and Horus.[413]

Howes agreed with Jung's views about the archetypal reality out of which the Christ myth comes, but not with his conclusion that Jesus was a figure of no significance. Her contribution, I believe, was to see how Jung's theory is lived out in a human life, how Jesus's life and teachings show us a way of living in relationship to the archetypal self. Jung saw the need for a new era to come, but he did not see how the life and teachings of the historical Jesus was pointing to that new era. Howes suggests that Jung, like Christianity itself, confused the man Jesus, and the projections on him:

Christianity has been and is a religion about Jesus or Jesus Christ. It has centered on the individual's experience of Christ as Saviour rather than on the relationship of the man Jesus to God. ... The human catalyst has been forgotten. ... Yet by this omission, is it not possible that Analytical Psychology has made somewhat the same mistake that Christianity made—that is, to equate the experience of Jesus and the experience about the projections *upon* Jesus as Savior? If the experiences are *not* the same—and I believe they are not— then many questions must be asked and answered.[414]

Not only did Jung not see the value of distinguishing the archetypal Christ from the human Jesus, like many historians today (as Hal Childs argues in *The Myth of the Historical Jesus and the*

Evolution of Consciousness), Jung didn't believe it possible to find such a figure. In "Answer to Job," he acknowledged the "special interest that attaches to the character and fate of the incarnate son of God,"[415] but then argued, as many have and still do, that it is "uncommonly difficult to reconstruct a biographical picture of Christ from the traditions that have been preserved. Not a single text is extant which would fulfill even the minimum modern requirements for writing a history."[416] Note that he conflates Christ and Jesus. About the impossibility of reconstructing a biography of this figure, he wrote, "The oldest writings, those of St. Paul, do not seem to have the slightest interest in Christ's existence as a concrete human being. The Synoptic Gospels are equally unsatisfactory as they have more the character of propaganda than of biography."[417]

Howes observed that Jung "*almost* seems to equate the dogmatic Christ and the person of Jesus."[418] For her, the Synoptic Gospels were far more than "propaganda." She agreed with Jung that through projection, the hero, in this case Jesus, was transformed in the eyes of his followers into something greater than human and "became identified … with the Christ image and the Self. He became the centre of the frame, the object of religious devotion. What he taught and lived became distorted and temporarily or permanently lost."[419]

It is my own view that Howes's insights about the value of the historical Jesus—that is, the role of the human in the human-divine dance—along with the unique method of working with the Synoptic Gospels that she and her colleagues developed, provide a way to see beyond the "Christian aeon" that Jung—and Howes—saw coming to its end.

Chapter 4

Was There a Historical Jesus?

One of my primary motivations for writing this book was to answer the question, "Why is Jesus so important to me today when I no longer consider myself Christian?" A related question is this: "What if there is no valid historical evidence to support all that we think we know about Jesus? What if, in fact, there was no historical figure at all, merely a great story woven about a charismatic hero?" Such questions would be shocking to believing Christians, and probably to many people who don't consider themselves Christians.

Scholars have continued to question whether there was a historical Jesus at all. I now turn to Childs, Wink, Israel Finkelstein, Neil Asher Silberman, Jan Assmann, and others to explore my own response to the question, "Does the Christian myth require a historical Jesus to retain the power of its message?" If not, what are the possible implications for a depth psychological understanding of the Christian story? What are the implications for the method of study of the Synoptic Gospels that Howes and her associates developed over the decades? Do the Jesus stories in the Christian myth maintain their transformative power if one does not accept the existence of a historical Jesus?

Albert Schweitzer

Howes's search for the historical Jesus followed the great wave of this quest that began with the Enlightenment and seemed to come to an end with Albert Schweitzer's monumental *The Quest of The Historical Jesus*, first published in 1905 and then in an edited version in 1913. In it, Schweitzer concluded:

> The Jesus of Nazareth who came forward publicly as the Messiah, who preached the ethic of the kingdom of God, who founded the kingdom of heaven upon earth, and died to give his work its final consecration, never existed. He is a figure designed by rationalism, endowed with life by liberalism, and clothed by modern theology in a historical garb.[420]

Hal Childs: Was Jesus a Historical Figure, and Does It Matter?

Is it possible to find a historical Jesus at all? Was there ever such a person? There are those who raise questions about the possibility of finding *any* such historical figure, and one of these is Hal Childs, longtime Guild leader and psychotherapist in the Jungian tradition. Childs worked with Howes for several decades in the study of Jesus from a depth psychological perspective, and for him the importance of *Records* seminars was to transform participants' relationship with the self, not to determine whether Jesus walked the earth or not. In fact, his "working hypothesis [is] that there never was a historical Jesus" and that Jesus is "a complete fiction or myth."[421]

Childs's position seems close to Jung's own: "It is not the historical Jesus who matters, but Jesus the resurrected, Jesus the Risen…. This Jesus is the revealer, that is, the voice of the self, the collective unconscious."[422] From Childs's point of view, the value of working with the Jesus myth is "not the recovery of the historical Jesus, but the transformation of the *historical image* of Jesus, because this is related to self-transformation."[423]

Howes, too, saw the *Records* as a method to propel the individual along the lifelong journey of individuation. And like Childs, she saw it as a method by which ego, the conscious individual, untangles its own identity from the person of a historical Jesus and from the archetypal Christ, arguing that the *Records* method can move us from our projections *onto* the myth of a historical Jesus and reclaim these numinous traits in ourselves. Childs explains, "The phrase 'the myth of the historical Jesus' is meant to unsettle the traditional and popular associations to the words 'myth' and 'history,'"[424] arguing that the view that history is true and myth is false comes from positivist Cartesian understanding,[425] which considers *knowledge* only that which is received from the senses and interpreted through reason (verifiable data), and continues in our belief systems today despite current insights that history itself is constructed.

Childs quotes philosopher and historian Peter Munz: "Sir George Clark once described history as a hard core of fact surrounded by a pulp of disputable interpretations. E. H. Carr, wittily and with greater perspicacity stood the statement on its head. 'History,' he wrote in *What Is History?* 'is a hard core of interpretation surrounded by a pulp of disputable facts.'"[426] Childs adds, "As Hayden White has noted, the term [history] is ambiguous because of a 'failure to distinguish adequately between an object of study (the human past) and discourse about this object.' The word history refers to both the reality of the past and those texts that are written about that past."[427]

Contrary to the positivist view, Childs argues, we cannot retrieve the actual events of the past, that history is not the reconstruction of "reality," but is constructed by language and the historian who uses it. "The general idea that the 'forthright empiricism' of historical method is somehow objective is actually faulty,"[428] he argues, quoting from Lionel Gossman: In the construction of historical accounts, "interpretation enters at every step along the way. ... Historical facts are not established from pure data—they are postulated to explain characteristics of the data. Thus the sharp division between fact and interpretation upon which the classical view insisted and which the revisionists have accepted, does not exist."[429] It's time, Childs writes, "to view history as myth" and to see history and myth as simply different kinds of narrative. We can gain much data about the events of the past, but it is the narratives that weave the events together and bring us what we think of as history.

Childs's views do not invalidate the Christian story or *Records* study. To the contrary, he finds the Christian story to be of great value because it indeed tells about a transformative event in the human psyche, an event that has been attached to a figure who became the historical Jesus:

> It is not the historical Jesus who matters but Jesus the resurrected, Jesus the Risen, the Living Jesus (Gospel of Thomas), the life-giving Jesus, the revealed Christ (Paul). This Jesus is the revealer, that is, the voice of the Self, the collective unconscious. This is not a historical figure, but a cosmic revelation, a mystical eruption and experience. This Jesus is the personification of a new access to God, or the collective unconscious. It is this Jesus that moved so many people, and prompted the creation of hundreds of gospel (good news) proclamations of this new revelation.[430]

This Jesus, as Childs writes, was not a historical figure whose life gave rise to a new myth "but a vast energetic system and field of potential building in the collective unconscious (in culture and history) that emerges simultaneously and independently in many different individuals, places and times."[431] The people of the time and culture out of which Christianity came, then, were responding to an "archetypal movement in the collective unconscious."[432] These thoughts echo Jung's: "Christ would never have made the impression he did on his followers if he had not expressed something that was alive and at work in their unconscious. Christianity itself would never have spread through the pagan world with such astonishing rapidity had its ideas not found an analogous psychic readiness to receive them."[433] And as Jung says in his letter to Upton Sinclair: "Thus it is the spirit of the time, the collective hope and expectation, which caused this astounding transformation and not at all the more or less insignificant story of the man Jesus."[434]

Paradoxically, Childs's view about the historical Jesus supports Howes's mission to understand how Jesus's teachings inform and enliven us today, but the historical-critical method that Howes believes could lead to a historical Jesus, in Childs's thinking, contributes only to the evolution of consciousness, not to historical truth.

Childs contends that our sense of who we are is bound up in history *as we know it*. When unexamined and accepted unconsciously, these are "true" stories, and within the Christian story the archetypal self is inextricably bound up with Christ, and with Jesus. The historical-critical work of *Records* study moves people to *question* the stories and ultimately to question their own relationship to Jesus, to the Christ, and to the self. In this way, the historical-critical work furthers the journey of individuation and the evolution of consciousness, which is the point.

In *The Myth of the Historical Jesus and the Evolution of Consciousness*, Childs presents another reason why historical-critical work is essential. What is needed "is not to abandon the historical critical approach to the figure of Jesus, but to create alternative myths within which it can operate."[435] Childs tells us that while biblical historical criticism has "disturbed and destroyed the faith of many in the gospels as accurate reports of Jesus' sayings and actions," at the same time it "shows us the creative power of narrative, and helps us to realize that each historical epoch has its own type of narrative with terms and meanings particular to it."[436] As a way to draw on the positive potential for historical criticism, he suggests a "phenomenological perspective" which "continues the tradition of scientific observation but [is] no longer under the illusion of the neutral, uninvolved observer. In this case, a critical historical criticism is undertaken by a self-aware observer who knows he or she is an involved and interpreting investigator. ... The objective otherness and autonomy of the collective unconscious is a respected partner in the work."[437]

A phenomenological perspective, in Childs's view as in Jung's, acknowledges the empirical reality of psyche. Not only sensory experience (which is the limit of acceptable data collection according to positivism) but "unconscious experience"[438] that comes to us in dreams and reflective imagination, is also a legitimate contributor to the phenomenological exploration of the Jesus myth.

Childs proposes that the historical-critical method can help construct new narratives and myths, thus contributing to the evolution of consciousness. In *Records* study, we are challenged, through the historical-critical work with the texts and many other techniques to question our own beliefs and assumptions about the story, about the man Jesus, and about ourselves. Out of hard critical thinking and considerable emotional anguish which arises when we meet the conflict between old beliefs and new, a new story can emerge.

The question whether the story arises from a "real" historical figure remains. It was not a question posed in *Records* seminars in the past. I wonder what responses would have come if it had been. Childs would respond that we cannot find evidence of such a person; what we have are the many narratives that have been told for two thousand years about a man named Jesus.

Walter Wink

Walter Wink, a longtime associate of Howes, came to a different conclusion from Childs: "We do not need 'a *final* truth of history,' but only approximate truth, backed up by evidence."[439] Wink acknowledges the postmodern critique that Childs raises, but does not deny the existence of a historical Jesus.

In his book *The Human Being*, Wink takes a view contrary to Childs's, arguing for "a myth of a human Jesus," This is an instructive lesson in how two people—Wink and Childs—can look at the same information and arrive at different conclusions. Wink agrees about the impossibility of finding the "real" Jesus. He writes, "Biblical scholars have been exceedingly slow to grasp the implications of the Heisenberg principle, that the observer is always a part of the field being observed, and disturbs that field by the very act of observation."[440]

Wink accepts the validity of contemporary scholars that all views are subjective, and every student comes with their own "interest" in the subject. He quotes Brian Stock, "Historical writing does not treat reality; it treats the interpreter's relation to it,"[441] and Wendy Doniger O'Flaherty, "All truly creative scholarship in the humanities is autobiographical."[442] He agrees with Childs's point that, as Wink puts it, "The past is not an object we can observe. It is an idea we have in the present about the past."[443]

However, in response to Childs's conclusion "that Jesus of Nazareth, as a real person who once lived but who now no longer exists, is unapproachable by historical-critical methods,"[444] Wink argues, "The text is a brute fact, not a Rorschach inkblot onto which any conceivable interpretation can be read. The great if limited value of the historical-critical approach is that it debunks arbitrary notions of what the text might mean."[445] He intends "to overcome the objectivist illusion that disinterested exegesis is possible; and to affirm the present meaning of the past by means of the most rigorous exegesis possible."[446]

To do such work, the scholar must acknowledge what Schweitzer saw as the motivating force behind the quest for the historical Jesus: "a modern longing to be encountered by the divine."[447] Wink's approach means acknowledging that "Every picture of Jesus that scholars produced was inevitably invested with that scholar's projections onto Jesus, positive or negative."[448] It is Wink's contention that "the quest for the *historical* Jesus has all along been the quest for the *human* Jesus."[449] It is a quest, he believes, that can be pursued through the method of historical-criticism which places upon the searcher rules and boundaries of what is and is not admissible evidence. And in contrast to Childs, Wink concludes, "The myth of the human Jesus cannot simply be spun out of the air, because that myth insists on the historicity of the human Jesus."[450] Wink accepts that historical research cannot find the "real" Jesus, but holds to his belief that there was a historical Jesus at the center of the story.

Finkelstein, Silberman, and Assmann:
Myth or History, Who Decides?

In reviewing archaeological findings, scholars Israel Finkelstein and Neil Asher Silberman found no evidence of the grand events reported in the Pentateuch, the first five books of Hebrew scripture, so they challenged the historical validity of treasured Bible stories "from Abraham's encounter with God and his journey to Canaan, to Moses' deliverance of the children of Israel from bondage, to the rise and fall of the kingdoms of Israel and Judah."[451] Based on the evidence they reviewed, they concluded that the first five books of the Bible were not written during the tenth and ninth centuries BCE during the (supposed) reigns of Solomon and David, but two and a half centuries later, "toward the end of the seventh century BCE," and that "it was an epic saga woven together from an astonishingly rich collection of historical writings, memories, legends, folk tales, anecdotes, royal propaganda, prophecy, and ancient poetry."[452]

> Much of what is commonly taken for granted as accurate history—the stories of the patriarchs, the Exodus, the conquest of Canaan, and even the saga of the glorious united monarchy of David and Solomon—are, rather, the creative expression of a powerful religious reform movement that flourished in the kingdom of Judah in the Late Iron Age.[453]

Finkelstein and Silberman did not intend to debunk this great epic, but to help us see it in a different light:

> The power of the biblical saga stems from its being a compelling and coherent narrative expression of the timeless themes of a people's liberation, continuing resistance to oppression, and quest for social equality. It eloquently expresses the deeply rooted sense of shared origins, experiences, and destiny that every human community needs

in order to survive. ... We can at last begin to appreciate the
true genius and continuing power of this single most
influential literary and spiritual creation in the history of
humanity.[454]

Finkelstein and Silberman see the Old Testament not as history, but as
a "literary and spiritual creation" no less powerful and significant.

Egyptologist Jan Assmann's mnemohistory, on the other hand, "is
concerned not with the past *as such*, but only with the past as it is
remembered."[455] For example, although we have no evidence that
Moses lived, because of the story and the tradition, we remember him
as a historic figure. In contrast, Akhenaton, the Egyptian king who
instituted a monotheistic religion in the fourteenth century BCE, "was
forgotten immediately after his death" because his religion spawned
no tradition. "Moses is a figure of memory but not of history, while
Akhenaton is a figure of history but not of memory."[456] We in the
European-Western tradition have lived in this "constructed mental or
cultural space" for two millennia.

Can we say that the Christian myth is memory not history, that
the entire story, even though set in a historical time about which there
is much evidence, is myth? That it is one of the great stories arising out
of the collective unconscious and woven, as Finkelstein and Silberman
say of the Torah, of "historical writings, memories, legends, folk tales,
anecdotes, royal propaganda, prophecy, and ancient poetry.[457]

These views help us think about the power of the Christian myth,
whether there is a verifiably historical Jesus at its center or not. While
many continue to find in the Guild's study of the Synoptic Gospels a
historical figure, a personality who preaches and teaches, lives and dies,
others may find a mythic Jesus no less compelling.

Finkelstein, Silberman, and Assmann argue that history derives
from written records, artifacts, legends, poetry, folk tales, and memory;
blurring the line between myth and historicity. That history is a
narrative about events—real and remembered—is a view these three

scholars articulate, suggesting that history is what we *remember*, which is what Assmann means by *mnemohistory*.

My own study leads me to see that Jesus, historical figure or not, is a rich symbol of a human being living in relationship to the archetypal self. He is the before and the beyond-Christianity that Howes spoke of. Each of us, I believe, has to come to our own conclusion whether he lived in history, and in this way, new narratives may arise out of the old Gospel accounts. But I'm getting ahead of myself. I've shared the theoretical overview of the quest I have been on my whole life, and in Part Two, I'll speak more—memoir-style—about the process.

Part Two

The Guild Seminars

Chapter 5

My First Seminar

A magic dwells in each beginning
and protecting us it tells us how to live.[458]
— Hermann Hesse

It was a rainy morning approaching the spring equinox of 1984, now thirty-seven years ago, when I arrived at my first Guild seminar. I had heard about the Guild for Psychological Studies for years, that it was dedicated to the study of the world's great myths, and that its core program, called *Records,* was a study of Jesus and his teachings from the perspective of Jung's depth psychology. The friend who had told me about it said it had changed her life. I couldn't imagine how such transformation comes about, but from the moment she told me about it, I knew I had to attend.

I was at a crossroads in my life. The Berkeley retreat house where I was codirector was about to close; our appreciation of silence, meditation, and reflection proved no match for our financial naiveté. I wanted meaning and direction for my life, and hoped the study of the life and teaching of Jesus at this Guild seminar would reveal it to me. It was not the Christ of Christianity I was looking for, but a man who seemed to know something I wanted to know.

Memoir

In Part Two of this book, I recount my experiences of *Records* seminars and other Guild events I attended. It is a *memoir*, as defined by William Zinsser: "The writer of a memoir takes us back to a corner of his or her life that was unusually vivid or intense … or that was framed by unique events. By narrowing the lens, the writer achieves a focus that isn't possible in autobiography; memoir is a window into a life." By sorting out memories and emotions they "arrived at a version of their past that they felt was true."[459]

In other words, it's a process of history and myth, facts and memories, not unlike the quest for the historical Jesus and the historicity of the Christian story explored in Part One. Looking through my journals, notes, and expressive art, I too am sorting through memories and emotions to understand how the seminars helped me weave together the many strands of thought, imagination, somatic experience, ritual, and play that made possible a new understanding of a familiar tale. In the sense that a therapist's case studies are "fiction"—the story of what was remembered of what was told to them by their patients[460]—so memoir is sharing memories of things past and the sense I made of them then and make of them now. Here, the client is both the seminar and myself, and I am creating this case study out of my own remembrances of events, emotions, and mnemohistory, a word coined by Jan Assmann: *mnemohistory* "is concerned not with the past as such, but only with the past as it is remembered."[461]

"In myths and fairytales, as in dreams," Jung wrote, "the psyche tells its own story, and the interplay of the archetypes is revealed in its natural setting, as 'formation, transformation / the eternal Mind's eternal recreation.'"[462] That can be said of the Christian myth too, with its interweaving of mythology and history.

Day One: Tuesday, March 13, 1984

The first day of my first Guild seminar began at 11 a.m. I arrived, breathless, a few minutes late. I was driving my VW Rabbit with Anthea, codirector of our Berkeley community. The Rabbit was crammed with my things for sixteen days. The plan was for Anthea to take my car after dropping me off. Uncharacteristically, I hadn't studied a map beforehand; I just blindly headed north toward the wine country. But somewhere past Calistoga I missed a turn, and we were running late.

I backtracked to Tubbs Lane, went past The Geysers, and began the ascent over Mount Saint Helena. The two-lane road wound its way upward through madrones and black oaks just beginning to leaf, many of the trees leaning over the road to form a canopy that was dripping from the spring rains. I've marveled at the beauty of this drive many times since: bright with color in the fall, majestically bare and bleak in winter, glowing with brilliant fresh shades of green in spring, and bathed in darker, cooling hues of green during the hot summer months. But that day, running late, I neither noticed nor appreciated the beauty, focusing instead on the twists and turns in the road. Thankfully, I wasn't behind any slow-moving cars.

The road to Four Springs is not well-marked, but fortunately we arrived in the nick of time at a small house I later learned is the caretaker's home. A sign alongside the road read: "Four Springs Keep Out. Dead End Turn Around Here." As an invited guest, I proceeded. The road became steep, and I swept past a mowed field that had been an orchard, drove between two stone pillars, and came to a halt in front of a large log structure. Our greeter, John, ushered me up the stairs and into the grand old living room, where a circle of faces gazed at me—three leaders, two other staff besides John, and eleven participants.

I've thought since how disruptive my arrival must have been. In those days, Guild seminars began *on time* or the whole group waited till the tardy members arrived. I don't know whether they followed the rule that morning or had given up and begun. I only remember the hustle and bustle of it all. I found a seat in the circle, took a moment to catch my breath and look about me, and began to take in the feel of the room, which would become so familiar in the next sixteen days and for the next twenty-five years. It took some moments for my heart to quiet and for me to sink back into relative invisibility after that grand entrance. I took notes that morning, and this is what I wrote:

Sacred Time, Sacred Space: These days here.
    What can this sense of sacred say to me?
    What in me needs to die so something new can be born?
    What is the new that needs/wants to be born?

Gate: We came through one as we arrived.
    What does this gate mean to you?
    (Choice, focus, beginnings and endings)

Epidaurus: Only those who know they are in need of healing are bidden.

Epidaurus was an ancient Greek city famed for its fourth-century BCE temple to Asclepius, the god of healing. I came to learn that the Guild often used this quotation in workshops, but these words only begin to capture the sense of what was brought forth in the hour we sat together before lunch. The leaders established the themes, which were sometimes articulated but always present. We had entered sacred time *(kairos)* and sacred space *(temenos),* "time out of time." For sixteen days, we would remain on these grounds, working individually and together to learn what in each of us was crying out for healing. *What brought us here? What needed to die? What needed to be born? Was it God? What did we mean by "God"? What was our understanding of our relationship to a man named Jesus? Who was that man? Who was he to me, to each one of us, now?*

I had barely noticed the gate as I rushed past it that morning. In later, dryer years, we'd go outside, walk between the stone pillars, and continue down the road a bit. Then we'd turn around to face the gate those pillars define, stand there for a moment, and *choose* to walk back through them, knowing we were choosing to embark on a journey that could and would take us into unknown, unexplored territory of our inner landscapes. But on that first rainy March day, we didn't go outside. We visualized the gates and imagined making the choice to pass through them and begin our journey.

That first time I entered the gate at Four Springs, I was approaching my fiftieth birthday. It was the beginning of a new stage of my life's journey and the end of a tumultuous three years, trying with others to keep alive a retreat house in Berkeley called The Desert. This three-story, shingle-sided home on a residential street was *a place in the city to enter the desert*. Spiritual seekers have always retreated in search of something. The Desert was conceived by dreamers who knew the value of silent retreat, but not much, I'm afraid, about finding funding. Anthea and I were the last in a short line of keepers of the retreat. Before leaving for Four Springs, we had accepted that we had to close The Desert, and I had no idea where my journey would take me. I hoped this seminar might help show me the way.

That first morning's seminar had ended with introductions. One of the leaders explained the process and then began. Turning to the person on her right, she said, "My name is Alice Newman," and then she asked, "And who are you?" That person said, "My name is …" giving her first and last name, then she turned to the person to her right and repeated, "My name is …" before asking, "And who are you?" And so, everyone introduced themselves around the circle, ending with the second leader, who said, "My name is Mary Edwards." She then turned to Alice Newman to complete the circle.

This welcoming tradition was a way to put names to faces. The formality of addressing one another by first and last names was followed whenever we referred to one another during seminar time. "As Elli Norris was saying, …" "As Alice Newman said, …" It was a way of acknowledging each person fully, and a habit that grew on me, so that today I still want to hear both or all the names of a person. It seems to convey a sense of the whole of them.

Not a Christian Anymore?

I don't call myself Christian anymore. Yet Jesus grabbed me as a child and stays with me as I move into old age. I find it embarrassing to speak of Jesus; I immediately feel the need to explain that I am not an evangelical Christian, not one who believes the Bible was dictated by God, not even one who knows what "God" is. I do not believe in Jesus Christ as my or the world's Lord and Savior therefore, I am not a Christian. Yet here is Jesus, still speaking to me after all these years. What's going on? Why does this figure called Jesus still grip so many of us, some who are still beneath the broad umbrella of Christianity, others of us who have left, some who were never under that umbrella, and still others who grew up Jewish or in some other faith tradition?

In those next sixteen days and for the decades that followed, I would find some answers to these questions, but not to all of them.

The Who and What of the Records Seminar

During a sit-down lunch on our first day together, our group of thirteen began to meet one another. Gradually, I came to understand that there were three leaders. Alice Newman and Patricia Wells had been associated with the Guild for decades though they were not much older than I. (Names of seminar leaders, staff, and participants have been changed out of courtesy, except for the three Guild founders who are well-known public figures.) A third leader, Julie Anderson, was called "Art Resource" or simply "Resource," the staff person who brought forth art materials for us to use not to create "works of art," but to express feelings and images that came as we worked our way through *Records*. Resource also placed artwork in the living room and in later years in a small building called the art meditation room, where she created whatever occurred to her that symbolized or expressed the passages we were working with. Next to the art meditation room was an art studio, where we could find various arts and crafts supplies to work with day or night. And Resource met with us individually to discuss our own artwork and what messages these expressions might be holding for us to see.

There were three more essential staff members. The cook, Anne Coles, had attended previous *Records* seminars and was both cook and participant in this one. The staff was completed with two "committee people," the pair who kept household logistics running—providing chairs and candles, making repairs, and building fires everything needed to keep a lodge and outbuildings, and the people in them, comfortable for sixteen days.

In those days, there was a committee man and a committee woman. The former was in charge of outdoor things and general maintenance, things that in 1984 were thought of as men's work. For the duration of the seminar, only the committee man was permitted to leave the grounds for errands, unless a medical emergency required someone to go to the clinic in nearby Middletown. John Noble, who had met us on arrival that morning, was the committee man and a leader-in-training.

The committee woman, Susan Greg, was in charge of indoor tasks—housekeeping, coordinating with the cook, making the rooms cozy with candles, flowers, and greenery, as well as shepherding us through our chores in the kitchen and grounds. She, too, was a member of the Guild leadership-training class.

Those rigid gender roles were loosened over the course of the next twenty years. Eventually this support staff position came to be called simply "Committee." One person, man or woman, took care of outside things; the other was the keeper of the house. Fewer fires were built in keeping with a higher environmental awareness. It remained the case, though, that only one "committee" would leave the property to get groceries, pick up mail, or purchase the *San Francisco Chronicle* (so we weren't entirely cut off from the outside world). But mail and the newspaper were not put out until social time just before dinner. The seminar and the silent time were not intruded upon. It was one of the committee people who made the rounds early in the morning to ring the wake-up gong and light the candle in the meditation room, as well as sound the good night gong at 10 p.m.

Individuals in Community

As "individuals in community," three or four of us on a rotating basis helped the cook and committee woman do what was necessary before the meal and clean the kitchen afterward. We also did "meditative work," such as bringing in firewood, feeding the cats, or sweeping the porches and patio. And we helped tidy the common rooms, the library, and the art room; clear the swimming pool of debris; and clean the bathrooms.

The outlying bathrooms, in a building that had a curved stick affixed to it in the shape of a serpent, were named Adam and Eve. Each had two toilet stalls, two sinks, a cramped shower, a row of pegs for towels, and two narrow shelves for toiletries. These rustic facilities were unfairly apportioned, since there were only two men among staff and attendees. Since then, the facilities have improved, and each cabin and each bedroom in the main house has a private bathroom.

We wrestled with the Synoptic Gospels and the leaders' questions and prompts in the seminar room circle, the living room, the grape arbor near the olive tree, at Standing Stones, a ten-minute walk away, and in the meadow near the lodge. We each brought our own life experiences and struggles to this work, not attempting to arrive at consensus but working as individuals in a group that was becoming a community.

Although we weren't seeking consensus, the leaders did have a focus that guided the work—the *historical* Jesus and his teachings informed by the depth psychology of C. G. Jung. Rather than a search for the Christ of faith, *our task was to tease apart, through close study of the Synoptic Gospels, the man Jesus from the story told about him.*

This perspective was stated in the brochure that each of us had received before registering and was made known in direct discussion with staff members. It became most apparent in the question-and-answer process of the seminar, as we turned to the question, By what name shall we call Jesus?

A Routine Day

At 6 a.m., a silent figure makes her way along the well-worn dirt trail from her cabin, past other still-dark cabins among madrones, manzanitas, oaks, and evergreens, past the seminar room and the library to a small building set near, yet slightly to one side of, the rest. She, or he, opens the wooden door and steps into the entrance hall, finds the box of matches, and continues into the meditation room—wood and glass shaped as an overturned arc, broad beams curving from each corner to meet at the center of the ceiling, tall windows facing west into the trees, a small, round, stained-glass window glowing when daylight comes on the remaining walls. In the center of the room there is a wooden stand, upon which sits an interlacing of metal strips that form a globe. Almost hidden at the top of the globe is a small trap door. The silent figure approaches the globe-sculpture, opens the tiny trap door, and lights the votive candle inside that will burn all day long, until the gong sounds at 10 p.m.

The silent figure leaves the meditation room and walks, more briskly now, to the lodge, climbs the steps to the broad porch, and rings the gong to begin another Guild seminar day, one sound for each of us in attendance. Then she or he cheerily rings the small bell, walking from cabin to cabin to bring forth the new day. A few of us are already up to get our morning showers in Adam or Eve before the others arrive. This is the ritual to begin each day.

Except for the bells and early morning birdsong, all is silent. Silence begins and ends each day. We don't even greet our cabinmates during that time, or so the rule says. The silence began the night before with the closing gong at 10:00, and will continue until the seminar begins at 8:30 a.m. This silence is, in itself, a presence, a time for staying present with whatever emotions, images, and thoughts are stirring, or just to do nothing.

We're silent at other times during the day, too. After the morning seminar, we observe half an hour of silence before lunch, and after the afternoon seminar, there's an hour of silence before we gather for socializing and dinner. In some seminars, half a day or an entire day is also given to silence.

At 7 a.m., a gong sounds to remind us that it's time to gather for the day's first circle. On pleasant days, we form the circle near the giant olive tree on the lodge patio; on rainy days we gather in the living room. We stand in silence until the morning reading—a poem or a short prose passage. It might be Kazantzakis's terrible message from the "Cry," which demands that the human "Stand up!" Risk all to take yet another step out of the primordial waters of unconsciousness.[463] Or it might be Secretary-General Dag Hammarskjöld's injunction, "You dare your Yes and experience a meaning. You respect your Yes and all things acquire a meaning. When everything has a meaning, how can you live anything but a Yes?"[464] Or it could be T. S. Eliot, Sheila Moon, Rainer Maria Rilke, Mary Oliver, David Whyte, Rumi, William Stafford, or any writer who stirs the imagination and addresses the questions that brought us here.

The reading done, we step apart to find a space for ourselves, and recorded music fills the air perhaps Carlos Nakai with his Native American flute, or Buffy Sainte-Marie reminding us, in her quirky way, that "God Is Alive," or Mahalia Jackson singing of the loss of Abraham, Martin, and John, or it might be Brahms or Fauré, Rutter or Taverner. Each of us responds as we wish, in movement or stillness, for five or ten minutes, then we go to the kitchen to pick up breakfast, find a place in the lodge or outdoors to eat in silence, and prepare for the morning seminar. Participants on morning crew clean and tidy the kitchen before rushing to seminar.

At 8:25, the gong begins to sound once a minute till 8:30, when everyone is supposed to be seated in the seminar room. The leaders sit to either side of the fireplace or sometimes randomly. Two people light the taper candles set on sconces above the fireplace, and the silence is broken with "Good morning!" Emerging from silence, we turn to the study of passages in the *Records of the Life of Jesus.*

Throughout the morning, each of us ponders the critical questions about sources, differences among the Gospels and why, and seeks the significance of each passage for ourselves. We begin with John the Baptist, who came preaching of baptism and repentance. On the following days, we meet Jesus, who comes to be baptized and then is driven or was he led? into the wilderness where he is "tempted by Satan."[465] Through the days of the seminar, we follow Jesus who calls his disciples to follow him as he preaches and heals or does he? and prays, and turns his face to Jerusalem to meet his final test. We will each engage our own understanding of what happened after the crucifixion.

After lunch there's time for swimming, a walk on Big or Little Circle Trail, sunbathing, napping, or dancing with abandon. Always at the center is *the work* of the seminar. Each morning we wrestle with the Synoptic Gospels and the questions raised and work with these ideas in the afternoons through mime, expressive art, or dialogue with inner and outer figures.

Some evenings are festive, some we gather and reflect on a question that touches our life, and on other evenings we'd hear from the original Guild leaders about the history of the Guild or just to listen to their stories. Now that the three are gone, we gather with the leaders they trained for movement or guided relaxation and shared massage, or simply to sit and listen to music and reflect on the day.

Slowly people begin to disappear from the group, going to the library, the art room, or the meditation room. Finally, we make it back to our cabins. The gong sounds at 10 p.m., beckoning silence till we begin a new day tomorrow.

Chapter 6

The Work of Discerning

I love the way in *Records* seminars we enter two lines of converging history, both the gospel story we're studying and the history of the Guild itself—the three women who founded it and the man who created the text we work with, *Records of the Life of Jesus*. Henry Burton Sharman, always called Dr. Sharman by Guild leaders and participants, used the question-and-response method that was always at the core of Guild seminars, although much has been added since Dr. Sharman's first Canadian retreats. Following is a story shared by one of the women who attended his 1919 seminar:

> "What are the names with which you are familiar by which the one who is the centre of our study is commonly known?"

> "The Master," "Our Lord," "Christ," "Lamb of God," "King of Kings" out they all came tumbling from the silent, terrified *Intellectuals*! Then: "What do the records give us as his name?" "Jesus: thou shalt call His name *Jesus*."

> "Then this is how he will be called by us until the records lead us toward some other designation. For us his name will be Jesus."[466]

When I attended my first Guild seminar and onward, these questions continued to be used to introduce us to critical thinking about Jesus and the Gospels.

On the afternoon of the first day of the 1984 seminar, the leader instructed us to write these words at the top of a sheet of paper: *Jesus, Christ,* and *Messiah,* and had us write a definition beneath each. I discovered how much I thought I knew and didn't. "Jesus, a man," I wrote down. I added descriptives like "wise and compassionate," "in touch with something greater than himself," and "followed his destiny to his death." I had no idea how to define *Messiah* and *Christ.*

At a later seminar, I wrote, "Messiah: a leader who will save us from the terrible world we're in. Christ: a divine being 'of God' who will enter this reality to save us." At another seminar, apparently in an angrier mood, I wrote, "Christ: some made-up dream created from our longing to be 'saved,' taken care of," adding, "I feel anger at the fundamentalists' demand that everyone should accept Jesus as Christ, Messiah, that is, our Lord and Savior." I was not alone struggling with definitions. Some of the other participants wrote: "Jesus: son of God," "Human being like us," "A man so receptive to divinity that he brought that divinity into the conscious world," and "Christ: son of God."

The leader helped us by explaining *messiah* comes from the Hebrew word for "anointed one," as the kings of the ancient Middle East were anointed with oil when they ascended their throne. And *Christ* is the Greek word for "messiah." "We'll refer to Jesus as *Jesus* in our historical work," said the leader. "We bracket *Christ*. Why is this important?"

Several people responded: "Christ is a faith statement, the belief that Jesus is the Christ, the one who is different from all others." "For some Christians, Jesus Christ has no faults." and "In some cultures, people just say Jesus Christ. That's his name."

"How do you feel about putting *Christ* in brackets for the time being?" asked the leader. Someone said, "Relieved." Another said, "Relieved, and yet I still feel a pull to Jesus Christ."

Just as participants at Sharman's seminars had been led to do so long ago, we focused on a man, Jesus the Jew; we did not begin with Jesus Christ. My challenge, as was each of ours for the rest of the seminar, would be to determine which name I believed was correct. Perhaps I'd even discover why my stomach clenched in anger when people said, "Jesus Christ."

The Records Book

After lunch on the first day of the 1984 seminar, I settled into Big Star, the cabin I'd be sharing with Mary Johnson, also from Berkeley, for the next sixteen days. Mary had attended previous seminars. Although we hadn't met before, our pairing was fortuitous, for we both brought skepticism sometimes and an irreverent sense of humor to the process.

Big Star was the largest of the cabins with windows on three sides and a small deck outside the entry. Propped up on my bed during afternoon quiet time, I could look out the window and watch the black oaks begin to put out their delicate pink leaves, raindrops hanging from their edges and captured in their folds. At times, I was startled by the harsh rat-a-tat-tat of the pileated woodpeckers that lived in the neighborhood, flitting from evergreen to evergreen, and in season, came to the grape arbor to harvest the fruit. A big show-off of a bird with a flashy red hood to set off its black-and-white costume, its raucous call think Woody the Woodpecker often lightened our arduous seminar work.

On the afternoon of our first day, we met in the seminar room. From the lodge, where we'd had lunch, we went down the stairs, across the dirt area where I had arrived so hurriedly that morning, over a small wooden bridge that spanned a tiny rivulet of water, and up three brick stairs into the wood-paneled seminar room. A fire was ablaze in the stone fireplace; two Navajo rugs lay on the wooden floor in the middle of a circle of wooden chairs, some with armrests, others not, all with cushions and small footstools to ease the hours we'd be sitting together.

After the opening ritual lighting the candles on the sconces, the leaders gave us each a copy of *Records of the Life of Jesus*. As noted, this book contains the Synoptic Gospels, Matthew, Mark, and Luke, in parallel columns. The Gospel of John is also in the book, but separate from the synoptics and not a part of *Records* study. Most scholars agree that John's account does not pretend to be historical; it presents what came to be the Christian vision of Jesus Christ. In contrast, Matthew, Mark, and Luke contain or may contain accounts of the historical Jesus.

The *Records* book I was given fit nicely on one knee with my notebook on the other. It was a hardcover, about six by nine inches and 239 pages of the fine print required to fit three columns of gospel text on one page. There were footnotes on each page that referred the reader to passages in Hebrew scripture to which the gospel text might refer or derive from, occasionally offered alternate translations of the original Greek, and sometimes commented on the sequence in which a particular passage appeared. It was the text that New Testament scholar Dr. Henry Burton Sharman compiled around the turn of the twentieth century. The copyright was 1917, and it has been reprinted many times since.

The Guild published this book in a larger format, about eight-and-a-half by eleven, in 1991, using the Revised Standard Version (RSV) of the Bible, updating Dr. Sharman's English Revised Version (ERV) of 1881, and using a larger typeface which makes it easier to read. There have been additions; perhaps most important are the references to parallels in the Gospel of Thomas, a non-canonical sayings Gospel that was discovered near Nag Hammadi, Egypt, in 1945. Otherwise, it's basically the same book Dr. Sharman compiled for use in his seminar method, which was the same at its core as the Guild's method.

Guild leaders refer to this as a modified Socratic approach in which the leader brings questions about passages in the synoptic stories intended to spark new ways of thinking. Questions are put *into the circle*, and responses are also put into the circle, without comment from Guild leaders. More responses are put forth; another question is posed; and more responses are given, all without comment or discussion.

Elizabeth Boyden Howes, who in contrast with Dr. Sharman was called by her first name by everyone at seminars, attended his seminar for the first time in 1931 and had been *gripped* by the story and the method, as she told us many times over the years. She had begun leading seminars following this method in 1934 and continued to do so until she was in her seventies. By that time, she and her colleagues had for some years been training a new generation of leaders to carry on the work. The three cofounders of the Guild, and many of the men and women who became engaged with them in *Records* study, have added insights and methods gained from Jung's depth psychology which were not a part of Dr. Sharman's approach, nor his interest. Succeeding generations have also added the study of other myths— first incorporated were Native American myths, one of Sheila Moon's great interests.

There is a picture of Dr. Sharman in the library at Four Springs revealing a proper gentleman wearing an early-twentieth-century gray business suit, a white shirt with a stiff collar attached by buttons, a necktie, and well-polished shoes, sitting upright in a rocking chair. According to accounts from seminar participants, he never rocked or even moved during the four-hour sessions he led on Jesus's life and teachings. This was a man of the old school, a man with a mission that for two decades led him to conduct seminars in the wilds of Minnesing, Ontario, reached only by train and for the final few miles, canoe.

That's the journey Elizabeth Howes made from Stanford University, where she was a student, in 1934. Fifty years later, I was participating in the work she and her colleagues had continued and expanded to include their own depth-psychology perspective.

Thinking

In 1984, I didn't know about the quest for the historical Jesus that began during the Enlightenment and continued among scholars till the present day. Some scholars believe it's possible to find a historical Jesus at the root of the stories; while others believe that Jesus Christ, the risen savior, is the center of the story. For the *Records* seminar and for me, it was Jesus we were interested in. Whether he was or thought he was Jesus Christ was a question we were confronted with many times each seminar. The search for this Jesus and what he taught was, I slowly learned, not simple.

It required first of all what the leaders called "critical work," paying attention to the possible sources of each Gospel and how each account was similar or different, then considering why that might be so. I saw no point in this, especially when the differences seemed to be just a word or two. It took years before I understood the crucial place of the critical work as I and my fellow participants sifted through the Gospel accounts for what *might have been* the original story, even the original thought, if not the words of Jesus.

We began the 1984 seminar by becoming familiar with the *Records* book and its organization. In a traditional New Testament, Matthew, Mark, and Luke are presented one after the other with chapters and verses within each. Matthew comes first, even though scholars today believe it was written between 80 and 90 CE,* after Mark's Gospel. Next comes Mark, believed to be the first of the Gospels, written around 70 CE. And third is Luke, written perhaps about the same time as Matthew.

My first Bible as a child was a King James Version, given me by my grandmother. It was leather bound, and the edges of the cover became dog-eared and worn, not from great use but from being moved from place to place, shelved in an upright position not intended for its soft edges. The words attributed to Jesus are in red, on gilt-edged pages.

* Guild custom follows current scholarly practice in using CE (Common Era) and BCE (Before Common Era), rather than the clearly Christian delineation BC (Before Christ) and AD (Anno Domini).

I loved seeing the red-letter words and believing Jesus really said these things. My name is embossed in gold on the cover.

I never knew, until at age fifty when I was handed the *Records* book, that the three Gospels don't begin in the same place and often don't even tell the same story. Matthew begins with the genealogy that leads up to Jesus. Luke begins with the story of Zechariah and Elizabeth, who in her old age conceived a child, John the Baptist. Matthew and Luke tell variations of the Christmas story. Mark says nothing of genealogy or of the birth stories. He begins with John the Baptist, who comes preaching repentance for the forgiveness of sins. Matthew and Luke tell a version of this story too the first time all three Gospel accounts are present together in the parallel columns of the *Records* book. I was nearly fifty years old, and I hadn't known that! Embarrassing. Grandma would be disappointed.

The way the *Records* book is laid out, it becomes obvious that the three Gospels are not identical. The Gospel passages are grouped into sections, and sections into portions, and it isn't until page 15 of the *Records* book that all three Gospels appear together for the first time. Each paragraph is given a letter—A, B, C, and so on. When I quote from the synoptics, I give both Gospel chapter and verse and *Records* section and portion. [467]

The leaders told us what most contemporary scholars believe about the sources for each of the Gospel accounts.[468] Mark, the earliest Gospel, is one of the sources for Matthew and Luke. Matthew and Luke have many passages that agree with each other but are missing from Mark, so biblical scholars hypothesized a source from which Matthew and Luke worked, known as the Sayings Gospel and called "Q," for *Quelle,* German meaning source. Although Q has not been discovered, scholars believe it is earlier than Mark. Luke also has material that is not in Mark or Matthew, and Matthew has some material that is not in Mark or Luke. Thus they conclude that there are two other source documents, one particular to Matthew and one particular to Luke.

If they are correct, there are at least four sources for the three Gospels: Mark, Q, Matthew's special source (M), and Luke's special source (L). Every time we began working with a new section in *Records,* the critical questions brought were: What is the source? Are the Gospel accounts the same or different? Why? If a story is omitted from one of the Synoptic Gospels, why might that be so? Working our way through much of Jesus's life and teachings, noting where the Gospel stories agreed and where they didn't and surmising why, and whether it makes any difference, was part of the work we did the next sixteen days.

Each day, we were assigned passages from the *Records* book to read the next day. Gathered in the seminar room each morning, we listened as the leaders brought questions about those passages and responded out of our own understanding. Our task was not to come to agreement or to argue with each other or even engage in discussion. We simply "put our answers into the circle." We would hear ourselves say what we thought in that moment, and we'd hear what others thought. This was the magic of the seminar process processing the questions that opened our minds to new possibilities, finding our own image of Jesus and what he might really have taught. This was a quest for the Jesus who appeared in the *Records* seeking the answer to the ultimate question: Who do *I* think Jesus was?

A Long Day's End

After supper the first day, we gathered in the living room, its wood-paneled walls and large windows reflecting the light from the ever-burning fire and candles, to view slides—images taken from a recent trip to Israel showing the desert John the Baptist and Jesus knew so well. This was not welcoming country. My notes from that evening:

"What kind of God would be here?" a leader asks.
She explains that this is the God who told Moses to say to Pharaoh: "I am who I am. Tell them, 'I am' has sent me."
The leader asks, "Is this a 'finished' God? Or is this a God in process?"
She asks, "Does God require relationship with us?"

I wrote a note to myself which I highlighted in red. "What would it mean to be a co-creator with God of this still-incomplete creation?" I replied, "Relationship."

Then a leader read a passage from Luke:

And behold, a lawyer stood up to put him to the test, saying, "Teacher, what shall I do to inherit eternal life?" He said to him, "What is written in the law? How do you read?" And he answered, "You shall love the Lord your God with all your heart, and with all your soul, and with all your strength, and with all your mind; and your neighbor as yourself." And [Jesus] said to him, "You have answered right; do this, and you will live."[469]

The leader asked: "Can you *love* the God we've been talking about with all your heart and all your soul and all your strength and all your mind?" "What does it mean to love yourself?" "What are clues that there is more to you than you know?"

The passage was familiar, yet I found these questions troubling: Who is this God? What would it mean to love that God with my *all*? What *is* that all? To love myself so I can love others? And to know there is more to myself than I know?

Another question was asked: "What other words come to you for 'God'?" The group's responses included, "Mystery, Life Force, Higher Power, Beloved Spirit, Energy, Sophia, Challenger, Essence, Divinity, Guide, and Unfolding Pattern of the Universe." We were not wed to a single definition of who or what God—who was central to Jesus's life and in some form to our own lives—might be. This God was central to our study, yet for each one of us He/She/It had a different form, or none at all. My mind reeled.

Chapter 7

Meeting the Three

As the evening seminar came to a close, we heard a car approach, then the sound of footsteps coming upstairs. The Guild's founding leaders, Elizabeth Boyden Howes, Sheila Moon, and Luella Sibbald ("the Three," as they were called) had just arrived from Europe via San Francisco International Airport. These legendary figures had touched the lives of hundreds if not thousands out of devotion, dedication, and skill. I learned a lot about these qualities as these elders assumed their roles the rest of the seminar.

We each met them, greeted by our first and last names in keeping with the tradition we'd learned that morning. "So, you're Elli Norris! I've been wanting to meet you! I'm Elizabeth Howes. ... I'm Luella Sibbald. ... I'm Sheila Moon." They had done their homework and were prepared to meet us. It never ceased to amaze me that they remembered the first and last names of everyone they met.

As the seminar unfolded, I learned more about these women. They were sitting together in a pub in Oxford, England in 1956 when they decided to form the Guild for Psychological Studies. Elizabeth had already been leading *Records* seminars since the 1930s, first in the Stanford area, then in the mountains of Southern California from 1942 to 1956, and then they moved to Four Springs. Sheila met Elizabeth in 1940 when she attended her first *Records* retreat and began working with her on seminars soon after. Luella joined them in 1946. Supported by a network of people who had studied with Elizabeth, they formed a nonprofit organization patterned after the guilds of the Middle Ages, a loosely affiliated, voluntary community seeking spiritual truths in this particular way.

Although I didn't know this story that evening, I knew as I looked into Elizabeth's craggy face, her straight gray hair cut in simple Dutch-boy style, middle height, still upright even though she was supporting herself with a cane, that this woman was a force of nature. *Records,* she often said, "grabbed me" young and never let her go. After decades of leading *Records* seminars and sitting in circles as a participant, she could still say, and mean, "Now that's interesting. I never thought of it that way before."

Luella, who like Elizabeth would soon reach her seventy-seventh year, was also lovely. Her white hair swept up and back in a stylish wave, her profile was patrician; her smile when turned full-face radiated delight, welcome, and pleasure. She was the softest of the three, and some say the warmest. At The Pines in Southern California, she had been coordinator for the seminars, although she was also a teacher in the San Francisco Unified School District and had a private therapy practice with individual clients, using sand play and other expressive methods. It was Luella who introduced movement and art expression to the seminars. In her middle years, she had studied astrology in Zürich with Gret Baumann-Jung, C.G. Jung's daughter. She loved telling us that Elizabeth had pooh-poohed astrology until Toni Wolff, one of Jung's foremost followers and also his muse, his mistress, told Luella that it was "unwise to let former interests fall back into the unconscious." She recounted this story in her book *Footprints of God: The Relationship of Astrology, C. G. Jung and the Gospels.*

Sheila was a poet and perhaps a mystic, and certainly the most reticent when we met that evening. Yet she revealed much of herself in her writings, most of all in *Dreams of a Woman: An Analyst's Inner Journey,* in which she analyzed her own dreams over a period of nearly forty years to see how they revealed her life course. She followed as well her love of Native American myth, which she wrote about in *A*

Magic Dwells: A Poetic and Psychological Study of the Navaho Emergence Myth and *Changing Woman and Her Sisters: Feminine Aspects of Selves and Deities.* Her love of *Records* seminars and the man Jesus are expressed in her poetry, particularly in *Joseph's Son.* Although I never struck up more than a casual relationship with her at seminars, it was she who became a model for me as I continued to struggle with my own journey. I think this was because of her writing, her solitary habits, and her love of nature.

As the evening of the first day came to a close, it was clear that the container (*temenos*) had been created the physical container of this place, the communal container of the participants, and the psychic container for the work we had begun. It was the sealed alchemical vessel in which we sought the true gold, the philosopher's stone, the self. We had begun to weave the tapestry of this *Records* seminar. The strand of loving God with *all* had been introduced, and questions had been offered, which we'd revisit throughout the seminar.

It was still raining as I made my way back to Big Star with Mary Johnson. Over the next sixteen days, we laughed and groused a lot, but on that evening we both were silent. My head, my heart, and my soul were full.

Chapter 8

Into the Depths

John the baptizer appeared in the wilderness, preaching a
baptism of repentance for the forgiveness of sins.[470]

And when he came up out of the water, immediately he saw
the heavens opened and the Spirit descending upon him like
a dove; and a voice came from heaven, "Thou art my beloved
Son; with thee I am well pleased."[471]

The Spirit immediately drove him out into the wilderness.
And he was in the wilderness forty days, tempted by Satan.[472]

I can now look back over five *Records* seminars and more than
quarter of a century of study and struggle, and see the vast course of
Jesus's journey from baptism in the Jordan by John the Baptizer to his
wrestling in the wilderness for forty days before setting out on his
mission to preach and teach, to his death on the cross. Stories from his
journey float up in my memory: calling his disciples poor, uneducated
fishermen to him, and they came without second thought; healing the
paralytic, whose friends had to break through the roof to get him into
the crowded room where Jesus was; the "sinner woman" who went
against all conventions of the time to enter the banquet room and
anoint Jesus's feet, and whose sins were forgiven because she loved

much; the parable about the kingdom of God I love best the pearl of great price; the mysterious phrases about the Son of man. Of course, the three times the question was asked, each time in a different way, "Who is this man, Jesus?" I reflect on the terrible final week when Jesus "turned his face to Jerusalem," was welcomed by the throngs on Palm Sunday, and condemned to death by crucifixion by the crowd on Friday at the instigation, so the story says, of the Jewish hierarchy, the "scribes and the Pharisees."

After years of discussion with others who have participated in and led *Records* seminars, I see how seeds of anti-Semitism were sown in this and other New Testament stories and that historical research shows a very different picture of the scribes and Pharisees suggesting Jesus himself was a Pharisee. We know now that Pilate, portrayed as a sympathetic figure who would have set Jesus free, was a tyrant, monstrous even by Roman standards.

I see how we studied certain passages as we worked toward understanding the story from new perspectives and still wonder why these passages and these questions and not others? And yet I know this study has given my life meaning. Finally, I remember the lesson to include opposites—my experience of the value of the work and my own doubts as I continue to question this journey. Doubting and questioning are creative acts that lead us onward.

Our work at the seminar that first day, and every year, began not with nativity scenes, the birth of a divine child, nor with the genealogy, but with the adult Jesus's baptism and experience in the wilderness. For some historical researchers—through critical study of the synoptics and other documents as well as through historical and archaeological research—this is the first part of the story backed by evidence.

Our journey to understand Jesus's life and teachings *psychologically* begins here as well; for in baptism and the wilderness, we see a man visited by something enormous, who hears the words, "Thou art my beloved Son; with thee I am well pleased."[473] How is Jesus to make sense of this? Go mad? Become a megalomaniacal cult leader? In the wilderness, Jesus faced his demons, and when he left the wilderness, he was neither mad nor megalomaniacal. He simply set out on his life work to preach "the Gospel of God."

My *Records* journal from 1984 shows a man coming up from the baptismal water, his arms outstretched, a great light breaking out of the dark blue sky, and out of the light a dove descending toward him. I placed this drawing at the beginning of my journal as a graphic expression of how I saw and felt Jesus's experience, marking the beginning of my intellectual, emotional, and psychological journey working with this story.

The Heavens Opened and the Spirit Descended Upon Him

The next day began, as always, at 7 a.m. We gathered at the olive tree in a silent circle to hear the morning reading. Sheila Moon read the third stanza of her poem "Prolog," her voice quiet, clear, low-pitched, and almost dry, perhaps the dryness of age.

There are a few who, during spans
of historical man's harvest,
have risked a fuller fruit, have
plunged to blind ground
and left behind the rasping years.
True was their descent, asked
by itself only, plumb line straight
smashing at midnight
in a bright bloody river of seed.
Such men have turned, have lent
their flesh to needs of earth,
to life wanting birth and tomorrow.
They are wanderers. They bear questions
fresh with asking and desire
toward always a farther garden.
They come from nowhere, their home
is sorrow, their eyes hear gold

and their ears see dreams.

. . . .

. . . What is this
they do? What breach in our walls
comes with their coming, to let
into our prison the smell of sun
and grass? Their existence tells
itself to ours through the crack.
One such was Jesus the Jew, bearing
his hours on his back,   pedlar
of choices and fisher for God.
Let him pass.[474]

I didn't understand all that she wanted to convey, but I was deeply moved. Sheila loved Jesus, and she seemed to know something about him that I didn't. What did she mean "pedlar of choices and fisher for God"?

Seven days a week, after a silent breakfast of cooked cereal, toast, hard-boiled eggs still hot, granola, fruit, juice, yogurt, and coffee or tea, which we ate alone, wherever we chose, we gathered in the seminar room. The bell began to ring at 8:25, one gong a minute till 8:30, calling us to the circle. We scurried from Adam and Eve, our cabins in the trees, or the lodge, leaving our shoes on the steps, finding a place in the circle, and waiting in silence for the seminar to begin.

On that first full morning, we dove into the *Records* book, beginning with the story that set Jesus's course for the rest of his life. We turned to page 15, Section 17 where we found the Gospel of Mark, along with Matthew and Luke. Sections 1-16 present the stories told by Matthew and Luke—the genealogy, the birth narratives, and Jesus's early years. Today, scholars regard this material as without historical basis. This mythic story of the divine child, the messiah foretold in ancient days, was not forgotten at our seminar, but we would enter its magical depths at another time.

Beginning on page 15, Mark, Matthew, and Luke tell of the same events—John the Baptist calling all the people to be baptized in the River Jordan—though each tells it a little differently. The leader asked what source or sources they each were using and what were the differences among their stories.

This critical work was the bane of many of the seminar participants. Who cares? But for many of us, it was the first time we'd considered that these are literary works that each of the Gospel writers constructed for his own audiences and purposes, *based on* written material and perhaps oral tradition he had at his disposal.

In Section 17, we saw that all three Gospels tell the same story, although not necessarily using the exact same words, and determined that Mark is the source for that part of the story. As the telling goes on, there are passages where Matthew and Luke agree, and we decided their account comes from Q. And there are passages which only appear in Luke, so they're from source L. There is one passage, about Herod imprisoning John, that Luke tells here, and Matthew and Mark tell later. All this becomes apparent in the *Records* book where the three stories are placed side by side.

In the Gospel of Thomas, saying 2, Jesus says, "Let one who seeks not stop seeking until one finds. When one finds, one will be troubled. When one is troubled, one will marvel and will rule over all."[475] Seeking answers to these critical questions did lead many of us to feeling troubled. And sometimes we marveled at what we found. What was being said here, and what was its significance for each of us?

We began to see the differences in the stories and to ponder whether it makes a difference in what Jesus might have meant. Here is an example. Matthew says that John came "preaching in the wilderness of Judea, 'Repent, for the kingdom of heaven is at hand.'"[476] Luke says that John "went into all the region about the Jordan, preaching a baptism of repentance for the forgiveness of sins."[477] And Mark tells about a messenger who will come to "prepare thy way."[478] Then, the three quote Isaiah, saying, "The voice of one crying in the wilderness: Prepare the way of the Lord, make his paths straight."[479] Then Mark says, "John the baptizer appeared in the wilderness, preaching a baptism of repentance for the forgiveness of sins."[480] This seems to be what Matthew and Luke have already said.

We compared Mark's words with Matthew's, then with Luke's. Both Mark and Luke say, "repentance for the forgiveness of sins." Matthew says, "repent, for the kingdom of heaven is at hand."[481] Mark is considered to be the earliest of the three and so perhaps closest to the events he is describing. What does *repentance* mean? We struggled with this, and then someone told us that the Greek word for *repentance* is *metanoia*, "coming to a new way of thinking." Does that add to our way of understanding John the Baptist's preaching?

In this detailed work we began to see a different image of Jesus constructed by each Gospel writer. In Section 17, we meet a John the Baptist who proclaims (Matthew and Luke) the "one to come" who will baptize not with water, but "with the Holy Spirit and with fire," and he will gather his wheat the good ones into the storehouse, "but the chaff he will burn with unquenchable fire."[482] Mark says that one will come after him, "mightier than I," one who will "baptize you with the Holy Spirit."[483]

We heard the longings of a people for a messiah to free them from oppression, bring them to a land of abundance, punish the wrongdoers, and reward the righteous. A leader asked, "What was that longing for?" and I responded, "For something that never was, the Garden of Eden. Innocence." "From what in the psyche might that longing arise?" the leader asked, and I responded, "A sense that I was once one with the *all* and now I'm separated." Today, I would add, a longing for wise leaders to bring an end to suffering and conflict, still yearning for someone, a wise one, someone *else,* to lead us out of chaos and into a place of peace and abundance. The leader then asked a rhetorical question. "How did Jesus relate to these images and longing for a messiah? How did Jesus see himself in relation to the Messiah?" These questions stayed with us throughout our study.

We moved from John's preaching to the next step of this story. The three Gospel writers tell us that John drew throngs of people to be baptized in the Jordan. What brought them there? What did they seek? In Section 18, we learned that one among those throngs was Jesus. This is the first time we met Jesus in Mark's Gospel. In my mind's eye I saw a wild man, John the Baptist, clothed in camel's hair with a leather girdle around his waist eating locusts and wild honey.[484] I heard his messages of wrath, of separating wheat from chaff. What does *metanoia* mean in my life?

And then we see Jesus coming through the crowds of people and plunging into the depths of the Jordan. Mark tells us, "When he came up out of the water, immediately he saw the heavens opened and the Spirit descending upon him like a dove; and a voice came from heaven, 'Thou art my beloved Son; with thee I am well pleased.'"[485] Matthew says, "This is my beloved Son, with whom I am well pleased,"[486] conveying a different sense. Mark's God speaks directly to Jesus, as does Luke's. Matthew's God proclaims to the crowds, as if they had all witnessed this event together.

The leader asked us, "What might have been Jesus's experience going into the waters? What might have been happening to him? To the 'heavens'?" Then the leader added, "Heavens opened could be translated 'the heavens were torn open.' The spirit descended upon him could be translated 'the spirit descended into him.' Does that change anything?"

All three Gospel writers said Jesus came and was baptized by John. Only Matthew adds, "John would have prevented him, saying, 'I need to be baptized by you, and do you come to me?' But Jesus answered him, 'Let it be so now; for thus it is fitting for us to fulfill all righteousness.' Then [John] consented."[487]

What does Matthew's narrative imply? That Jesus knew the important role he was to play? Does including this passage change the story? Some in our group saw no difference; others surmised that Matthew wanted us to believe that Jesus knew he was "the one to come."

Before the seminar ended for the morning, the leader posed one more question, "What questions would this baptism have raised for

Jesus?" I imagined Jesus asking, "What now? What is being asked of me? Can I do it? How?"

The Wilderness

On the morning of the third day, Sheila Moon read to us again at the olive tree, this time a quote from Herman Hesse's *Magister Ludi*: "As every blossom fades and all youth sinks into old age, so every life's design, each flower of wisdom, every good, attains its prime and cannot last forever. At each life's call the heart must be prepared to take its leave and to commence afresh, courageously and with no hint of grief submit itself to other, newer ties. *A magic dwells in each beginning and protecting us it tells us how to live.*"[488] The last sentence became a comfort and a guide for me.

That morning, we "went into the wilderness" with Jesus. I knew Jesus had been forty days in the wilderness, that Satan had tempted him, and that he had said no. I didn't know what those temptations actually were; I assumed they were "bad" in some way, that Satan was "bad," and that Jesus, a man of integrity, had turned him down like an upright man saying no to bribes from the mob.

Our study opened me to seeing this experience in a human way, likening it to a traumatic psychological experience with all the doubts and questions that follow. It offered me another way of thinking about Satan and his role in the story, and of the Spirit that drove—or led—Jesus into the wilderness "to be tempted," as Matthew put it.

Studying Jesus's experience in the wilderness made it clear why we'd been introduced the day before to the messianic yearnings of the Jewish people. In Matthew, John rails against the "brood of vipers" who think they can flee "the wrath to come." He proclaims, "The axe is laid to the root of the tree," and those that do not bear good fruit will be "cut down and thrown into the fire."[489] Luke says much the same; they both speak of this messiah's winnowing fork that will separate the wheat from the chaff. All three Gospels have John preaching that someone mightier than he will come "to baptize you with the Holy

Spirit." Matthew and Luke add, "and with fire."[490] This study of
messianic yearnings is an essential strand of the *Records* study, perhaps
the warp of the tapestry we were weaving.

John's apocalyptic vision is one of messianic hopes and longings.
Apocalyptic refers to a soon-to-occur end of the current order, the
splitting of good from evil, and the creation of a new order all under
the control of a supernatural God. As we worked with the baptism
story, the leaders guided us to earlier passages to find other messianic
hopes. One is the longing for a messiah who will free his people from
oppressors and rule over them in peace and harmony so they may
worship their God without fear.

Matthew begins his Gospel with genealogy,[491] telling us that Jesus
Christ is the son of the great King David. Luke also tells of the coming
of a mighty ruler in the Davidic line.[492] The angel Gabriel tells Mary
she will bear a son: "He will be great, and will be called the Son of the
Most High; and the Lord God will give to him the throne of his father
David, and he will reign over the house of Jacob forever; and of his
kingdom there will be no end."[493] A footnote in the *Records* book
informs us that this hope comes from II Samuel, who reports that God
tells David his kingdom will be without end. Luke weaves this theme
throughout his Gospel, drawing on Hebrew scripture to affirm the
message that someone will come to carry on the line of David, and that
this one will be Jesus. Matthew tells the story of the wise men who
came to see the baby Jesus, drawing on Micah 5:2 to say that a great
ruler will come out of the land of Judah.[494]

We studied Hebrew scriptural passages that speak of a third
messianic hope, the longing for the one to come who would
accomplish all these things. Amos conveys a land of plenty: "'I will
restore the fortunes of my people Israel, and they shall rebuild the
ruined cities and inhabit them; they shall plant vineyards and drink
their wine, and they shall make gardens and eat their fruit. I will plant
them upon their land, and they shall never again be plucked up out of
the land which I have given them,' says the Lord your God."[495]

Could we feel these yearnings in ourselves, the longing for a good and wise leader, for a land of plenty? Could we feel a longing—or a terror—that there would be a time of judgment and that we would be among the wheat and not the chaff? Later in the seminar, we revisited this yearning when John the Baptist, imprisoned, sent his disciples to ask Jesus, "Are you the one?" But on the second day, we didn't know about this. That morning we focused on the wilderness and its trials. The stories of Jesus's wilderness sojourn are gathered in Section 20 of the *Records* book.

The contrast between Mark and the other Gospels is startling. Mark begins, "The Spirit immediately drove him out into the wilderness. And he was in the wilderness forty days, tempted by Satan; and he was with the wild beasts; and angels ministered to him."[496] That's all Mark says about Jesus's time in the wilderness. Matthew and Luke fill in what happened during the forty days. We suggested they both used Q as their source because of the similarities in their stories. A leader reminded us that Q is thought to be earlier than Mark, so perhaps Mark didn't know about Q. And why do Matthew and Luke tell the story using different words and in a differing sequence? All of this provoked thought as we made our way through the stories and were encouraged to reach our own conclusions. The leaders didn't tell us answers if there were answers. We had to think it all through for ourselves and come to our own conclusions.

Mark's brief telling is usually referred to as the "temptations," but the Guild leaders suggested we think of it as the "issues." Temptations implies that what Satan offers is inherently evil. What does he offer? Mark says that after Jesus's baptism, the Spirit "drove" Jesus into the wilderness. Matthew says the Spirit "led" Jesus into the wilderness "*to be tempted* by the devil."[497] Luke says it was the *Holy* Spirit who "led" Jesus. Mark and Luke say *tempted* whereas Matthew says *to be tempted*. Mark names the tempter "Satan," while Matthew and Luke say "the devil." Is there a difference?

A leader asked, "Do you think Jesus was 'led' or 'driven'?" Sometimes when I find myself in a "wilderness," I'm driven there by trauma. Other times, I feel as if I've been led there. What was Jesus's experience? He'd just gotten the message that he's God's beloved son. What do you do with a message like that? It's a time for a pause, for solitude, time to wrestle with the questions that have come: *What does it mean? How will I realize this in my life?* Perhaps Jesus *fled* to the wilderness to struggle with these feelings. But the story says the Spirit led or drove him there and this is where he meets Satan, or the devil, who is there to help him struggle for answers. Why would the Spirit want Jesus to face Satan at that moment? Why did the Gospel writers weave their stories that way? And why did Jesus say *no* to Satan's temptations?

The first exchange between Jesus and the tempter offers Jesus if he is the Son of God the chance to transform stones into bread. He could feed all the people of Israel, yet he declines. Matthew draws on Deuteronomy for Jesus's words: "Man shall not live by bread alone, but by every word that proceeds from the mouth of God."[498]

According to Matthew, the devil then takes Jesus "to the holy city, and set him on the pinnacle of the temple," and promised Jesus if he is the Son of God that if he throws himself off, angels will prevent him from striking the stones with even his foot.[499] Why not accept the protection of angels? Yet Jesus again says no. "Again, it is written, 'You shall not tempt the Lord your God.'"[500]

Luke tells a similar story, but in the opposite sequence. Then Matthew and Luke both tell about the third exchange between Jesus and the devil, wherein Jesus is offered rule over all the kingdoms of the world. "All these I will give you, if you will fall down and worship me."[501] And again, Jesus says no, this time, in Matthew's account, with great force. "Begone Satan!" he says, "for it is written, 'You shall worship the Lord your God and him only shall you serve.'"[502]

The devil says to Jesus, "If you are the Son of God . . ."[503] before offering the power to turn stones into bread and the protection of angels, and Jesus says no. In the third exchange, the devil makes this offer, "if you will fall down and worship me."[504] And here Jesus says, "Begone Satan! for it is written, 'You shall worship the Lord your God and him only shall you serve.'"[505]

The leader asked us, "Why did he call the tempter Satan here and not earlier?" Perhaps, I thought, because Satan has asked Jesus to bow down and worship him, and he could only be true to the God he served.

The leader posed another question: "What is Satan's function?" Someone responded, "To make the choices clear." A second person said, "Satan is taking Jesus on a journey, internal or external, through the minefields of possibilities." A third offered, "Satan is an agent of God, of change." I was reminded of the serpent in the Garden of Eden, another tempter who initiates a great journey. But that's another story, which we would get to soon.

After we'd worked on these "issues" as a group, the leader asked, "Was he turning down all messianic expectations?" Today, I think yes. He declined the opportunity to change stones into bread to provide food for the hungry, to be protected by angels and defy natural law, and to be ruler of the world. Surely a messiah would choose these things, but Jesus said no. He stayed true to the God he knew.

Then the leader raised more questions: "What is the relation between Satan and Spirit? Satan and God?" But before we could respond, the morning seminar drew to a close, and the leader sent us out with more questions to reflect on: "What does Jesus have as he leaves the wilderness that he didn't have before? What comes up in you as you watch him leave the wilderness? Is there something in this passage for you?"

I knew that something immense had happened to him, and there was much for me here as I dealt with my own choices. We would engage with that question again when Jesus speaks about the narrow gate and doing the will of God.

I came to Four Springs that March with a love of Jesus, a man I wanted to know better. But these questions weren't drawing me closer to him. I was troubled if not angry, and I asked myself (notes from my journal), "Why am I feeling so heavy, sluggish, unwell, and inattentive. I don't know where I belong. I don't want to be doing this work. It's not clarifying anything for me, it's "mudifying" my brain. I just want to take a nap."

Chapter 9
Ministry and Miracles

Still overcast and cold, but spring is all about. My body longs for the sun's warmth, my soul longs for the sun's light. Does my soul long for you, too, my God?

It's confusing to confront my mixed motivations. Why am I here? Who am I? Who is Jesus? How can I live a secular life? How can anyone not know God is all about us, that God is?

Studying Sharman's text this way is confusing. Are we trying to describe Jesus or, from our own experience as humans, to "feel into" his life and experiences? To know? To be in his shoes? Or, as Mary put it, to get in touch with the archetypes?

How do I relate Jesus's teachings to the issues I'm struggling with right now? What are my *issues*?

Individuation: Knowing myself as distinct from expectations, real or imagined, of others. Freeing myself from others' energy. Believing in my own worth/value, my own unique contribution, feeling whole in myself.

Knowing my relationship to God, knowing what God wants of me.

I wrote this entry in my journal on the fourth day of the seminar. Now, rereading those words I wonder, What did I mean by *God*? After all these years, I finally understand that I am not "Christian" in the sense most people use the word. I have moved quite a distance from the God of my childhood and from the God of the monotheistic religions, a father figure "out there." Is it that the word *God* no longer has meaning for me at all? I don't think so. I think "the mystery of the Cosmos the mystery that life *is*" is what I now call "God." Jung used the word *self* to express *the image of God,* which he said is all we can know of God. And he used the word *self* for the wholeness of being human. Can I replace *God* in what I wrote in 1984 with *self*? Jung's word *self* suggests that this image of God is the *all* we can know.

Jesus's Ministry

So far during my first *Records* seminar, we followed Jesus through his baptism into the wilderness, two enormous events that began his ministry. Next we turned to just what his ministry was, and as always we sifted through the words of Matthew, Mark, and Luke, the storytellers, in search of what might have been the earliest telling and thus perhaps the clearest picture of who this man was.

We gathered in the seminar room. The leaders lit the tall taper candles, and one leader asked, "With *what* did Jesus leave the wilderness experience?" Many responses were offered: "Readiness, purposefulness, not knowing how his experience would translate into action." "A sense of relationship with God leading to joy." "A sense of being a container of conflicts and opposites." "That the relationship was to something within himself, not outside." "A sense that nothing is finished."

I could understand most of these responses, but not the ones about "being a container of conflicts and opposites" and "that the relationship was to something within himself, not outside." I still wasn't connecting with the seminar method, even though I knew it had come from Jung and Howes. I wasn't sure I agreed with the worldview behind it, and one evening after hearing so much talk of archetypes, I stormed out of the lodge, muttering to myself, "Archetypes! Eternal patterns! Plato's forms! Who believes in things like this today?" I certainly didn't. It was one thing to read Jung's ideas about psyche, the collective unconscious, archetypes, individuation, and the ego-self axis, but quite another to live life conscious of these concepts' implications.

Yet it was in such notions that I began to see a glimmer of hope that my life was of value and had something to do with the evolution of consciousness and even the evolution of God. I asked myself, Can I substitute *self* for *God*? Is this evolution of self really about the evolution of humanity?

I thought of one of the morning readings we'd heard, the words of Nikos Kazantzakis: "Blowing through heaven and earth, and in our hearts and the heart of every living thing, is a gigantic breath a great Cry which we call God." And then, in a few paragraphs, he sketched the terrible Cry, the terrible God, who demands that life rise up from plant to animal to human and, in Kazantzakis's vision, something beyond.

"Leave the mud, stand up, give birth to your betters!"
"We don't want to! We can't!"
"You can't, but I can. Stand up!"
And lo! After thousands of eons, man emerged, trembling on his still unsolid legs.[506]

The passionate, God-struck Kazantzakis then proclaimed that the Cry demands that the human leap into the abyss of whatever the human is capable of being next.

The leader's reading of Kazantzakis stirred me to tears and rebellion, and I joined the many creatures crying out, "I can't! I don't want to!" I was agitated, rebellious, and angry, during much of those sixteen days. My worldview, no matter how unsatisfactory in bringing meaning to my life, was easier than taking on a new one, even if it held the promise of a richer life. This was a struggle between my own opposites, but I didn't have the words or the understanding yet. On the first day, the leaders had asked, "What needs to die in you?" I was beginning to have suspicions, and I was not giving in easily.

Next we studied Jesus setting forth on his ministry. We made a quick survey of the passages that show, first, Jesus's spreading fame as he preached and healed throughout Galilee; then we looked over passages that showed the opposition beginning to rise against him.[507] Who was the man in these writings?

Mark says it most clearly. Jesus's disciples say to him, "Every one is searching for you,"[508] and Jesus replies, "Let us go on to the next towns, that I may preach there also, for that is why I came out."[509] Preaching and teaching "is why I came out." Luke uses these words, "I must preach the good news of the kingdom of God to the other cities also; for I was sent for this purpose."[510] Mark says, "For that is why I came out," and Luke says, "I was sent for this purpose." What is the difference? Sent by whom?

And what does Jesus the preacher say and do? After Herod arrested John the Baptist, Jesus went into Galilee "preaching the gospel of God, and saying, 'The time is fulfilled, and the kingdom of God is at hand.'"[511] We noted the end of that sentence, "repent and believe in the gospel," is considered a later addition. It isn't included in Matthew or Luke.

Then he preaches in Nazareth, his hometown, where the people wonder at "the gracious words which proceeded out of his mouth; and when they say, 'Is not this Joseph's son?'" Jesus responds, "Truly I say to you, no prophet is acceptable in his own country."[512] And the people became angry, and "rose up and put him out of the city." They would have thrown him off a cliff, "but passing through the midst of them he went away."[513] Why did they not accept his authority? Matthew and Mark tell a similar story later in which Jesus teaches in the synagogue of his home country. The people are astonished and they ask, "'Is not this the carpenter, the son of Mary and brother of James and Joses and Judas and Simon, and are not his sisters here with us?' And they took offense at him."[514] The story tells us, "he could do no mighty work there

… And he marveled because of their unbelief."[515] Did people have to see him a certain way in order to be healed?

He taught with authority at Capernaum, and the people marveled. And a "man with an unclean spirit" cried out to him, "I know who you are, the Holy One of God."[516] And Jesus replied with a rebuke and drove the unclean spirit out of the man, saying, "Be silent!" The people were amazed and asked "among themselves, 'What is this? A new teaching! With authority he commands even the unclean spirits, and they obey him.' And at once his fame spread everywhere throughout all the surrounding region of Galilee."[517] What did people say about him? Were they wondering whether the unclean spirit was right, that Jesus was the Holy One of God? And why does Jesus say, "Be silent!"?

We looked ahead for clues. Mark writes that so many from Galilee are following Jesus that he tells his disciples to "have a boat ready for him because of the crowd, lest they should crush him, for he had healed many."[518] Mark continues, "And whenever the unclean spirits beheld him, they fell down before him and cried out, 'You are the Son of God.' And he strictly ordered them not to make him known."[519] Twice, we heard the unclean spirits call Jesus "Holy One of God" or "Son of God," and twice, he told them to be silent, not to make this known. Why did he want them to be silent? Did he believe they would remain silent? Who was this man Jesus?

Matthew tells this same story, and Luke includes parts of it in another story. But Matthew adds a prophetic passage from Isaiah 42:1-4. After Jesus has healed people and they followed him, Matthew says, "This was to fulfil what was spoken by the prophet Isaiah: 'Behold, my servant whom I have chosen, my beloved with whom my soul is well pleased.' Isaiah says more about the wonders this servant will perform; he will bring justice 'and in his name will the Gentiles hope.'"[520]

Why is Matthew talking about the Gentiles? Isn't Jesus preaching and teaching among the Jews, his own people? Could Matthew be calling up images of the messiah and one who will speak not just to Jews but to the whole of humankind? We held the question. Whether

Jesus was or thought he was the messiah followed us through our *Records* study.

Next we studied the stories about Jesus calling his disciples. It appears in the first chapter of Mark, the fourth chapter of Matthew, and not until Luke's fifth chapter, and Luke gives a different account. In Mark and Matthew, Jesus sees Simon and his brother Andrew fishing in the sea of Galilee and calls out, "'Follow me and I will make you become fishers of men.' And immediately they left their nets and followed him."[521] Then Jesus called two more brothers, James and John, sons of Zebedee, "and they left their father Zebedee in the boat with the hired servants, and followed him."[522] The leader asked us, "Why did they do that?" and we could only speculate: They'd heard stories about him. They heard him preach or knew someone who was healed. Still, to leave your livelihood and your father to follow him?

Then we turned our attention to Luke, that when Jesus came upon the fishermen cleaning their nets, he went into Simon's boat and "taught the people from the boat." As soon as he was done speaking, Jesus commanded Simon, "Put out into the deep and let down your nets for a catch."[523] Simon protested that he and his men had been fishing all night without success, but even so, he did as Jesus said. They let down their nets and brought them up nearly full to breaking, enough fish to fill two boats. This, our leader told us, is called "the miraculous catch of fish."

Then Simon, who Luke now calls Simon Peter, "fell down at Jesus' knees, saying, 'Depart from me, for I am a sinful man, O Lord.'" And Jesus replied, "Do not be afraid; henceforth you will be catching men." And as soon as the men brought their boats to land, "they left everything and followed him."[524]

The leader asked, "What are some possible reasons the fishermen followed Jesus, according to Luke?" People suggested, "They'd heard him teaching and were impressed." "They were astonished by this miraculous catch of fish."

The word *miracle* had been used, and the leader asked, "Luke's telling is an account of what?" "A great catch of fish," someone responded. Next, the leader asked, "What are all the possibilities accounting for this event?" Not *miracle* but *event*. We gave some possibilities: "Jesus had extraordinary powers. Chance, coincidence. An elaboration of a simpler event. Luke made it up." *Why?* To make a point." *What point?* Synchronicity. *What's that?* Perhaps it was added by a later editor of the Gospel account.

Then the leader asked, "*How do you define miracle?*" Supernatural. *What does that mean?* The leader brought up the wilderness passages where the tempter offered Jesus the power to turn stones into bread and commanded Jesus to cast himself from the pinnacle, that the angels would save him. *Would these acts have been miracles? Why would Jesus say no to a miracle then, and now perform one?* Then came the test. *Which of these would you choose?* I said nothing. It was all too much to think about.

The leader moved on. *What did Simon Peter say to Jesus?* He said to go away, for he was a sinful man. *And what did Simon Peter do?* He followed him. *What was going on?* He was torn, ambivalent. Something in him longed to follow Jesus; something felt he was not fit to. *What was Jesus to Peter in this moment?* A miracle worker. A wisdom teacher. A man of God. *What was Peter afraid of?* Finally, this question landed in me. What is that Peter-attitude inside me? What happens to me when I'm in the presence of a truly great value?

Next, we explored these questions somatically. The leader read, "Depart from me, for I am a sinful man, O Lord," and asked, "Do you want him to go away? If he does, what are your feelings?" I fell to the floor and covered my head with my arms. "Depart from me, O Lord. I am a sinful woman. I am not worthy for you to call me. Not me, Jesus. You know my weaknesses and failings. I can't do what you ask. You ask too much."

I wrote in my journal: "Do I want him to go away without me? Can I remain behind and watch Jesus walk away? Yes I can, and I feel great sadness and loss as I turn back to my ordinary life." As I revisit those words today, I still struggle with self-doubt, even knowing the value *Records* study has brought to my life. In that mime, I let Jesus walk away from me, and here I am decades later still wrestling with him. In the 2003 *Records* seminar when the leader asked about Simon Peter's response, one participant said, "Simon Peter was projecting onto Jesus what he couldn't accept in himself." Is that me? I often think others are more advanced than I am, that they know more and understand better.

Another question many leaders have asked over the years is, "How do you respond if you are called to the 'higher value'?" Elizabeth Howes, Luella Sibbald, Sheila Moon, and the leaders they trained used this phrase to mean "in service of something greater"—God, the will of God, the self. When confronted with that "higher value" in the form of Jesus, Simon Peter said, "Go away! I'm not worthy!"

"What do you know of that in yourself?" has been the follow-up question, not for the ego alone but for the ego in relation to self. My ongoing struggles in the face of the Cry to stand up for myself, to be myself—have expressed themselves as self-doubts and wrestling with Jesus. In 1984, I let that Cry in the person of Jesus walk away from me, and I'm still struggling with the implications.

Opposing Jesus

That was only part of what we studied that morning. After looking at the accounts of ordinary people who came to hear Jesus preach and teach and heal, we turned to a passage in which there was opposition to Jesus's works and words. Jesus invited Levi, son of a tax collector, to follow him and they ate with a group of "tax collectors and sinners." The "scribes of the Pharisees" were there too, and the scribes raised a serious question: "Why does Jesus sit with sinners and tax collectors?" And Jesus said, "Those who are well have no need of a physician, but those who are sick; I came not to call the righteous, but sinners."[525]

Then we come to the mysterious phrase *Son of man*. When his disciples harvested grain on the sabbath, Jesus was questioned by the Pharisees. "Look, why are they doing what is not lawful on the sabbath?"[526] and Jesus replied, "The sabbath was made for man, not man for the sabbath; so the Son of man is lord even of the sabbath."[527]

Matthew and Luke, for the most part, follow Mark here. But they leave out the verse, "The sabbath was made for man, not man for the sabbath," and go straight to "For the Son of man is lord of the sabbath."[528] The leader said *Son of man* could refer to humankind in general or Jesus only. If it is a quality of Jesus only, is Jesus referring to himself as messiah? If it's a quality in all humans, it would, of course, include Jesus. This simple phrase that Mark writes but Matthew and Luke don't ("The sabbath was made for man, not man for the sabbath.") makes a difference in considering these possibilities. There is some relationship between *man* and "Son of man" here.

In 1984, I wrote to myself:

Is this a statement about a new level of consciousness, an evolutionary step, in which each person has a relationship with God and can make choices in a different way than before (the rule of law)? "Something unique in each person" would be what Son of man refers to. ... Who were the Pharisees and scribes? I don't know, yet my instant reaction is negative. They are the bad guys. They must be bad guys if they raise questions about Jesus!

The leader provided more information. The Pharisees were devoted to upholding the Torah, the "Law," the first five books of the Old Testament. Some Pharisees interpreted this narrowly, for they were upholding something of tremendous value to them. According to their beliefs, to associate with sinners was to defile oneself. The leader asked, "Who might be considered sinners by today's norms?" "The unemployed, the godless, street people, gays, minorities." "And who might society judge as non-sinners?" "Employed, comfortable, hard-working folks; straights; those in the majority."

A leader informed us that the word *sinner* comes from the Greek "to miss the mark" or "miss the target." "Given this meaning, who do *you* judge as sinners?" "Those who judge, those who glorify themselves, murderers, those who torture, rape, politicians who support war."

The leader pushed onward: "Which of these come from your 'moral self' and which from your 'self-righteous self'? What aspects of yourself does your self-righteous side judge?" My responses all had to do with the *shoulds* of my life. I should do this, I should accomplish that.

Perhaps my growing awareness of how I miss the mark and judge myself leads us to the next passages that still speak deeply to me today: the healing of the paralytic and the forgiveness of the "woman of the streets."

Chapter 10

Who Forgives? What Heals?

The afternoon and evening of Day 4 were devoted to the story of the paralytic, the "palsied one" whose friends, with great effort, brought him to Jesus when he was preaching at Capernaum, a fishing village on the northern shore of the Sea of Galilee, a fertile mountainous region in the north of today's Israel. Jesus was born in Bethlehem, brought up in Nazareth, and preached in Jerusalem, and in the years of his Galilean ministry, he lived in Capernaum. "And when Jesus saw their faith, he said to the paralytic, 'My son, your sins are forgiven.[529] … rise, take up your pallet and go home.'"[530] We meet this theme again in Luke's story of "a woman of the city, who was a sinner"[531] who enters a banquet room to weep over Jesus and anoint his feet with oil. And he says to her, "Your sins are forgiven," and then, "Your faith has saved you; go in peace."[532]

To this day, these two passages speak to me. What is the connection between sickness and sin, the relationship Jesus draws between healing and forgiveness? Who, really, does the healing?

The Paralytic and His Friends

By the time we come to this story, Jesus had been baptized, met the challenges of the wilderness, and begun his ministry teaching throughout Galilee, calling his disciples to him and drawing great throngs. People came to hear this man who "speaks with authority" and be healed of their many ailments. Now, when he returns to Capernaum, word gets out; Jesus is home! Many come to hear him, a full house.

Mark says, "And they came, bringing to him a paralytic carried by four men."[533] Surely, they were friends or family members, though the story just says "men." The room was so filled, the men climbed onto the roof and made an opening in it, through which they lowered a pallet on which the paralyzed man lay, so he could be close to Jesus. "And when Jesus saw their faith, he said to the paralytic, 'My son, your sins are forgiven.'"[534] Is that what they came for? The story says they brought the paralytic, but doesn't say why.

The scribes in the crowd were shocked: "Who can forgive sins but God alone?"[535] to which Jesus replied, "Which is easier, to say to the paralytic, 'Your sins are forgiven,' or to say, 'Rise, take up your pallet and walk'?"[536] Then Jesus used a phrase that we continued to work with throughout the seminar: "But that you may know that the Son of man has authority on earth to forgive sins … rise, take up your pallet and go home."[537] And the man did, and those present were amazed and glorified God.

Why did the four men bring their friend? We assume to help the paralytic find healing, but that was never said. The men went up on the roof and made a hole to lower the paralytic into the crowded room below. We pondered the meaning of *sin* and the relationship between sin and illness. One participant offered that sin was breaking religious laws, that illness was punishment for sinful behavior. What did people do to be forgiven their sins? There were prescribed ritual steps, not easy for the poor to comply with.

I was beginning to see how different Jesus's message about forgiveness was from this. No ritual—simply, "Your sins are forgiven," and the man was healed. Jesus doesn't say the man's sins are forgiven because of his faith. Mark writes, "And when Jesus saw their faith, he said …" Jesus didn't use the word *faith*, though. He said, "My son, your sins are forgiven." Who did the forgiving?

The scribes got upset, seeing this as blasphemy! But Jesus hadn't said, "I forgive" or "God forgives." He used the passive voice: "Your sins are forgiven." The leader asked, "What might the paralytic have heard?" "Son, you are whole. Daughter, you are healed, free of guilt. You're okay."

Jesus perceives the questions of the scribes and asks if it's easier to say, "Your sins are forgiven," or "Rise, take up your pallet and walk?" Then we come to the Son of man statement, which seems to draw a connection between forgiveness and healing: "'But that you may know that the Son of man has authority on earth to forgive sins, ... I say to you, rise, take up your pallet and go home.'"[538] The leader queried us about the relationship between the two statements. Same? Different? Does the sequence matter?

Then we turned to the "Son of man" phrase. We had encountered it earlier when Jesus was charged with working on the sabbath, and he replied, "The sabbath was made for man, not man for the sabbath; so the Son of man is lord even of the sabbath."[539] Here, in the paralytic story, Jesus is claiming that the Son of man has authority to forgive sins! And he tells the man to get up and walk. Forgiveness and healing go hand in hand, and this Son of man can cause it to happen!

The leader reminded us that *Son of man* can refer to a quality that is in Jesus only, to Jesus as the Messiah, or to a quality that is in each person, available to humankind in general. She pushed us to choose among these possible meanings. I wondered, "Do I have the power within myself to forgive my sins and heal myself? Am I in touch with the healing process within me?" A decade later, I wrote, "Today I hear this as the Son of man is in Jesus, in the paralytic, and in each of us."

The man rises, picks up his pallet, and leaves, and the people are astonished and glorify God. The leader asks, "Who do they glorify?" The text says God (not Jesus). Matthew says they "glorified God, who had given such authority to men."[540] Why does he say this? Mark and Luke don't.

"What do you see as the role of Jesus in the whole process?" I spoke of *empowering.* "Jesus was empowering the paralytic to find *his own* authority, to lift his own pallet and walk," and the leader asked, "What part of you might be 'paralyzed'? How do you experience that part? What does it mean to pick up your pallet?" We wrote our responses, then shared them with the group.

The leader continued to pose questions: "How would you characterize Jesus in this story? What impresses you about him? What questions have still not been answered?" Today, I characterize the Jesus in this story as a man who trusts his own wisdom, a man in touch with, as Jung calls it, the *self,* all that a human can be. Jesus knows about forgiveness and healing because of the relationship between his ego and self. "What questions are still unanswered?" *Is this man the messiah? Who did Jesus think he was?*

In seminars I later attended, we shared our responses in small groups. "What is the wound in you that paralyzes you? What does this wound need now?" At other seminars, we acted the story out, miming each part, guided by these questions: "Who are the four friends who carry you to be healed? What is your paralysis? What is it like to hear, 'Child, your sins are forgiven. Pick up your pallet and walk'? What does it mean to carry your own pallet, your own bed? How do you experience that?"

All the seminars I attended drew on a "knowing" the body could express silently or through expressive art. That evening, the medium was a ball of clay out of which "the wounded one" emerged from our hands unguided. Jung wrote, "Often the hands know how to solve a riddle with which the intellect has wrestled in vain."[541] The riddle for that evening was, "Who is this wounded one in each one of us, and how might it be healed?" The leader instructed us to let our hands, not our heads, do the work. We worked in silence until a piece of music began, and then we rose to *carry* this wounded one, this ball of clay that had transformed itself into some shape, to whatever or whoever is the healing one for us.

Was it Jesus? An object, a symbol that carried healing powers for us? My journal notes that day read, "Healing the palsied one, working the clay. The tortured body struggling to be free. The friends who came to carry him to the healing place." Then I named four women who have influenced my life.

> So many nature images, other friends the owl, Pegasus, the lake on the way to Muir Pass, green moss on the trees here at Four Springs. The wet, shiny red of a gnarled manzanita trunk. Manzanita berry blossoms, like tiny bells.

> The clay work very satisfying. I kept my eyes closed mostly and let the clay and my hands guide me. Began feeling the clay needed nurturing it was cold and needed to be warmed, massaged. When I looked at it, I saw my wounded self. There was a strength in its suffering bowed but not defeated. Striving to stand upright. Beauty in its strength even though contorted.

Even now, I can reenter the silence of that evening. I can pick up another ball of clay and let my wounded part, whatever it is on a given day, reveal itself and then guide me to the healing power, the healing value, to do its work. As in 1984, I find it in the love and support of friends, in the healing power of nature, and in communion with that God I am coming to call the self.

The Woman Who Anointed Jesus's Feet

Another numinous, sacred "time out of time" moment came the evening we worked with the story of the "woman of the city, who was a sinner." She entered the banquet hall of the Pharisee where Jesus had been invited to eat. It's a familiar story, told in this way only in Luke.[542] All those men reclining at their tables, being served by slaves, and here enters a sinner woman! Brazen! Courageous! Driven by a yearning for … something? What?

She is bearing an alabaster jar filled with precious ointment, goes to where Jesus is reclining at the table, and bathes his feet with her tears. She then dries them with her hair, and anoints them with the precious ointment. And Jesus says to her, "Your sins are forgiven.... Your faith has saved you; go in peace."[543]

But first he has to contend with the criticism of Simon, the Pharisee who invited him to the dinner. Surely, a true prophet would know what kind of woman she is. Jesus responds with a story. Two men owe money to a creditor. One owes five hundred denarii, the other fifty, and neither is able to repay it. One denarius was a laborer's daily wage; these are no small debts. And the creditor forgives both. Jesus asks his host, "'Which of them will love him more?' Simon answered, 'The one, I suppose, to whom he forgave more.' And [Jesus] said to him, 'You have judged rightly.'"[544]

Jesus turns to the woman and continues to speak to Simon, reminding Simon that when Jesus entered the house, nobody bathed his feet, but the woman did so with her tears. Simon gave him no kiss, "but from the time I came in she has not ceased to kiss my feet."[545] Simon did not anoint Jesus's head with oil, but the woman anointed his feet. "'Therefore I tell you, her sins, which are many, are forgiven, for she loved much; but he who is forgiven little, loves little.' And he said to her, 'Your sins are forgiven.' Then those who were at table with him began to say among themselves, 'Who is this, who even forgives sins?' And he said to the woman, 'Your faith has saved you; go in peace.'"[546]

Does he mean that because she had sinned much and been forgiven that she loved much? Or had she loved much and because of that, had been forgiven? Which comes first, love or forgiveness? Had she forgiven herself, or had Jesus forgiven her? He doesn't say, "I forgive you," or "God forgives you." He says, as he said to the paralytic, "Your sins are forgiven." To the disabled one he said, "Take up your pallet and go." To the woman he says, "Your faith has saved you; go in peace." What does he mean by *faith*? Faith in what, in whom?

We worked with this passage in every *Records* seminar, and different leaders brought it in differently. On an evening in 2001, we had dinner in the cabaña, the covered area next to the pool, reclining on mats while "servants" passed finger food to us. After dinner, we all became servants to clean up the kitchen. When the work was done, we wandered in silence, then returned to the cabaña. By now dusk had fallen, and in the liminal light of evening we entered a contemplative and ritual exploration of the story we had been discussing. My notes tell me we were wordlessly invited to enact pivotal aspects of the drama:

> Roger, the steward, greeted each guest and brought her or him to another "servant" at the pool who bathed their feet and dried them while another "servant" anointed their foreheads with oil. Then Roger took each to "Simon," who greeted them with a kiss on each cheek and showed them to a cushion. At this point, only one table remained in the cabaña to symbolize the meal, a lantern, bowl, and pitcher on top. We sat on cushions all around.
>
> When we were all gathered, the leader began the story. Her pace was relaxed, leaving much time for reflection and imagination. After setting the scene, she began the questions, followed by a pause for response.

The leader asked us to envision the scene, to see this woman *who was she?* coming to the banquet where no righteous woman would be welcomed. What brings her? What is she feeling? How does Simon the Pharisee respond? What does Jesus say? What does he do? Does he forgive her? If not, what happens? What is the relationship between forgiveness and love? Which comes first? What about faith. In some way, the woman's faith saves her. Faith in what, in whom?

What might this woman represent in ourselves? The responses were slow in coming, and as the evening wore on, they were even fewer. But the leader was steadfast and let the space be.

After that, one by one in silence, we rose and went out of the banquet hall and became that woman of the city. Each of us approached and stood with an alabaster jar of ointment, looking into the room filled with those important enough to eat at the Pharisee's house knowing that Jesus, too, was there. Each chose to enter and approach the empty mat, representing where Jesus reclined, and acted out the story as we were moved to do so. We each heard Jesus's words, then went outside to become ourselves again and return to the banquet hall. One by one we did this until all who wished to do so had enacted the story.

I felt a tremendous yearning to be close to Jesus. Something about him drew me. He represented something I couldn't name, but I knew I had to enter that room, break all the rules, and express my love for him. Not Jesus Christ, but simply Jesus, a wise teacher who lived and taught long ago. What in me does Jesus represent and hold? Do I believe myself to be a "sinner" longing for forgiveness? I certainly have regrets, the "if-onlys" of a lifetime. The Greek word for *forgiveness* connotes "release," "to break the bonds." Call my regrets and if-onlys "sins" or "missing the mark," the story tells me that it is only I who can release me, only I who can pick up my pallet and walk. My notes recall my own longing to be close to Jesus and reconciled with myself:

I felt that forgiveness came out of her act of tears, kisses, anointing. And that act came out of love. She was forgiven she was reconciled with her "self." Yes, that's it. All of her was reconciled, in tune, harmony, rhythm, with her inmost being, her essential nature.

And Jesus entered into complete relationship/harmony with her.

I wonder … is this what being in the kingdom of heaven is? To be totally at one with oneself? No, not with "oneself," but "one's little ego self totally at one with the self."

Chapter 11
Myth or History: Finding Great Truths

In every *Records* seminar, we hold the tension between myth and history. Is the Christian story, or parts of it, historically true? Or are they myths—fabricated, but true on different levels? Did the events happen in real time and space, or are they about great patterns of reality that are "true," but not necessarily historical? Are they myths that tell us about life, death, rebirth, and creation? Some stories, scholars agree, are mythic; others may have happened. Whether myth or history, when we look through the lens of depth psychology, we "see through" the stories and find truths about our own lives.

In the Beginning

On the morning of Day 5, we worked with the difficult passages about the narrow gate and doing the will of God. That afternoon, we turned to the story of the creation of the earth and all who live upon it, and of the man and woman who were driven from the Garden of Eden in shame.

Years later at a different seminar, we were asked, "What is the earliest story you remember from childhood?" Others recalled children's stories, fairy tales, and myths. I remembered my mother reading the book of Genesis to me *over and over*. I would lie in my cot on our long screened-in porch in Porterville, California, and she would read from the King James Bible:

In the beginning God created the heaven and the earth. And the earth was without form, and void; and darkness was upon the face of the deep. And the Spirit of God moved upon the face of the waters. And God said, "Let there be light"; and there was light. And God saw the light, that it was good: and God divided the light from the darkness. And God called the light Day, and the darkness he called Night. And the evening and the morning were the first day.[547]

Day by day, the earth was created with the waters and heaven, and all the plants and animals, and the lights in the sky, sun and moon and stars. God created fish and birds and every living creature. And then he created "man in our image, after our likeness. … So God created man in his own image, in the image of God created he him; male and female created he them."[548] All was created by the evening of the sixth day, and God rested on the seventh day.

I did not notice that the story then seems to start over again as Mother continued reading. "The Lord God made the earth and the heavens, And every plant of the field before it was in the earth, and every herb of the field before it grew: for the Lord God had not caused it to rain upon the earth, and there was not a man to till the ground."[549]

And again God created man, but this time from the dust of the ground and his own breath. Then God created a wonderful garden for the man to live in, filled with "every tree that is pleasant to the sight, and good for food; the tree of life also in the midst of the garden, and the tree of the knowledge of good and evil."[550] I heard God's injunction to eat of every tree in the garden, "but of the tree of the knowledge of good and evil thou shalt not eat of it: for in the day that thou eatest of it thou shalt surely die."[551]

God creates a companion for Adam out of Adam's own rib. The serpent comes and tells the woman, who doesn't have a name yet, it's not true that she and Adam will die if they eat of the tree of the knowledge of good and evil. "Ye shall not surely die," the serpent says. "For God doth know that in the day ye eat thereof, then your eyes shall be opened, and ye shall be as gods, knowing good and evil."[552] And she did eat, and Adam ate. "And the eyes of them both were opened, and they knew that they were naked; and they sewed fig leaves together, and made themselves aprons."[553]

The Great Fall! God soon discovers their perfidy. Adam blames the woman. The woman blames the serpent. God curses the serpent, places a burden of pain on the woman, and sentences Adam to a lifetime of toil until he shall "return unto the ground; for out of it wast thou taken: for dust thou art, and unto dust shalt thou return."[554] Now Adam gives his wife a name, Eve. And the Lord makes them clothes. Then he casts them out of the garden. Why? In God's words:

> Behold, the man is become as one of us, to know good and evil; and now, lest he put forth his hand, and take also of the tree of life, and eat, and live for ever: Therefore the Lord God sent him forth from the garden of Eden, to till the ground from whence he was taken. So he drove out the man; and he placed at the east of the garden of Eden Cherubim, and a flaming sword which turned every way, to keep the way of the tree of life.[555]

I was caught up in the mystery of this great creation story. "In the beginning God created the heaven and the earth. And the earth was without form, and void; and darkness was upon the face of the deep. And the Spirit of God moved upon the face of the waters."[556] I don't know what the words meant, but I had an image of a great darkness, this vast deep and yet filled with waters visited by the Spirit of God, and I fell into the image. And then the Garden of Eden in my mind's eye it was beautiful beyond belief. My heart broke when the man and the woman were sent out of the garden into a harsh and cruel life.

Night after night, Mother would come with her Bible, sit on the side of my bed, and ask, "What shall I read tonight?" and I would say, "Read the creation story again." And then I would ask, "Where is the

Garden of Eden?" "Nobody knows," she would say. "Can they really never return?" "Nobody knows," she would answer again.

I've loved that story all my life, not questioning the different creation stories it contains, even the different stories of the creation of the man and the woman, not questioning that the serpent was an evil creature and that Eve had done a terrible thing. How I puzzled over why God had not wanted the man and the woman, who God created, to be "like us." Why not? And who is this "us"? I thought there was only one God. And later, why did God not want his creatures to live forever? I grieved that they had been sent away from their perfect garden.

I met the story again at my first *Records* seminar. I was living in Berkeley, and some students at the Pacific School of Religion, a liberal seminary on "Holy Hill," told me that the serpent was not evil, that temptation was part of God's plan, and that the story was not a "fall." But I hadn't thought about it seriously. On the afternoon of Day 5, that all changed.

The leader read us the story and brought questions. My journal entries are mostly words and drawings: Beginnings. A great dream. Inner symbols. Light/dark, day/night. I drew the yin/yang symbol, then wrote more words: The Spirit impregnated the waters. "Let us make man in our image, after our likeness; ... male and female, he created them."[557] God as a "we." The feminine adds *relationship*.

I have more drawings one labeled the Tree of The Knowledge of Good and Evil, the other The Tree of Life. Beneath the Tree of The Knowledge of Good and Evil sketch, I wrote, "A step in our evolution to know good and evil. Differentiation." And beneath the Tree of Life I wrote, "Singleness." *Does God know what God is doing here?* Is God newly conscious? Not having a plan? I must see the trees in myself, the serpent within myself.

Sheila Moon, sitting among us, asked, "Can the serpent be seen as creative, rather than negative? Myths of every culture include a serpent who is wise."

I asked myself, Is God inviting us to participate with him or her in evolving this creation to be co-creators with her or him? Otherwise, we are like the animals and do not know who we are.

Another drawing: the cherubim that the Lord set at "the east of the Garden of Eden" with "a flaming sword which turned every way, to guard the way to the tree of life."[558] The way into the garden wasn't sealed with a gate, simply cherubim. My Oxford Bible told me that cherubim were "guardians of sacred places," winged creatures, half-human and half-lion like the Sphinx of Egypt. "A flaming sword ... was placed near the cherubim to remind banished man of the impossibility of overstepping his creaturely bounds."[559]

Next we were asked, "How do I linger in the garden?" I wrote, "Letting others make decisions; not taking responsibility; not accepting my role as participant or co-creator." Then Sheila Moon brought a question: "Do you have the spunk to fight your way back?" I'd never considered such a possibility since I had asked my mother, so long ago, "Can we ever go back?" The leader pursued this idea. "What might it be like to return?" I wrote, "Having experienced much and gained wisdom, I can now *choose* to eat of the tree of life." Today my answer would add delight, amazement, and fear at what eating of both these trees might bring. I can't avoid eating of the tree of the knowledge of good and evil. I have already done so; I am no longer innocent. Would I choose to eat of the tree of life as well?

"What part of this myth most touches you?" they asked, and I wrote, "The need to leave the garden to gain wisdom; the potential to return. How I want to remain a child, innocent in the garden." A leader quoted Dag Hammarskjöld: "You dare your Yes and experience a meaning. You repeat your Yes and all things acquire a meaning. When everything has meaning, how can you live anything but a Yes?" Another quoted *Codex Bezae,* a fifth-century gospel account: "On the same day, seeing someone working on the sabbath, Jesus said to him, 'Man, if indeed you know what you are doing you are blessed; but if you do not know, you are cursed and a transgressor of the law.'"[560] I am reminded of, "'The sabbath was made for man, not man for the sabbath; so the Son of man is lord even of the sabbath.'"[561] Hearing Hammarskjöld's *yes* and Jesus's knowing what you are doing, I began to see and fear that *it is all about conscious choice.*

A leader asked, "What has happened to God in this incident?" Someone responded, "If we are made in the image of God, the way to know what we are like is to look at ourselves. Now God can look at us to know God's self. And to know God, we look at ourselves."

The next question was, "What image stays with you?" Someone responded, "That God didn't have anyone to relate to until Adam and Eve were banished from the garden. Now the question begins to stir in us of what God is about."

Is this garden life? Is the choice to eat of the tree of the knowledge of good and evil anything like the choice to enter the narrow gate? Is knowing what I am doing when I choose to eat, rather than betraying God, doing the will of God? Doesn't God know what God is doing? Doesn't God know the whole story? Do I mean by 'God' *life* itself?

The English essayist John Middleton Murry wrote, "The will of God that is known beforehand ceases to be the will of God."[562] Jung spoke to this same idea: "God is the name by which I designate all things which cross my willful path violently and recklessly, all things which upset my subjective views, plans, and intentions and change the course of my life for better or worse."[563] There is no plan, no grand design written down by the great author; there's just life in its complexity, joy, tragedy, and unexpectedness. Is this garden, this *life*, what Jesus was talking about when he spoke about the kingdom of God that is here and now, spread out among and between us, within and without us, if only we have eyes to see and ears to hear?

Another Creation Story

On Day 2, we looked through our newly acquired *Records* book and saw that only Matthew and Luke tell about the birth of Jesus and what happened before and after. Mark says nothing of genealogy or

Bethlehem, wise men or shepherds in the fields. He begins with the baptism.

That evening we gathered in the living room. Votive candles were glowing on each window sill and in front of the fireplace as we visited the familiar Christmas story of Mary and Joseph's journey to Bethlehem for the birth of the child called holy. History or myth? Does it matter? We worked on the birth story as a way to look at ourselves and to consider Mary, Joseph, and the child as qualities in us.

Over the years I learned that not all the leaders bring this material in the same way. Some tell the story, some read it. One leader told it as a dream, and then we each brought our own memories of the story as if we'd dreamed it ourselves. As though analyzing a dream, we "remembered" the main characters—Mary, Joseph, the child, the inn that was full, and the innkeeper who offered a crib in the stable. There was the stable, the manger, the animals in the stable, the donkey that carried Mary, the shepherds with their sheep, the angel who told them, "Be not afraid," the star that shone over the manger, the wise men with their gifts who followed it "from the East," and Herod the King, who wanted to destroy the child.

Then we began exploring each figure. The leader asked, "What are Mary's qualities?" People responded, "Innocent. Fresh. Undamaged. Full of life. Deep. Vulnerable. Strong." The leader asked, "What is it like to experience these things in yourself?" It was startling to consider that the qualities of Mary were in me, and I wrote, "The inner virginal needs protecting."

Next the leader asked, "What are the qualities of the child?" and someone responded, "Divine and human." The leader then asked, "What comes together in a new consciousness?" and I wondered, "Are we talking about a new consciousness in the human? In me?"

The father not Joseph but the father as the story tells it was next. The leader read, "The Holy Spirit will come upon you, and the power of the Most High will overshadow you."[564] Then she asked, "How do you respond to this father?" and my notes say, "Whew. That's tremendous!" The leader likened this Holy Spirit's action to inspiration, as *breathing* (literally) into one's soul, and she asked, "What happens when there is inspiration but it does not take root?" I wrote, "I know too well what happens a death happens."

Joseph, the earthly father, was examined too. The leader asked, "What are his qualities?" I wrote, "Loving, caring, heeds the irrational, protects the New Thing; he knows when to protect and when to retreat. He listens to dreams the ones Matthew tells." In the first dream, the angel tells Joseph to take Mary as his wife even though she was pregnant; in the second, an angel tells Joseph to take his child and the mother to Egypt to escape Herod; and in a third dream when, after Herod's death, the angel appears to Joseph and tells him to return. And he returns with Mary and Jesus to Nazareth. "What do we know of this Joseph in ourselves? What do we need from this inner Joseph?" Perhaps this quality of Joseph's that he listened to dreams impressed me in 1984 because I was still wary of the power of dreams. My doubting Thomas was very present, and yet here was Joseph, listening and acting, saving the child and his mother from destruction the good father.

In this way, we worked with each character in the story the animals and the stable, which remind us of our instinctual natures; the shepherds, simple people who also listen to the words of the angel who brings them good news and who go to see for themselves; the wise men who follow a star, not knowing what it means or where it would lead; the star itself. "What star has guided you on your own journey?" a leader asked. And we meet Herod, and consider, "What attitude within and outside you slaughters the new?" I knew that one well, the one who plays it safe, "thinks it through" for a long time before acting or not guarding against spontaneity the one who is fearful of change. I knew, as well, the harsh critic who would kill the new idea at birth.

We brought all these figures and their qualities into the circle, and each of us looked within ourselves, meeting each image as a familiar, unexpected, or unwanted part of us. I began to see the Christian birth myth as a story about humanity, birthing the *new thing* in each of us, responding to the "higher value" and the call of the self. I experienced it as psyche telling us about ourselves.

The leader continued, "When have you been aware of an important birth in you? Of a real change in consciousness? What might you call the *new thing* born in you during this seminar?"

I have before me a drawing of the new thing I made at a recent *Records* seminar, a childlike drawing with blotches of purple, green, and yellow, a red line that meanders through and around the blotches, a stream of gold, and sparkles. In my journal that day, I wrote, "*What fun!* A playfulness came into my dribbles and splotches that delights me. Spontaneity, color *space* glitter unknown and unexpected and happy with it! There's no up or down, right or left. It's a work in progress." As is my life.

Chapter 12

Choosing Life

On the fifth day of the seminar, we studied "The Sermon on the Mount." Only Matthew and Luke tell this story, and our critical work concluded that both of these Gospel writers were drawing from the hypothetical source Q. While Matthew presents 110 verses in three chapters, Luke's account has just twenty-nine. Some of Luke's verses parallel Matthew's sequencing, others appear here and there in different chapters of his Gospel. And while Matthew begins by saying, "Seeing the crowds, he went up on the mountain,"[565] Luke says, "And he came down with [his disciples] and stood on a level place."[566] So, according to Luke, it's not exactly "on the Mount."

In this great sermon, we hear Jesus's "Blessed are" the poor, those who mourn and are meek, who hunger and thirst after righteousness, who are merciful and pure of heart, who are peacemakers, even those who are persecuted for righteousness's sake and are reviled "on my account."[567] Luke says, "on account of the Son of man."[568]

It's in this sermon that we hear what Jesus has to say about anger, lust, and evil, about loving one's enemy, not being public in one's devotions, judging not lest ye be judged. It's here we find the "mote and the beam" story (King James Version's translation—translated in the New Revised Standard Version as "Why do you see the speck that is in your brother's eye, but do not notice the log that is in your own eye?")[569] It's here Jesus says, "You therefore must be perfect, as your heavenly

Father is perfect."[570] And in this sermon, Jesus speaks the Golden Rule, as Hillel had spoken earlier: "So whatever you wish that men would do to you, do so to them, for this is the law and the prophets."[571]

Three days of seminar are devoted to the Sermon on the Mount. One of the leaders cautioned us: "This is powerful material. It deals with forces, powers, energies that simply *are*, that simply exist." Yes, the Sermon on the Mount includes orations on lust, anger, judgment, these oft-violent human emotions that exist within each of us, whether we acknowledge them or not. In these three days, we were asked, allowed, and forced to look at them in ourselves and perhaps to accept their reality and find new ways to deal with them. All the passages in the Sermon on the Mount teach us about life and death.

Three passages speak of a narrow gate that leads to life, and few are they who find it; of "doing the will of God," not merely saying *yes*; and of building a house on rock, not sand. There is a fourth passage about choosing life that's found elsewhere in the Gospels: "Whoever seeks to gain his life will lose it, but whoever loses his life will preserve it."[572] These are not merely theoretical; they can illuminate our lives.

Coming to terms with being lesbian was for me an example of choosing life, one of the many ways the life and teachings of Jesus speak to me. My coming-out story illustrates the interplay of what I learned through *Records* study with the choices I've faced and made in my life. On the third Sunday of January 1987, the pastor of Trinity United Methodist Church in Berkeley had his usual "altar call Sunday." We had joked about calling it that. It was a part of services in earlier days of the church when people were invited to come forward and pledge their lives to God and Jesus Christ. In our liberal church, one's religious beliefs were no longer a matter of public discourse. Instead, this was a day when members of the congregation were invited to come forward to share activities, causes, issues, or personal concerns they wanted others in the church to know about.

That Sunday, Ron's sermon was based on Moses saying to his people, "I call heaven and earth to witness against you this day, that I have set before you life and death, blessing and curse; therefore choose life, that you and your descendants may live."[573] Ron's message was that it isn't always easy to choose life or even to know which is the choice for life and which is for death.

Our church administrative council, of which I was a member, was facing a crucial vote the following Thursday as to whether to become a Reconciling Congregation, adopting a policy welcoming all people, including gay men and lesbians today it includes bisexual and transgendered individuals to full participation in all aspects of the church, including ordination. For some weeks in preparation for this vote, another church member, a straight man, and I had led a study group about sexuality and homosexuality and what various Bible scholars say about them. I had not come out to this group. I was still living in the closet, except with my closest friends and in communities of gay and straight people that felt safe. Ron, our pastor, was one of these friends. He knew his congregation was divided on the issue. Welcome gays into the church community, okay, but ordain them? No, that's going too far.

Was it coincidence that the reading for this particular "altar call Sunday" was Moses's "choose life" injunction? Today, I call it synchronistic. In any case, Ron made the most of it. He told about a man with terminal cancer. Should he go through what would be painful treatments that might prolong his life? Which is the choice for life? He told about a woman with several children who found she was once again pregnant and to deliver the baby could endanger her own life. Abortion? Which is the choice for life? And he told about a gay man who lived closeted in fear of being found out. To come out or not? Which is the choice for life?

I sat torn to come out as lesbian and say, "We are here! How can you not accept us in all the work of the church?" Or remain silent, even while advocating that we become a Reconciling Congregation? The fear of a lifetime first, that I "was one," a queer, and second, that I would be found out rose in me as I sat listening to Ron's sermon. Yet by the time he had finished and invited everyone to come forward, I knew which was, for me, the choice for life.

Others went forward with me that day. One woman invited people to join in a peace march; another recommitted himself to working with the homeless. I waited until last. Then I held tight to Ron's hand as I looked out over the congregation and told them why it was important to me for our church to become a Reconciling Congregation. When I returned to my seat, I was engulfed in hugs and words of support. Four days later, the administrative council voted yes, and Trinity joined many other United Methodist Churches in welcoming the gay and lesbian community in all aspects of the church. This is not, I need to make clear, the official position of the United Methodist Church or of some other mainline Protestant denominations, and certainly not the Roman Catholic Church. I also need to make clear, it was not my coming out that swayed the vote. The council would likely have voted yes whether I had spoken or not. But if I hadn't spoken, it would have been (for me) choosing the wide gate that leads to destruction.

I came out at Trinity United Methodist Church in 1987, three years after my first *Records* seminar. I did not come out to people at the seminar for many more years. Fear is a terrible thing. Even as I began to write this chapter, reflecting on passages in which Jesus speaks about life and death, I had not intended to tell this story. But as I was writing, I realized I had to come out yet again. Something in me is crying out to be heard: "Don't you see! Don't you see how crucial it is to choose life and how hard it is?" We all have closets and too often think we're "gaining" life by staying in them, when if we look more deeply, we are destroying life.

I spoke of the passage about loving God with all in an earlier chapter. Clearly, it has more to teach me:

> And behold, a lawyer stood up to put him to the test, saying, "Teacher, what shall I do to inherit eternal life?" [Jesus] said to him, "What is written in the law? How do you read?" And [the man] answered, "You shall love the Lord your God with all your heart, and with all your soul, and with all your strength, and with all your mind; and your neighbor as

yourself." And [Jesus] said to him, "You have answered right; do this, and you will live."[574]

The leader asked, "What might it mean to love with all your heart and soul and strength and mind?" And she asked, "What clues do you have that there is more of you than you know?" This unknown realm makes itself known to me in dreams and guided imagery, where I meet figures "who" reside in me, sometimes to my surprise or even horror. I get clues to the unknown parts of myself in words I say that I hadn't intended, a "no" when I meant to say "yes," and the "yes" that bursts out of me, surprising me even when I know it's the right "yes." A leader asked, "What would it mean to love your God with *all* of you?" Not just the good stuff, but the stuff we don't want to know about ourselves.

Some days later, we worked with another passage about the heart. "Hear me, all of you, and understand: there is nothing outside a man which by going into him can defile him; but the things which come out of a man are what defile him."[575] Mark gets quite specific a few lines later when he says, "What comes out of a man is what defiles a man. For from within, out of the heart of man, come evil thoughts, fornication, theft, murder, adultery, coveting, wickedness, deceit, licentiousness, envy, slander, pride, foolishness. All these evil things *come from within*, and they defile a man."[576]

The passage we worked with first said to love with *all* your heart, soul, strength, and mind. Jesus says that while knowing that evil along with good resides there, we are to love God with it all. "Resist not evil." Turn the other cheek. Go the extra mile.[577] I always thought these words were telling us how to deal with others. Does "resist not evil" also mean not denying what exists in our own heart, becoming conscious of what Jung calls "the shadow"? Then what?

Jesus asked, "Why do you see the speck that is in your brother's eye, but do not notice the log that is in your own eye? Or how can you say to your brother, 'Let me take the speck out of your eye,' when there is the log in your own eye? You hypocrite, first take the log out of your own eye, and then you will see clearly to take the speck out of your brother's eye."[578] I understand this passage to be about projection.

In Matthew, it says, "You, therefore, must be perfect, as your heavenly Father is perfect."[579] I always heard this as a harsh and impossible injunction. And yet in the *Records* seminar we learn that the word that has been translated "perfect" could alternatively be translated "complete, whole, fulfilled, all-inclusive."[580] If Jesus is teaching us how to live, he's saying we need to bring our *whole* being to God, and that his Father in heaven is also whole.

Is this the God I know? I don't think so. The God of my childhood was good and loving, until He failed to answer my prayers to heal my sister. So, for many years, there was no God for me, and yet something in me yearned for such a Being. It was a book that leaped out at me in a bookstore that opened my thoughts again: *The Problem of God,* by Jesuit theologian John Courtney Murray. I realized, perhaps for the first time, it's okay to question God, that blind faith is not required or even desired. So I returned to questioning; and it was questioning that brought me to Four Springs. And I found at Four Springs that I was not alone in questioning, and seeking new words to express what God was for me, and for all of humankind.

On the first night of the seminar, we put other words for God into the circle: "Mystery, Life Force, Higher Power, Beloved Spirit, Energy, Sophia, Challenger, Essence, Divinity, Guide, Unfolding Pattern of the Universe." Mystery was a good one for me, and also Energy and Unfolding Pattern of the Universe.

My thoughts returned to the young man's question, "What shall I do to inherit eternal life?" What does Jesus mean by *life*?

Enter by the narrow gate; for the gate is wide and the way is easy, that leads to destruction, and those who enter by it are many. For the gate is narrow and the way is hard, that leads to life, and those who find it are few.[581]

Every one then who hears these words of mine and does them will be like a wise man who built his house upon the rock; and the rain fell, and the floods came, and the winds blew and beat upon that house, but it did not fall, because it had been founded on the rock.[582]

Not every one who says to me, "Lord, Lord," shall enter the kingdom of heaven, but he who does the will of my Father who is in heaven.[583]

I've worked with these three passages at *Records* seminars, in training and in life, but the questions don't stay answered. What is the narrow gate that leads to life, and the wide gate that leads to destruction? How do I choose which to enter? What does it mean to *do* the will of God? How? Is it not enough just to love God with all? Is this *love* more than an emotion? Who is "God" and what is "the will of God"? What is the kingdom of heaven I can enter if I can figure out how to do God's will?

Regarding the passage about the narrow gate that is difficult and few find it, the leader asked, "What are the contrasts here?" People respond: "The narrow gate and the wide gate, life and destruction, many and few, easy and hard, find and not find, enter and not enter."

"What are other words for *destruction*?" the leader asked. A flood of words came from the circle: "Disconnection, death, despair, meaninglessness, addiction, stagnation, emptiness, ruin, anxiety, loss of self, living a lie, a living death, unconsciousness, suicide, chasing after worldly success."

"What is the end result of these outcomes?" "Death, a living death."

The leader pushed us onward. "What might lead one to enter the broad gate?" "Unconsciousness, busyness, going along with the crowd, not even realizing one has chosen the broad gate."

"What might Jesus mean by *life*? What might *life* be as an outcome of choice to enter through the narrow gate?" And the responses: "Feeling loved, being in harmony with nature, including the light and the dark, continuous new birth, meaning and purpose, beauty, joy, and vitality, childlike quality, play, compassion, creativity."

"Given the two choices, which do you choose?" No one chooses destruction. Then the leader asked, "What is the narrow gate? Is there more than one gate in a lifetime?" I rephrase this to mean, "Do we make the choice to enter or not more than once in a lifetime?"

I say the narrow gate is choice, choice that can be painful, terrifying, and even threatening to life as we've known it. And we're faced with these ethical and moral choices daily. How then shall we live?

The leader continued, "'Those who find it are few.' Why?" People responded: "Distraction draws energy away, comfortableness, lack of consciousness, liking the broad way, liking destruction." Our work on this passage ends with a rhetorical question: "What is the experience of destruction that we know and find attractive and are able to contrast with *life*?" I know one example all too well. For years, silence, despair, and depression were more bearable than what I feared would happen if I came out as a lesbian. It is a stunning question and a shocking answer. I wonder how often I still choose unconsciousness, a life that seems easier and even more pleasant than entering by the narrow gate Jesus is talking about.

We went on to a passage about building your house on rock instead of sand. The leader asked, "What are the options?" and we responded, "House on rock, house on sand." She continued, "And the outcomes?" We said, "Survival or destruction." "What are the rain, the wind, and the flood symbolically?" "The vicissitudes of life, natural disasters, broken relationships, death itself." "Which house do you choose? What are the ways we build on rock? What are the ways we build on sand?" Sometimes, we think we're building on rock only to find it crumbling beneath our feet. The leader posed another question: "Who chooses?" My answer then and today is that *each of us chooses*, not God and not Jesus. I don't always know if I've made the right choice until time provides the answer.

Next, we turn to the passage in which Jesus states, "Not every one who says to me, 'Lord, Lord,' shall enter the kingdom of heaven, but he who does the will of my Father who is in heaven."[584] A leader reminds us that Matthew, a Jew, would not use the word *God*,* but we, not constrained, will, and so will speak of "the kingdom of God" and "the will of God." And in this passage, Jesus says we must *do* the will and not simply *say*, "Lord, Lord." Someone pointed out that Matthew said, "Do the will of my Father which is in heaven," not "Do the will of Jesus." Jesus separated himself from God. We "do the will" of God, not of Jesus.

The leader asked for synonyms for *will*. We respond: "Intention, yearning, plan, purpose, bidding, central value, need, vision, evolutionary pattern, natural laws, passionate desire, and heart's desire." Many of us also expressed a force, an energy, an emotion that we experience in ourselves. Others spoke of something *given* by God or by nature itself.

As she had earlier in the seminar, the leader asked for other words for *God*. Some were the same as earlier, others different: "Great Mystery, Divine One, Source of All, Holy One, Other, Dynamic Unfolding Pattern of the Universe, Truth, Reality, Life Force, Love, Sum of the Whole, the Nothing That Wants to Become Something (after Meister Eckhart), Ground of Being, the Behind Which There is Nothing, the One from Which the Many Come."

Then we were instructed to bring forth words for *kingdom of heaven* or *kingdom of God*. We thought that the Jews of Jesus's time would consider the kingdom of heaven to be: "Abundance, freedom from oppression, a kingdom on earth in which they are free to worship their God, a kingdom in which only the wheat and not the chaff are to be found." These were the messianic hopes we kept finding as we journeyed with Jesus.

But what about our *own* words for the kingdom? What does this phrase mean to us? An answer was forming in my mind and became

* Jewish culture judges it forbidden to pronounce God's name ("*Yahweh*"). In prayers it is replaced by the word *Adonai* ("the Lord") and in discussion by *HaShem* ("the Name").

clearer on another day. The leader asked, "Who is it who will enter the kingdom now?" The text was clear: Not the ones who say "Lord, Lord," but the ones "who *do* the will of my Father who is in heaven."

Next, we were given the task of "filling in the blanks for 'doing the ____of____.'" Over the years, I've made many attempts: "Live out the central value of the Source of All. Do the desire of the Holy One. Live out the deep yearning of the Great Mystery. Do the heart's desire of the Mystery, of the Source of All, of the Cry." "Listen, discern, resonate with."

I'm still not satisfied. I haven't said what I want to say. I feel a great yearning in myself that comes from something greater than me, something I call "Mystery" or "Self" or "Cry." To "do the will" is to respond to that self, that Cry, by doing what it cries out needs to be done. Say *Yes* to life. Say *Yes* to the narrow gate. Be mindful of what is needed in the now and say *Yes* to it then *do* something! *Speak* the truth, even when it goes against convention, political correctness, or our own fears. *Join* a cause that demands your attention. *Make* the hard choices and live with the consequences. At bottom, "doing the will" often means going against things my ego personality longs for, whether it's a passive unconsciousness or frantically in response to obligations. "Doing the will" is being conscious. Being mindful. It's not what a God "out there" wants, even doing what Jesus says. I do it because it is the true thing for me to do. Is this what it means to love God with *all* my heart and soul and strength and mind? "Don't just say you love me. *Show* me."

The leader asked, "When faced with a situation that requires choice, what factors go into choosing the will of God? What are the criteria for discerning the will of God?" This question remains with me. I ask myself, "Is it enough that I feel it in my body, that I *know* it's right? I do make some choices on that basis, but surely there are additional criteria. One afternoon in 1984 as we gathered in a circle with Elizabeth Howes, someone asked her, "How do you determine the will of God?" She gave a variety of answers, including, "Commitment that no matter what emerges, I'll do it. Ask what's the best in the total situation I'm in. Have I given up holding on to the outcome and am just open to the answer? Jesus in Gethsemane was open even though he hoped it would go differently. It's not the natural process. 'Doing my thing' may come from my center, but 'Doing my thing' may also be an unexamined response."

Another leader said it differently: "I choose the most creative action, the one that will as far as I can see serve life. The choice that may bring healing to the situation." That rang true to me.

How one determines the will of God has no right or wrong answer, only guidelines for fumbling our way to the best choice we can make in a given time and situation. It is I who must choose. I think of Middleton Murry's comment, often brought to *Records* seminars, "The will of God that is known beforehand ceases to be the will of God." Thanks a lot, God! Thanks a lot, Life!

Another passage, known as the Great Paradox, also expresses what Jesus tells us about life. Luke said it most simply, "Whoever seeks to gain his life will lose it, but whoever loses his life will preserve it."[585] This teaching is contained in all three Gospels, with variations, and was a great awakening for me. Matthew added, "for my sake."[586] Mark (or perhaps a later edition of Mark) added, "for my sake and the gospel's."[587] Even Luke adds, elsewhere, "for my sake."[588] We did the critical work. Did the earliest version include these additions? We chose Luke's simplest statement, although to understand it is far from simple: "Whoever seeks to gain his life will lose it, but whoever loses his life will preserve it."[589]

As we did with each of the teachings about life and death, we listed the opposites, but this time we also took the saying apart, working each half independently, because the connotations of "save/lose life" are different in each.

"Whoever seeks to gain his life will lose it." The leader asked, "What's the goal here?" *To gain life.* "What's the method?" *To seek to gain it.* "And what's the outcome?" *Losing life!*

"What does it mean to 'lose life'?" My response was, "Meaninglessness; without vitality or mobility; living by rote; no connection to core; without the aliveness of the creative mind or imagination." The leader asked, "What does it mean to seek to 'gain one's life'?" Our responses:

"Control it. Hold onto it. Seek to know the will of God beforehand. Take the mystery out of life. Do things for someone else's sake. Think that what I *know* of life is all there *is* to life." Her next question was, "How do we do this in our own lives?" "By keeping busy, seeking success for ego's sake, trying to control the course of one's life, keeping silent when speaking out is what's needed."

Then we turned to the second half of the teaching: "Whoever loses his life will preserve it." We followed the leader again, "The goal?" *To save life.* "The method?" *Lose life.* "The outcome?" *Preserve life.* "In this context, what does *life* mean?" Our responses: "Feel the adventure of it. Know its uniqueness. The dance. Joyfulness. See its unlimited possibilities. Be excited and relaxed. Know and be connected with one's purpose and be juicy with it."

Of course, this is the choice we would make! And yet how hard it is to know how to "lose life" and then make such a choice. Someone in the circle brought an image from something Elizabeth wrote, "Whosoever shall lose his life shall save it ... places the highest value on the psyche as the container of divinity. It might read, in a free rendering, 'Whosoever will allow the rigid boundaries around his own psyche to drop, will find a vitality of life inside.'"[590]

For me, the idea of "rigid boundaries around the psyche" broke apart the paradox of Luke's statement. All my life I had built walls around my innermost self to protect it from the hurts of the world and from my fears of being fully myself. I knew too well how these walls cut me off from what I long for most life. I didn't tell my mother I was lesbian for another year after coming out at Trinity. I was as panic-stricken as I had been in front of a congregation of people. Homosexuality was not okay in her mind, and my coming out to her was wrenching for both of us. Often, in the remaining three years of her life, she said, "I love you, honey, but I can't accept your lesbianism." And yet, she said at other times, "I feel like we've been closer these past years. I don't know why." I did.

Chapter 13

The Kingdom of Heaven Is Like …

Every morning to greet the new day, I still light the candle on my altar, a ritual that grew out of many Guild seminars addressing the need in me to connect with that something greater than myself. Call it "self," as Jung often does, but more often I simply call it "mystery" or "pattern of life." Each day as I light my candle, I greet the many objects on my altar that speak to me of the mystery of life—that life *is* and I *am*. I say *Yes* to life and all it will bring this day. Is this what is meant by "entering by the narrow gate"? Perhaps it is.

Among the objects on my altar is a small pearl in a gold setting with a pinpoint of a diamond. It rests in a tiny white seashell I picked up somewhere. I purchased the pearl after a *Records* seminar to help me remember one of my favorite parables: "Again, the kingdom of heaven is like a merchant in search of fine pearls, who, on finding one pearl of great value, went and sold all that he had and bought it."[591] This little pearl reminds me that there is something of such value we would sell all we have in order to obtain it. We can't just look at and long for it; we have to *do something*. "Not every one who says to me, 'Lord, Lord,' shall enter the kingdom of heaven, but he who does the will of my Father who is in heaven."[592]

To me, the pearl and the kingdom are related, perhaps even the same. What does Jesus mean by this "kingdom"? He speaks of it in parables, and after several of them he says, "He who has ears to hear, let him hear."[593] Apparently, not everyone has "ears to hear."

What images does Jesus conjure in these parables? There's the farmer who sowed seed. Birds ate some of the seeds, some fell on rocky soil, some fell among thorns, and some fell on good soil and brought forth a bounty.[594] His disciples were puzzled, and Jesus said to them, "To you has been given the secret of the kingdom of God, but for those outside everything is in parables."[595] I quote Mark and Luke here. Matthew's words are slightly different. But why is the secret given only to his disciples and not to "those outside"? And who would be called *disciples* and who would be *those outside*? Jesus called his disciples to him; is it only these who were his disciples, those who are *inside*?

Early in the seminar, we'd worked with another difficult passage, where Jesus's mother and brothers are "standing outside" the place he is preaching and want to talk with him. Mark writes, "And a crowd was sitting about him; and they said to him, 'Your mother and your brothers are outside, asking for you.' And he replied, 'Who are my mother and my brothers?' And looking around on those who sat about him, he said, 'Here are my mother and my brothers! Whoever does the will of God is my brother, and sister, and mother.'"[596] We'd heard this before: Those who *do the will* are in the kingdom, while his biological mother and brothers, who are outside, are *not* in the kingdom. Those sitting around Jesus *are* his family!

In Mark's telling of the parable of the seeds, Jesus refers to the "twelve," but Matthew and Luke say the "disciples": "To you has been given the secret of the kingdom of God, but for *those outside* everything is in parables."[597] Luke simply says, "to them," and Matthew says, "for others." So who's in and who's out? Apparently, *everyone* who "does the will of God" is inside, and those who do not even his mother, brothers, and sisters are outside.

Jesus's messages are simple but not easy. He continues his commentary saying the *seeds* represent "the word"[598] or "the word of the kingdom"[599] or "the word of God."[600] Are these really Jesus's words, or those of Mark, Matthew, and Luke? Jesus doesn't usually explain what he says. Someone at seminar noted that this is an *allegory*, unlike Jesus's simple storytelling. But whether he said it or some editor added it later, it is a great parable. Watch where you sow your seeds. I am reminded of Jesus's teaching to build your house on rock, not on sandy ground.

There's another seed parable in Mark. Jesus says, "The kingdom of God is as if a man should scatter seed upon the ground, and should sleep and rise night and day, and the seed should sprout and grow, he knows not how. The earth produces of itself, first the blade, then the ear, then the full grain in the ear. But when the grain is ripe, at once he puts in the sickle, because the harvest has come."[601]

Is this an apocalyptic message, or is Jesus just saying, simply yet mysteriously, "This is how the kingdom is." The image of *harvest* is often associated with the apocalyptic end-time, when God intervenes in history and separates good and evil; but in the context of the parable, Jesus seems to be saying that it requires a man to scatter seed, and it requires the night and the day and a natural process by which seeds sprout and wheat comes to harvest. He doesn't say God does it; it's just the course of nature.

Matthew tells a different version. His is about sowing "good seeds," but in the night, his enemy came and sowed weeds among the wheat, so when the seeds came up, there was wheat and there were also weeds. His servants ask whether they should dig up the weeds, and he says no, because that might also damage the wheat. Let them all grow together, "and at harvest time I will tell the reapers, 'Gather the weeds first and bind them in bundles to be burned, but gather the wheat into my barn.'"[602] Is this apocalyptic? Sure sounds like it. Mark's telling says everything is harvested together; it doesn't mention weeds or an enemy coming in the night. Is Matthew's kingdom different from Mark's?

Then there's the wonderful parable about the mustard seed, which the three Synoptic Gospels tell using similar words. Mark begins, "With what can we compare the kingdom of God, or what parable shall we use for it?"[603] Then he speaks of "the smallest of all the seeds on earth,"[604] and yet it grows into a great shrub that gives home to "the birds of the air."[605] Matthew tells it much the same,[606] while Luke sequences it differently in his Gospel.[607]

Then there is the parable about the woman and the leaven, which I love almost as much as the pearl of great price: "The kingdom of heaven is like leaven which a woman took and hid in three measures of flour, till it was all leavened."[608] Luke places it near the story of the mustard seed, while Mark doesn't have it at all.

From these parables, what can I say about the kingdom of God? With the exception of Matthew's "morality play" in which the weeds are bundled and burned before the wheat is harvested, reminding me of John the Baptist, the kingdom sounds like a rather natural place whose way life *is*. The course of events is here and now, and humans can take part. Is that what Jesus is saying? Is the kingdom of God like seeds that grow of themselves and are harvested in the natural course of things? Is it something tiny that grows to be a haven for the birds of the field? Is it like leaven, small in amount yet transformative?

Or is it like wheat and weeds that grow together and won't be separated till harvest time? Like seeds sown on good or bad ground, with the expected consequences? Didn't the Jews expect a separation of good from evil, or a land flowing over with milk and honey, a land governed by a good and wise leader in which they would be free from oppression, free to worship their God as they saw fit, a kingdom still *to come*?

Matthew's parable of the wheat and chaff seems to be the exception among these parables. The reapers, Matthew recounts, are angels who will gather the weeds and burn them. "The Son of man will send his angels" to throw the weeds into the fire, and "there men will weep and gnash their teeth," but "the righteous will shine like the sun in the kingdom of the Father."[609]

It's noteworthy that Mark and Luke don't include this, and even Matthew follows this apocalyptic as I hear it account with two parables of the kingdom with a very different image. The first is, "The kingdom of heaven is like treasure hidden in a field, which a man found and covered up; then in his joy, he goes and sells all that he has and buys that field."[610] The second, the one I began this chapter with, is, "Again, the kingdom of heaven is like a merchant in search of fine pearls, who, on finding one pearl of great value, went and sold all that he had and bought it."[611]

These parables speak not of fire and brimstone, but of a kingdom of such enormous value that one will sell *all* to acquire it. A man finds a treasure hidden in the field that he wasn't even aware of. The merchant finds the perfect pearl. One is looking, one is not; but both recognize the value when they see it, and they are willing to give all to obtain it. Am I willing to let go of all I have for such a treasure, for the kingdom of heaven? Or do I choose the wide gate that leads to destruction?

It seems to me Jesus is talking about *life as it is*, and yet *lived in an unordinary way*. What must I sell (give up) for it? How shall I live to dwell in this kingdom? My thoughts turn to the Sermon on the Mount. Is Jesus saying ... if one is meek, if one mourns, if one hungers and thirsts after righteousness ... if one deals with anger and lust in a different manner than the culture says, if one turns the other cheek against evil acts if one loves her enemy and prays for those who persecute her for righteousness' sake ... Is he saying these are the ways to *do* the will of God? So many lessons in the Sermon on the Mount beseech us to be aware of the narrow and wide gates, and the consequences of choosing one or the other. No wonder Jesus says that few find and enter the narrow gate, the one that leads to life. Today I hear *life* and *kingdom* as one and the same, and I hear Jesus saying the gate that leads to the kingdom is narrow. It is a hard way to live. And if I want it, I must sell all.

These questions came to us on the very first evening when we worked with the passage about loving God with all one's heart and mind and strength. Now as I ponder these parables, the same questions arise, although I have more information than I did on the first day. But is it enough to tell me what this *all* might be, and to whom I am to sell it?

Searching through my seminar journals, I came upon a guided meditation that Elizabeth Boyden Howes called simply, "The House." She led this exercise in 1984, after we worked with the "sell all" parables. The spring rain had finally changed to the dry warmth of early California spring, and we were gathered in the grape arbor in our usual circle. Elizabeth introduced us to "The House" and all its rooms. Of course, this was more than an ordinary house. As Elizabeth spoke, I became startled, shocked, and anxious about all it implied: "Consider yourself a house you've been trying to run all these years with limited success. And now you are going to sell this house and *give it over* to another. *Give over ownership* to this Being we call God. Is it a single act? A decisive and choice full act?"

Yes! I wrote in my journal. She continued, "And are you selling more than you know your unknowns too. You're not to get *out* of this house. God wants you in it as its Steward. Now it's time to explore it and see how it really is, to discover more and more of the *all* [that one is selling]. Not just for the sake of the inner, but for the sake of the outer world too."

Then we visited each room of the house. My notes:
Living room Most in contact with the outer world. People come and go. We put certain things in the living room to express a certain image to people who come in.
Dining room Eating room. How do we eat? Gobble? Dawdle? Do we add a candle?
Kitchen Where the food is transformed. How do we relate to cooking? To the kitchen? Are we impatient?
Bedroom Place of intimacy, of sleep, where we make love.

Elizabeth guided us onward, through the bathroom, the closets, the attic, and the basement.

As we wander through the house, we may become aware sometimes of a darkness, a shadow. Other times, of a green thread, the Holy Spirit, present in the house. One day we will come upon a room we've never known was there. From it has come the fog and the green thread. Jung calls this *the self,* Jesus *the kingdom of God.* Call it "the image of God in our own Depths." Then we will know more about the relationship of all the rooms. But we can't just rush to this Central Room without first relating to all the rooms; one can become lost in it. It is a room of tremendous power. One can become inflated in that room.

Then she spoke of the outcome of choice, saying,

What comes as outcome comes as soon as one makes an act of will. The process then may be long, but there is joy in the first act, as the man who found the treasure in the field felt joy. When we completed our tour of The House, Elizabeth brought the hour to a close: "During the quiet hour, see how to make these images more yours, to make the process and the outcome clearer for you in your own life.

I was moved to tears. The work with "The House" unleashed emotions that had been brewing for days, stirred by the work with Jesus's teachings. I had come to this seminar longing for something, something that would show me the direction of my life now that my work at the Desert Retreat would soon end and I'd be at a crossroads once more. I wrote in my journal: "I am in awe of what Jesus seems to be calling us me to do. What is this commitment? What is this kingdom?"

More Parables

Two days later, we read more parables about the kingdom of God: A sleeping friend who must be harassed to wake up to help his friend who comes at midnight.[612] A vineyard owner who asks his sons to work in his fields. One says yes and doesn't do it; the other says no but then does as he was asked. It is he, the one who "repented," who Jesus says did the right thing.[613] A man who invites all to a banquet, but when the first-invited say no, the host says these will not taste of his banquet.[614] A rich man who rewards those who wisely use the talents he has given them ten talents to one, five to another but says of the one who buried his one talent that it will be taken from him and given to another.[615]

Another parable tells of wise and foolish maidens. Jesus begins, "Then the kingdom of heaven shall be compared to ten maidens who took their lamps and went to meet the bridegroom. Five of them were foolish, and five were wise."[616] The maidens called wise took enough oil for their lamps to last until the bridegroom arrived. The maidens called foolish did not take enough oil, and they had to go buy more as the bridegroom arrived. But "the door was shut," and the Lord they cried out to would not open the door. He said, "Truly, I say to you, I do not know you."[617] I was left with a lot to consider and more images of God. One thing I note now as in the parable of the banquet, if you don't accept the invitation, if you aren't prepared when the party begins, you don't get a second chance. Is Jesus talking about life as it is? We spent half an hour or longer with each parable, exploring the nuances of meaning and how each parable speaks to us today. The one that startled me most was about a sleeping God, a story Luke tells.

A man arrives at his friend's house at midnight. His friend welcomes him into the house, and because he has no food, goes to the house of *his* friend to ask for bread. Jesus asks, "Which of you who has a friend will go to him at midnight and say to him, 'Friend, lend me three loaves; for a friend of mine has arrived on a journey, and I have nothing to set before him'?" But the friend answers, "Do not bother me; the door is now shut, and my children are with me in bed; I cannot get up and give you anything."[618]

The leader asked, "What happens in you when you hear this?" I was puzzled. Isn't this about an all-giving, all-loving God? Others asked, "Why didn't the host have bread in his house? How dare the friend with food refuse to get up and help!" The leader then read the final sentence: "I tell you, though he will not get up and give him anything because he is his friend, yet because of his importunity he will rise and give him whatever he needs."[619]

In my *Records* book, I underlined "because of his importunity," and noted that importunity means "shameless persistence." What? The friend gives the bread, not out of friendship but because of his friend's "shameless persistence"?

We imagined each character as an aspect of ourselves: the friend who comes at midnight, tired and in need; his friend who knows where to seek what is needed; and the third, a sleeping friend who does not want to be disturbed but finally complies. I can find each of those "persons" in myself, certainly the sleeping one who doesn't want to be disturbed. But how is this parable about a sleeping God that must be importuned? It was a new way for me of thinking about God, the slumbering giant who cries out to us, as Kazantzakis proclaims, and yet who also needs us to wake Him, or Her, or It from sleep.

This story helps me understand Jung's "evolution of consciousness" and the crucial part we humans play. In *The Undiscovered Self*, Jung writes of "that infinitesimal unit on whom the fate of the world depends." We must be the host friend who is awake, who knows what is needed and goes for help; we require even the needy friend who comes in the middle of the night and asks for our help. And we need that God, sleeping though he is, because he does have the bread that is needed. So we must persist.

After we made our way through these parables, the leader asked, "What spoke to you most?" Someone responded, "Recognizing the door will be closed if I just slop through life, not really preparing myself and feeling everything will just be all right. It won't if I don't do my part." I responded, "My kinesthetic knowing that I am a participant with God in co-creating this existence. That God needs me needs me choosing, looking at the dark, using it to create myself anew. Life is a feast. All is prepared. My friend wants, needs me to come."

Then we turned to one more statement about the kingdom of God: "Being asked by the Pharisees when the kingdom of God was coming, [Jesus] answered them, 'The kingdom of God is not coming with signs to be observed; nor will they say, "Lo, here it is!" or "There!" for behold, the kingdom of God is in the midst of you.'"[620] A *Records* book footnote to Luke's passage informs that "in the midst of you" can also be translated "within you." Another reference[621] refers us to passages in the Gospel of Thomas: "It will not come by watching for it. It will not be said, 'Look, here it is.' Or 'Look, there it is.' Rather, the father's kingdom is spread out upon the earth, and people do not see it."[622] And elsewhere in the Gospel of Thomas, Jesus says, "If your leaders say to you, 'Look the kingdom is in heaven,' then the birds of heaven will precede you. If they say to you, 'It is in the sea,' then the fish will precede you. Rather, the kingdom is inside you and it is outside you."[623]

So I ask myself again, Is Jesus talking about life? Life as it is? And is it here and now if only I open my eyes to see it? I say Yes, this kingdom that is all about us, within and among us, is life itself. So, is life all the abundance, the joy, the vitality, and the sadness and grief and despair worth selling all? Is it worth knowing when I stand before the narrow gate and the wide gate, and choosing *consciously* which way to go? I say Yes, yet this examined life is not easy.

A day or two after Elizabeth led us through "The House," I wrote, "If God didn't need me, I wouldn't have been born." Elizabeth said it, and she believed it. Jung calls us "that infinitesimal unit on whom the fate of the world depends." Elizabeth and Sheila call us "essential choicemakers." I came to the 1984 seminar seeking meaning in my life; I left with the belief that life needs me, and each one of us. I still "fall asleep"; I still sit passively as something of great value calls out to me. Perhaps that, too, is part of life, of being human, and being aware of *all* that is me—the yes and the no.

Chapter 14

Gathering Strands

I carried my childhood image of Jesus with me into adulthood, the image from my book of Bible stories for children a kind and gentle white man seated amid a horde of children, beckoning all to come to him. Perhaps I was five, maybe a little older. Was this the image I brought to Four Springs? Perhaps, but the one I found at Four Springs was much more complex: sometimes gentle as that childhood Jesus; sometimes "beside himself," in Mark's—and only Mark's startling and puzzling little story;[624] sometimes a man who healed and forgave or did he? Most powerfully, he was a man who spoke about a way of life and how to live it, and it was not an easy way, and not always or ever obvious.

I see now that throughout the days of every *Records* seminar, I gathered strands and wove an image of Jesus for an adult Eleanor, a grown-up image. I didn't recognize the strands at first. But through revisiting my seminar journals and the passages themselves, the strands began to reveal themselves: the strands of place and people; of the Guild's particular method of living and studying together; the stories of preaching and teaching; the threads of healing and forgiveness; the strands that carry Jesus's messages about life and how to find it; and the ones that speak of the kingdom of God. All these passages and strands are part of the tapestry taking shape in my mind and heart. And there are three more essential strands.

The first is the messianic strand, about the existence of a messiah who will deliver his people from oppression. The second is the Son of man strand, expressed by that mysterious phrase that only Jesus uses in these Gospels. And the third is the Spirit strand. It takes me to the trials, the crucifixion, the empty tomb, and what happened after that. As the days of the seminar went on, these strands intertwined in ways that have helped me discover who this man Jesus is for me. Discerning and then weaving these strands, though, has been a labored and tortuous journey.

The First Strand – Messianic Longing

How many times in the Gospel accounts does the question "Who is this man?" arise in one form or another? Is he "the Holy One of God,"[625] as the man with an unclean spirit cried out? Is he "the Son of God,"[626] as the unclean spirits themselves proclaimed? And how did he reply? "Be silent," he said, and "strictly ordered them not to make him known."[627] Why not? It was a response that presaged those he offered as the story continued.

We met the messianic hopes and expectations on Day 2 when we read the story of John the Baptist preaching repentance for forgiveness of sins, foretelling the coming of someone "mightier than I," who "will baptize you with the Holy Spirit."[628] We met it again the next day when we heard how Jesus, after his baptism in the Jordan, was driven or led into the wilderness where for forty days he was offered powers that would have saved his people. And he said no, "Begone, Satan!"[629]

The clearest expression of the messianic hope, the yearning for a leader to deliver the Jewish people from oppression, came on Day 7 when we encountered John the Baptist, now in prison, who sent his disciples to ask Jesus, "Are you he who is to come, or shall we look for another?"[630] This was not just a question of strategy if you're not the one, let's go to Plan B. I can still feel the depth of yearning in John's question, and the yearning in myself for someone to deliver me and the world from destruction.

Jesus gave an enigmatic response. He spoke of all the things that had happened: the blind receiving their sight, the deaf their hearing, the dead raised up. And he continued, "And blessed is he who takes no offense at me."[631] A footnote tells us that this can also be translated, "who is not caused to stumble in me" or "who finds no obstacle in me." What would make Jesus an obstacle? If he were "the One," he would not be an obstacle. Why didn't he answer John's question?

On Day 10 of the seminar, the question "Who is this man?" arose again, this time asked by Jesus himself.

> And Jesus went on with his disciples, to the villages of Caesare'a Philip'pi; and on the way he asked his disciples, "Who do men say that I am?"
>
> And they told him, "John the Baptist; and others say, Elijah; and others one of the prophets."
>
> And he asked them, "But who do you say that I am?"
>
> Peter answered him, "You are the Christ."
>
> And he charged them to tell no one about him.[632]

Three stories we had worked with earlier offered more food for thought about who Jesus was. The first is the story, as Matthew and Mark tell it, about Jesus coming "to his own country" Nazareth and teaching in the synagogue. People are astonished. "Where did this man get all this? What is the wisdom given to him? What mighty works are wrought by his hands!"[633] And then they say among themselves, isn't this the carpenter, son of Mary and brother to several? "And they took offense at him."[634] And Jesus says, "'A prophet is not without honor, except in his own country.' ... And he could do no mighty work there ... and he marveled because of their unbelief."[635] But Matthew says, "And he did not do many mighty works there, because of their unbelief."[636] Okay, which is it? He *could* not or *did* not do mighty works?

The leader guided us with pointed questions: "What is the source of this story?" Mark is, and Matthew follows him for the most part.

Luke tells the story differently and at a different place in the Gospel. Does Matthew have the original telling— "*did* not do"—and Mark changed it to "*could* not do"? Or does Mark have the original, and Matthew changed it? I chose Mark, the earliest source. It fits the image of Jesus and the process of healing and forgiveness that had been growing in me since our study of the palsied one and the sinner woman.

The leader asked, "What is the implication of 'he could not do'?" Someone responded, "He is not all-powerful. He can't always do mighty works." The next question was, "What is the implication of 'he did not do'?" Some responded, "He could have done it if he wished." "He is all-powerful but chose not to do mighty works in this situation." Today, I add, "Healing takes two people a giver and an openness to receive." The leader posed a final question: "Where does the responsibility for healing lie?" In my notes, I wrote, "The receivers must come bearing their own belief. But is it only their belief, does Jesus bring healing power, or does he crystallize the receiver's own healing power?"

We worked with two more stories before coming to Jesus's great question, *"Who do men say I am?"* First, Mark:

> The Pharisees came and began to argue with him, seeking from him a sign from heaven, to test him.
>
> And he sighed deeply in his spirit, and said, "Why does this generation seek a sign? Truly, I say to you, no sign shall be given to this generation."
>
> And he left them, and getting into the boat again he departed to the other side.[637]

Matthew adds this familiar passage:

> He answered them, "When it is evening, you say, 'It will be fair weather; for the sky is red.' And in the morning, 'It will be stormy today, for the sky is red and threatening.' You know

how to interpret the appearance of the sky, but you cannot interpret the signs of the times. An evil and adulterous generation seeks for a sign, but no sign shall be given to it except the sign of Jonah."[638]

Luke's account is similar to Matthew's, but later in his Gospel.[639]

We counted the number of times "no sign" and "no sign except the sign of Jonah" appear. We commented that Jonah was a prophet who declined the call before ending up in the belly of a whale for three days and nights, when he repented and took up his task.

"Which version do you think is earlier?" we were asked. "Which version do you think is more authentic?" I decided that the story evolved from the simple "no sign" to the more complex "no sign but Jonah." However you read the response, though, what is it that the Pharisees are seeking? Mark's account, which Matthew repeats, says they are seeking a sign from heaven to test him. For what? To know whether this is really the Messiah? And he simply says, "No sign shall be given to this generation."

The leader asked, "What is Jesus's image of the kingdom of heaven?" My thoughts returned to the parables about the kingdom of God: "No trumpets blowing; the kingdom is a pearl, a treasure to be found here and now."

Revisiting these passages today, I'd add that the signs from heaven are those we find all about us, the red sky at evening and at morning. I'm struck by these words about Jesus: "And he sighed deeply in his spirit, and said, 'Why does this generation seek a sign? Truly, I say to you, no sign shall be given to this generation.'" He sounds weary, or is it despair that his messages are not being heard, that his listeners cannot read the signs that are all about them and seek instead a sign from heaven?

"Who do men say that I am?" Jesus asks. I see a man who can do no mighty works without some "special" relationship with others, a man who declines to say *he is* the sign of heaven or even that there is such a sign. Why does he ask this question? Those in the circle responded, "Are people understanding who I am? How do they see me? Do they say I'm the Messiah? The Son of God?" Someone else wondered aloud, "Is he asking himself 'Who am I?'" I felt him as the questioning human being who, even though he's had the baptism and the wilderness experience, is still struggling with this revelation and the question, "Who am I?" Or, "Does anyone out there get the point?"

We worked with his disciples' responses—that people say he is John the Baptist, Elijah, or another of the prophets. So Jesus asked again, "But who do you say that I am?" Is he testing them, trying to discover what they have received from his teachings? Then Peter replied, "You are the Christ." What is Peter seeing or hoping for in Jesus? Surely he longs for the "one to come." The seminar leader asked, "What kind of Christ is Peter seeing?" and people responded, "King. Warrior. Separator of righteous and unrighteous. Provider of abundance. Restorer of the kingdom. Daniel's 'Son of man in heaven.'"

Then she asked, "What in psyche wants Jesus to be 'the one'?" I wrote, "Life is too hard. Somebody make it safe; take away the burdens."

Next she asked, "What do you imagine Jesus felt when he heard Peter's response: 'You are the Christ'?" Responses varied: "Dismay that this is how the disciples saw him. He began to 'get' that he is the Christ. Maybe he didn't know his role yet, didn't believe there was such a thing as a messiah at all, yet he wondered how it was that he had such authority and power."

Then we moved to Jesus's statement: "And he charged them to tell no one about him." A footnote in the *Records* book says that the Greek for "charged" also implies "rebuked." The leader asked us, "What is the tone of this?" Some responded, "Authoritative." Others said, "Angry. Firm, very firm."

Jesus still had not said yes nor no. "Why?" the leader asked. "He himself was unsure. He wanted each to make up their own mind. He knew he is the Christ, but he didn't want others to know it yet. He knew he is not the Christ but didn't want to say so yet. He knew he isn't, but he also knew he's bringing something new. He didn't want to be put into old categories."

The leader asked, "Which do you choose for yourself?" My response was, "He knows he's not, but he also knows he's bringing something new" into the world, some new consciousness. The leader asked, "Why doesn't he answer yes or no?" and I wrote, "If he did, he would cut off each person's seeking, questioning, holding the tension that can lead to the third point."

This concept of a "third point" was new to me at my first seminar. I was struck by the belief, which comes from Jung, and Elizabeth spoke of it often, that when the tension of two opposites is held and held and held eventually a new, unexpected resolution will arise out of that tension. Jung called this the "transcendent function," a naturally occurring psychological process in human beings. So, as we pondered our answers to the question, "Why does Jesus not say yes or no?" rather than rush to either yes or no, we were to hold the tension of these opposites until a new understanding emerged, some new image of Jesus or what he represents. Is it true? Did he really think that if he declined to answer, his followers would struggle and find their own answers? The story says he "charged them to tell no one."

Twice more Jesus was faced with the question of who he is: at the trial before Herod the priest and again before Pilate the Roman authority. Many other events will occur before we come to those final days.

Second and Third Strands – Son of man and the Holy Spirit

And he began to teach them that the Son of man must suffer many things, and be rejected by the elders and the chief priests and the scribes, and be killed, and after three days rise again. And he said this plainly.

And Peter took him, and began to rebuke him. But turning and seeing his disciples, [Jesus] rebuked Peter, and said, "Get behind me, Satan! For you are not on the side of God, but of men."[640]

What is this about, and how does it relate to the second and third strands I've been weaving for decades now—Son of man and Holy Spirit. In this passage, is Jesus forecasting that he will suffer and die and rise again? Peter says, "You are the Christ," and Jesus rebukes the disciples "to tell no one." What's going on between them? What is Jesus saying?

On Day 4 of the seminar, we read: "The sabbath was made for man, not man for the sabbath; so the Son of man is lord even of the sabbath."[641] And we worked with the passage about healing the palsied one, in which Jesus says, "The Son of man has authority on earth to forgive sins."[642]

What does Jesus mean when he says, "Son of man"? I learned later that *Son of man* was a phrase spoken only by Jesus.[643] The leader proposed four ways we could understand Jesus's meaning:

1. Jesus is speaking of himself: I *am* lord of the sabbath; I have authority to forgive sins.
2. He's speaking of humankind in general.
3. He's speaking about a *quality* that's only in him.
4. He's speaking of a quality that's within all humankind.

I wrote in my journal: "Is this about a new level of consciousness, an evolutionary step in which each of us has a relationship with God and can make choices from a different place than following a strict rule of law? So, I think 'something unique in each person' would be what Son of man refers to."

Where else does Jesus speak about the Son of man? On Day 8, we read a story in which Jesus healed "a blind and dumb demoniac," and was charged of an offense by "the Pharisees" according to Matthew, or "the scribes" according to Mark, or "some of them" according to Luke. Mark says, "And the scribes who came down from Jerusalem said, 'He is possessed by Beelzebul, and by the prince of demons he casts out the demons.'"[644]

Beelzebul, our leader explained, is the name of a god opposed to Yahweh regarded as "the prince of demons." A leader asked, "Of what is Jesus accused?" The text tells us, "Healing a blind and dumb demoniac." Her next question was, "What do the scribes, following Mark, call the source of Jesus's actions?" In other words, who do the scribes think is the source of the healing? In the text it says, "Beelzebul, or the devil." Jesus responded, "How can Satan cast out Satan? If a kingdom is divided against itself, that kingdom cannot stand."[646]

Jesus tells the scribes it's not Beelzebul that brought this healing. Then who did? Jesus responds circularly: "Truly, I say to you, all sins will be forgiven the sons of men, and whatever blasphemies they utter; but whoever blasphemes against the Holy Spirit never has forgiveness."[647] Is he saying that the Holy Spirit is the source of healing and that the scribes are thus blaspheming the Holy Spirit, an act that "*never* has forgiveness."

The leader asked us, "What does Jesus mean by *blasphemy*?" and offered three possibilities:

1. The scribes *denied* the Holy Spirit.
2. They called the Holy Spirit *evil*.
3. They were not *related* to the Holy Spirit, which is a psychological view.

In this way of reading, Jesus believed that the scribes knew the healing power came from the Holy Spirit and said that it came from Beelzebul, an act that "never has forgiveness."

Right after Mark and Matthew say blaspheming against the Holy Spirit "never has forgiveness" Matthew, but not Mark, says, "And whoever says a word against the Son of man will be forgiven; but whoever speaks against the Holy Spirit will not be forgiven."[647] Luke, rather than "speaks against," says "he who *blasphemes* against the Holy Spirit will not be forgiven."[648]

We moved from Mark's statement that the sons of men who blaspheme against the Holy Spirit will never be forgiven, to Matthew and Luke saying something similar but with a significant nuance anyone who speaks against the Son of man will be forgiven, but not anyone who does so against the Holy Spirit.

So who or what is this Son of man? The one who has authority even over the sabbath. The one who has authority on earth to forgive sins. If this Son of man is a special quality in all of us, if I blaspheme against this quality, that may be forgiven, but if I blaspheme against the Holy Spirit, it's unforgivable. *Just what is this Holy Spirit?*

In this way, the strand of the Holy Spirit entered my tapestry. But we had met Spirit before. Where? On Day 3, we read the story of Jesus's baptism by John, and Jesus "saw the heavens opened and the Spirit descending upon [or into] him like a dove; and a voice came from heaven, 'Thou art my beloved Son, with thee I am well pleased.'"[649] And immediately the Spirit "drove him out into the wilderness." Matthew says the Spirit "led" Jesus into the wilderness. Luke says, "And Jesus, full of the Holy Spirit … was led by the Spirit."[650]

There is another passage that can help us understand what is meant by *Spirit*. Matthew and Luke both include it, although in different places in their accounts. In both, Jesus is speaking to his disciples. Luke says, "And when they bring you before the synagogues and the rulers and the authorities, do not be anxious how or what you are to answer or what you are to say; for the Holy Spirit will teach you in that very hour what you ought to say."[651] Matthew says, "It is not you who speak, but the Spirit of your Father speaking through you."[652]

So this Spirit is greater than any individual human. Perhaps it's the one the Creation story speaks of: "And the Spirit of God was moving over the face of the waters."[653] *Spirit* here can also be read as "wind" or "breath," the creative force present as God was creating the heavens and earth.

Medieval German mystic Jacob Boehme wrote, "The Holy Spirit is the creative force which drives us by anxiety to a new birth." So, to blaspheme this Spirit, to reject, deny, and betray the guide of my life will surely lead to my destruction. It may be to deny life itself, an act that will never be forgiven. Using psychological language, if I blaspheme (or speak against) this voice from the self, this creative force greater than my ego self, I damn myself to hell on earth. Neither God nor the self will have damned me. I'll have brought about my own destruction.

At seminar one year, the evening before working with these passages about blasphemy and forgiveness, we enacted the "sinner woman" story. Where had her forgiveness come from? Not from Jesus or from God as the story is told. Jesus says, "Her sins … are forgiven, for she loved much."[654] Her forgiveness came from something in herself, her own love. So, why will the sin of blaspheming the Holy Spirit never be forgiven? In my journal that year I wrote, "I related back to last night's experience in which forgiveness is an inner reconciliation of … my little ego self with Other? So how can that reconciliation occur if I'm denying the power of the Holy Spirit?"

Was this the answer to the question about the Holy Spirit? Is it a great creative force that exists "from the beginning" and a guide that will teach me what to say in the presence of authority? Is it the self? A messenger from self to my ego self? Jesus makes it clear that the Holy Spirit is not the Son of man when he says one can speak against the Son of man, but not against the Spirit. What does this tell us about Jesus? In my reading, he is not saying *he* is the Son of man, and he is certainly not saying he is the Holy Spirit. Yet he was so attuned to Spirit he could answer the scribes' accusations with wisdom and clarity.

When a leader asked, "How did he come to this clarity about himself?" I remembered a story in Mark in which Jesus did not have this clarity, or so it seemed: "Then he went home; and the crowd came together again, so that they could not even eat. And when his family heard it, they went out to seize him, for people were saying, 'He is beside himself.'"[655]

This story shows a side of Jesus we don't see anywhere else. What caused the people to say, "He is beside himself"? Personally, I think he was—quite simply—"beside himself," as humans can be when we're overwhelmed by the experiences of life. I love this story! But I digress.

Returning to the passage quoted earlier:

And he began to teach them that the Son of man must suffer many things, and be rejected by the elders and the chief priests and the scribes, and be killed, and after three days rise again. And he said this plainly.

And Peter took him, and began to rebuke him. But turning and seeing his disciples, [Jesus] rebuked Peter, and said, "Get behind me, Satan! For you are not on the side of God, but of men.[656]

I continue to think this "Son of man" is a special quality in humans that suffers many things in a lifetime, even feeling it has come to a death. And it rises again; life goes on.

We explored this statement about rising on the third day, turning back and forth in the *Records* book to look at three other places Mark wrote about rising again.[657] Matthew always follows Mark in these four instances but Luke does so only twice. Then we turned to two related passages in Luke (but not in Matthew or Mark), which probably come from document Q. Neither of these passages refers to death or resurrection.[658] Were the references to death and resurrection originally in Mark, and then Matthew followed him but Luke left them out? Or were the references added later to Mark and Matthew?

How might we decide? We could count the number of passages in which *the resurrection* is present and those that don't contain them. It turns out it's *in* more passages than it is *not*, but counting passages doesn't really help us make a determination. Q is earlier than Mark, so wouldn't it be in Luke's story if he's using Q? And if he isn't using Q, where did he get his story? Did he make it up? Why not follow Mark, as he does so often elsewhere?

Then I remembered other differences among the Gospel accounts. Mark did not include the birth narratives or the appearances after the crucifixion (which Luke and Matthew do). Mark ends with the story of Mary Magdalene, Mary the mother of James, and Salome going to the tomb where Jesus had been laid to anoint his body. But what they find is an empty tomb and a "young man sitting on the right side." And he says to them, "He has risen, he is not here; see the place where they laid him."[659]

The young man says to tell his disciples that Jesus is going on to Galilee and they will see him there. But the women "said nothing to any one, for they were afraid."[660] According to most scholars, this is the end of Mark's Gospel.[661] If Mark says that Jesus predicted his resurrection, why is his only reference that Jesus is going on to Galilee? Why doesn't he tell about other appearances, which are told in Matthew and Luke? Did he not know about them? Did he know about them but not tell about them? That isn't likely.

Let us draw on another criterion to consider whether Jesus predicted his resurrection: consistency. Which accounts are more consistent with the image of Jesus I had been weaving from Day 1? Would the Jesus who says no to the tempter in the wilderness speak of his death and resurrection? The one who never gives a straight answer to the question, "Who is this man?" What about the man who never says, "I forgive," or even "God forgives," but always, "Your sins are forgiven"? And there are those several passages in which he says, "No sign [from heaven] shall be given to this generation"[662] or "No sign ... except the sign of Jonah,"[663] and similarly although in a different context in Luke.[664] What does he mean, "No sign shall be given"? What were the Pharisees asking for? A sign that he was the Messiah? A sign from God? And he says, "No sign." Would a man who says these things be the Messiah? Would he predict his own death and resurrection? I think not.

But the Son of man, if it's "something within each person," does suffer many deaths in a lifetime. This Son of man rises up and staggers on once more. And sometimes it does die, as Jesus did, Bonhoeffer, and Martin Luther King Jr. did. Name your heroes and heroines who gave everything for their causes; some indeed did die and their work lives on.

Matthew and Mark say, "And Peter took him, and began to rebuke him. But turning and seeing his disciples, [Jesus] rebuked Peter, and said, 'Get behind me, Satan! For you are not on the side of God, but of men.'"665 *Why did Peter rebuke him?* In 1984, I wrote, "I think this Son of man is in all of us, and all of us who know that our 'sonship of man' must be prepared to let go of the old order held by the elders and scribes. Peter says, 'This is too hard!' The wrath of society will come down on you and me and all of us." I think also that Peter does not want Jesus, who he now thinks is Christ, to suffer and die. But why wouldn't he want him to rise again? And why did Jesus rebuke Peter so harshly? Is it because Peter called him the Christ (the Messiah)? Or because of what Jesus says about the Son of man? And what does Jesus mean when he says Peter is not on the side of God, but of men? Today I think Jesus is charging Peter for not understanding that the Son of man must indeed enter by the narrow gate, which leads to life but may first lead to death. And in my understanding today, this Son of man is *in* Jesus, *in* Peter, and *in* us all.

Right after Peter says to Jesus, "You are the Christ." Matthew's Gospel continues:

> And Jesus answered him, "Blessed are you, Simon Bar-Jona! For flesh and blood has not revealed this to you, but my Father who is in heaven. And I tell you, you are Peter, and on this rock I will build my church, and the powers of death shall not prevail against it.
> "I will give you the keys of the kingdom of heaven, and whatever you bind on earth shall be bound in heaven, and whatever you loose on earth shall be loosed in heaven."666

There's no doubt in Matthew's telling that Jesus is praising Peter for his vision. What a difference between this account and Mark's, which Luke follows. Here is the famous image of Peter as the rock upon which Jesus's church will be built, a church of which only Matthew speaks, and the recognition of Peter as the one who will be given the keys of the kingdom. What a contrast to how Jesus speaks to Peter after Peter rebukes Jesus for saying the Son of man will suffer, die, and rise again. "Get behind me, Satan!"

And what about Matthew's reference to *church*? Have we heard any reference to church before? No, but there is one later in Matthew, the story of working for reconciliation when "your brother sins against you."[667] Go to your brother, but if he doesn't listen, take witnesses with you and go again. "If he refuses to listen to them, tell it to the church; and if he refuses to listen even to the church, let him be to you as a Gentile and a tax collector."[668] Surely, these passages are excellent arguments for the establishment of the Christian church. Mark and Luke say nothing of them. Did Jesus say it? If not he, where did these statements come from? Matthew himself or later editors? They were, of course, weaving their own tapestry for others to see.

I began this chapter in search of answers to the question "Who is this man?" So many strands came together on Day 10 that I still haven't finished with the question. Twice more Jesus was asked who he is: during the trial before Herod: "Are you the Christ?" and at the trial before Pilate: "Are you the King of the Jews?" And how does he respond? Does he say yes? Does he say no?

Chapter 15

Jesus's Final Days

In this chapter, we walk with Jesus through the final week of his life and look closely at the questions we've raised thus far and at what happens next. I have been avoiding writing this. It's difficult to struggle with so many passages, do the critical work, and seek their meaning for today. And it's hard to watch Jesus greeted with "Hosanna," then betrayed, arrested, derided, mocked, crucified, and laid in the tomb. Is this history or myth? I'd call it "mythic history" a true story that speaks to all the betrayals, trials, crucifixions, and resurrections that occur every day in our lives. It's a story about all of us.

On seminar Day 11, we read (in Luke) that Jesus "set his face to go to Jerusalem."[669] We meet a man resolute in his purpose, yet of sorrows. Jesus says, "How often would I have gathered your children together as a hen gathers her brood under her wings,"[670] but the people would not hear his message. We ponder Jesus's command, "If any man would come after me, let him deny himself and take up his cross and follow me."[671] And we pondered the great paradox, "Whoever seeks to gain his life will lose it, but whoever loses his life will preserve it."[672]

We struggle to understand what it means when Jesus "was transfigured" before his disciples Peter, James, and John, and akin to the baptism story a voice spoke, "This is my beloved Son; listen to him."[673] And Jesus once again "charged them to tell no one what they had seen."[674]

We study Jesus's charge, "You hypocrites! You know how to interpret the appearance of earth and sky, but why do you not know how to interpret the present time?"[675] And then he asks the question, which comes to me again and again in my daily life, "And why do you not judge for yourself what is right?"[676]

We worked with more passages on Day 11: Jesus is warned to flee because "Herod wants to kill you," and he replies, "it cannot be that a prophet should perish away from Jerusalem."[677] As he struggles toward Golgotha to be crucified, Jesus says to the wailing crowd of women, "Do not weep for me, but weep for yourselves and for your children."[678] And, "I came to cast fire upon the earth; and would that it were already kindled! I have a baptism to be baptized with; and how I am constrained until it is accomplished!"[679] This statement still baffles me. Surely he is saying he has a destiny to live out and it must be done, and yet how hard the road. And there is this heartrending passage in Luke: "And when he drew near and saw the city he wept over it, saying, 'Would that even today you knew the things that make for peace!'"[680]

Who is the man we see? A man of compassion, resolute, troubled and sorrowing, and even angry. A man who had a great message for his people and was not heard. What is being added to my tapestry with these passages? Jesus's message is still with us and still being heard today. For many, he is the Christ, the Messiah. Yet I still wonder, What kind of messiah would tell his followers to be silent, to tell no one,[681] even when Peter says, "*You are the Christ*"?[682] What did Jesus say to the Jewish authorities?

There are two trials. The first is before the Jewish authorities. All three Gospels have the high priest ask Jesus, "Are you the Christ, the Son of God?" In Matthew, Jesus responds, "You have said so."[683] In Luke, his words are similar, "You say that I am."[684] In Mark, Jesus responds, "I am,"[685] which can also be translated, "Am I?" The fifth-century *Codex Bezae* has Jesus say, "You have said it."

On Day 14, we looked at the next trial, the one before the governor of the Roman province of Judaea, Pontius Pilate, who asks, "Are you the King of the Jews?" In all three Gospels, Jesus responds, "*You have said so.*"[686]

"The texts contain a bias against 'the Jews,'" the leader of one seminar pointed out. "We need to be careful about broad statements against all Jews." In the stories of the trial before the Jewish authorities, the Son of man emerges once more, but a very different Son of man from the one discussed earlier: This Son of man will be "seated at the right hand of Power, and coming with the clouds of heaven."[687] A footnote informs us that these words derive from Psalm 110:1, "A Psalm to David," and from the apocalyptic book of Daniel 7:13. But in the Gospel account, the words are put on the tongue of Jesus himself. *Did he say these words?*

Even in my first *Records* seminar, I came to see the Son of man as a quality within each human being, not a savior or a word Jesus would use to refer to himself. When I met this phrase again a decade later, still pondering what it might mean, I wrote cryptically, "The New Being within ... who chooses the life committed to the journey of consciousness." I hold to this belief that he was referring in all these passages not just to himself, but to a quality that is within each of us.

Why then is there such an apocalyptic message as the story moves toward the crucifixion? I believe the Gospel writers tell us this to claim that Jesus *is* the apocalyptic Son of man of whom Daniel speaks. The Gospels want to foretell the resurrection of this one man who is, for them, *the Messiah*. Did Jesus think or say that?

"Taking all his responses," the seminar leader asked, "how has Jesus answered?" Except for Mark's questionable telling, Jesus doesn't give a clear response. It's always, "Am I?" or "You have said so," never a clear *yes* or *no*. How would the story be different if he had? These are crucial questions. First, why did he not say yes? We put out possibilities: "He wasn't the Messiah. He knew he was, but didn't want to say so. He didn't know whether he was, or not he was still wondering." Much of Western history interprets his response to be "yes"; a great church has arisen out of that belief and kept the story alive for two thousand years.

The response I choose remains, "He knew he was not." In 1984, I wrote in my journal, "What did he say to himself? Did he see himself as Messiah? I don't think so. I see his message as giving each of us the way to know the kingdom of God within. There is no King who can give the answer, rule the territory." Today I'd add, "I see his message as giving each of us a way to know the Son of man within."

And why did he not say no? What would have happened in human experience what would have happened to the story if he had? The longing would not die; the search would continue. Something in us longs for a savior. John the Baptist asks Jesus, "Are you he who is to come, or shall we look for another?"[688]

The leader pushed us further: "What do you think is Jesus's answer to the question, 'Art thou the Christ?'" I think it's no. Yet he chose not to say it and thus save himself. He could not say yes, because he knew it wasn't so. Why couldn't he say no? When Elizabeth Howes told us, "If he'd said yes or no, we wouldn't be sitting here now," a flash of insight came over me: *The Son of man, that unique quality within the human being, is the fulfillment of that messianic yearning!* That messiah is not "out there" in Jesus Christ or any other messianic figure. It is here within me, within each human being. And Jesus wanted each one of us to know it. He could not say no because to do so would be to deny the reality of that Son of man.

I've searched through Elizabeth's writings to understand what she might have meant. She did believe that Jesus was aware of the new consciousness coming alive in humanity. He could not say no, because that would have denied this. "Jesus knew his inward relationship to the Christ image and knew it as a present numinous factor in the psyche of each man. He did not identify himself with it as later Christianity did. He did not say he *was it*, but he could never deny it as real and alive because it was exactly what he had touched."[689] We can't know, of course, whether this is so or not. We can't know what Jesus really thought. But the story in all its iterations does tell us that he did not say yes, and he did not say no. To me, and apparently to Elizabeth

Howes, this indicates that the Son of man that special quality that is *within each one of us* is alive.

The leader asked, "What was Jesus related to that led him to say neither yes nor no?" I remember Jesus's teachings about the narrow gate, about doing the will of God, about the Holy Spirit who will teach you what to say, and I know that whatever allows us to make our choices to enter or not, to do the will or not, is what led him to say neither yes nor no. Something had to die so that the messianic hope would become the Son of man come alive in each human being.

After years of pondering "Why didn't he say yes or no?" I think I have finally come to an answer that is true for me. An ancient way of thinking and believing that a messiah would arrive on white clouds to separate the righteous from the unrighteous had to die. But the unique quality that Jesus calls the Son of man continues on in each human being; it does not die. It leads us to choose the narrow or the wide gate, to discern what is the "higher value" and live it out or not. Being conscious is a burdensome responsibility most prefer to avoid, and it was soon placed on (projected onto) one man, Jesus named Christ.

Where are the disciples? Where is Peter? As Jesus stands before the chief priests and is condemned by them "as deserving death," Peter is warming himself at a fire. When he is asked by those around him whether he knows this man, he says no. "I neither know nor understand what you mean."[690] And "I do not know this man of whom you speak."[691] After his third denial, "he broke down and wept."[692]

We mimed this scene, denying three times that we knew him. At the time, I wrote, "I could deny him; I shut my mind off from knowing, from feeling my love for him. And when the cock crowed and I remembered what Jesus had said, I wept, knowing I have denied what? Jesus? Myself? The Son of man within myself?" The leader asked, "If we don't carry our own process, what happens?" A great possibility in me dies.

The Crucifixion

The events of the crucifixion and burial are recounted at times with slightly different language, at other times using the exact same language by the three Gospel writers.[693] Certain passages come to mind—how hard it was for Jesus to carry his cross and Simon of Cyrene helped him; soldiers nailing him to the cross at Golgotha between two thieves; taunts of the soldiers and of many who passed by; darkness "over the whole land" from the sixth until the ninth hour;[694] and Jesus's anguished cry, "My God, my God, why hast thou forsaken me?" as Mark and Matthew tell it,[695] or "Father, into thy hands I commit my spirit!" as Luke tells it.[696] All three Synoptic Gospels tell us, "And the curtain of the temple was torn in two."[697]

We worked with so many questions, plumbing the depths of our own consciousness, as this work demands. "For whom might there have been a darkness on the land?" For those who had placed their trust in this man as their messiah. And for the women who "came up with him to Jerusalem," followed him to the cross, and were "looking on from afar."[698] Yes, the women were there, but the Gospels don't speak of any of the men. Today, I add that there is a darkness over the world whenever something of great value is violated, when the world itself is betrayed.

Was it betrayal that Jesus felt when he cried out, "My God, my God, why hast thou forsaken me?"[699] This is the first line of Psalm 22, a prayer for deliverance, for help from God. A leader asked, "What do you hear Jesus saying about God and about himself? Is he absent from God? Is God absent from him?" Someone responded, "He feels God has left him, not that God isn't." Another person responded, "It's a lament on deep abandonment—by God." Another said, "He spoke so often about the kingdom of God *here and now*, and in this moment Jesus does not feel God's presence." And another: "God is present in our depths." Someone asked: "Was this a moment when evil was encountered so completely that it engendered a shift in Jesus's image of God?"

JESUS'S FINAL DAYS   231

Then the curtain was torn in two. What might this signify? One person responded, "The old law was torn; the new is coming." I recalled that at the baptism the heavens were rent asunder and something new was born. Was that happening here? With the death of Jesus, was something new being born?

In Luke's account, Jesus cried out, "Father, into thy hands I commit my spirit!"[700] Do I think he said that? Not really; I go with Mark's account, perhaps the earliest, certainly the simplest. He "uttered a loud cry, and breathed his last."[701]

The leader referred to the Passover passage in which Jesus, passing the bread and wine to his disciples, tells them he will not drink of the fruit of the vine "until that day when I drink it new in the kingdom of God."[702] Then the leader asked, "What might the fulfillment be on the cross?" I said it was, "a marriage between the Son of man and God. Incarnation is fulfilled."

Then the leader asked, "What might it have meant for God, for Jesus to be this loyal to God?" I responded, "Everything. One's Beloved Son has fulfilled his *all*." I wrote a note in the margin of my journal: "A marriage between the Son of man and God." Jesus sold *all*; he loved with *all*. He fulfilled his human destiny.

The leader asked, "From our study of *Records,* who or what was responsible for the death of Jesus?" Some responses came from the circle: "Jesus. Son of man. The people's fear and blindness. God." The leader asked, "What in the teachings of Jesus aroused the authorities to kill him?" People responded: "The way he redefined the laws. Breaking social custom. Living boldly, led by his relationship to God."

Pushing onward, the leader asked, "What did Jesus teach about evil?" One person responded, "Resist not; turn the other cheek." Jesus did not deny the existence of evil; he offered a way of meeting it. The leader posed another question: "What is Jesus doing with the problem of evil?" My response was, "He's including evil it's in all of us, the authorities and everyone, including me." Someone else responded, "When he says, 'Resist not,' he is undermining the one who does evil to you. Was he that conscious?" The leader referred to Nelson Mandela in jail, the truth commissions in South Africa that exposed the terrible evils done there, and asked again, "Was Jesus that conscious here?" Could he have lived as he did and not known what he was doing?

After we had worked our way through the story of the crucifixion, we took some moments of silence to become aware of our own feelings. We imagined we like the women who looked on from afar were seeing this man nailed to the cross, dead. "Some are in tears," I wrote. It was a time of grief as each of us imagined what in the story and in ourselves had died.

The leader reminded us of this passage: "If any man would come after me, let him deny himself and take up his cross and follow me."[703] There is scholarly debate about whether Jesus really said this. It's in all three Gospels, but at that time the cross was used only to execute criminals or seditionists. So what might this reference mean, symbolically? We responded: "Intersections. Meeting of opposites. Balance. Where human and divine meet. A dynamic process. Bridging polarities." Then we were asked, "What would it mean to pick up our cross each day?" by which the leader meant, working with our own opposites consciously. My response: "I feel it as an exciting adventure, because I'm willing to love what I see as a negative. Yet many times I feel it as burdensome and want to go unconscious."

Reading Jesus's words, "Pick up your cross and follow me," we imagined ourselves standing before the cross on which Jesus hangs dead. Then the leader asked, "What does it add to your understanding of this passage that there is a human being on the cross?" My response then was, "It's about risking your whole life." Now I'd add, "If you take up this particular cross, if you live your life trying to 'do the will,' choose the narrow gate, it leads to this cross, possibly to death, perhaps of some belief or attitude or way of life; perhaps even death to life itself." The leader said, "For 2,000 years, worship has focused on Jesus on the cross. What is the new meaning for you when you look at this man on the cross?" I wrote, "To live one's life in its *all* will lead to a cross, to many crosses."

The Burial

Next the Gospels tell us that "Joseph of Arimathea, a respected member of the council, ... took courage and went to Pilate, and asked for the body of Jesus."[704] Pilate granted his request, and Joseph of Arimathea wrapped Jesus in a linen shroud and laid him in the tomb "hewn out of the rock; and he rolled a stone against the door of the tomb."[705]

And "Mary Magdalene and Mary the mother of Joses saw where he was laid,"[706] just as they had been there at his crucifixion, "looking on from afar." The leader asked, "What does it say that it is the women who are there, not the men?" People responded, "It's the women who are steadfast in tragedy, who ponder in their hearts, who are true to the relationship"; and "They heard him in a way the men didn't." The scene was set for the next morning, when it would be the women, again, who bring us either to the end of the story or its continuation.

Chapter 16

The Empty Tomb

And very early on the first day of the week they went to the tomb when the sun had risen.[707]

On Day 15, after we'd gathered in the seminar room, the leader set out a painting of the women weeping at the tomb where Jesus had been lain. We sat in silence, attending to the feelings roused by the painting and what it conveyed. Then the leader asked for a word to express our thoughts or feelings. I wrote *bereft*, then *compassion, a kinship with these women*. After others responded, the leader said, "All these feelings are with us as we move to the text."

The accounts of what happened on the Sunday morning after Jesus was laid in the tomb are in all three Gospels,[708] but they aren't the same. Who went to the sepulcher (a small room or monument cut in rock or built of stone in which a dead person is laid or buried)? Matthew and Mark say it was Mary Magdalene; Matthew adds, "and the other Mary"; Mark says, "Mary the mother of James, and Salome." Luke says, "the women."

Then, all of them tell us that the stone that had enclosed the tomb had rolled away, and all recount that someone an angel, a young man, two men told the women, "He has risen," or in Luke, "Why do you seek the living among the dead?" In Matthew and Mark, the women are told that Jesus "is going before you to Galilee." In Luke, "two men" remind the women that Jesus had said he would rise on the third day. In all three accounts, the women are instructed to tell the disciples.

The Circle of Life and Grief

Matthew says that the women go with fear and great joy to tell the disciples and on the way, they meet Jesus, who instructs them to tell "my brethren to go to Galilee, and there they will see me."[709] Luke says nothing about meeting Jesus. In Luke, the women tell "the eleven," but "these words seemed to them an idle tale, and they did not believe them."[710] And Mark says, "And they went out and fled from the tomb; for trembling and astonishment had come upon them; and they said nothing to any one, for they were afraid."[711]

We worked our way through these passages: Who appears? To whom? And says what? All three Gospels say the tomb was empty, and the leader asked, "What are possible explanations for this?" We responded: "The body was stolen, perhaps by authorities. He wasn't really dead, but he was revived. That this myth was told later not historically true. That he had in fact risen."

The leader commented that Christianity has believed for two thousand years that Jesus rose from the dead. She asked, "If Jesus did rise from the dead, what is its significance?" I wrote, "Enormous implications for one's image of God. This is a God that intervenes in this reality." The leader continued, "If you do not hold to the resurrection of Jesus from the dead, then what do you think happened? Which of the possibilities do you choose, at least for now?" I wrote, "I play with the thought that he, like the yogis, was not dead but in deep trance and rose again to be seen by his followers. But would he have done this? I don't think so." Now I lean toward it being a myth added later. But something extraordinary did take place, and it changed the disciples' consciousness. Later, people explained it as a story of physical resurrection.

At my first *Records* seminar in 1984, I chose the possibility that the stories about resurrection and the appearances afterward were myths created by the Gospel writers; they weren't historically true. I did not choose the possibility that he rose. Two years later, I discovered that something in me held a very different belief. I digress now to tell that story because it shows so clearly how little our conscious selves know about the *all* of ourselves. It also illustrates the power of the Guild process to lead or drive one toward confrontations between conscious and unconscious beliefs.

In 1984, I believed that Jesus had died and did not rise from the grave. In 1986, I attended a seminar that began on Palm Sunday and ended the following Sunday, Holy Week, and I was confronted with the astonishing fact that something in me did not believe he died or rose at all.

In this eight-day seminar, we followed Jesus from his baptism to his death, and worked, as always, with questions of *what happened next*. On Day 7, we worked with the passages about the trials. Then the leader said, "We now come to the death of Jesus," and I wrote, "I've never really believed in his physical death. I've always believed in the resurrection. I think this is about not accepting my own mortality and therefore needing to live my own myth now."

That in itself was startling, but what startled me even as I reread this statement was my lack of affect, as though I was simply stating a fact. Did I really have no emotional reaction to this discovery? The next day as we worked again with the women who saw Jesus laid in the grave, the feelings came. The leader asked, "What does it add that it is the women who are there?" and people responded, "Faithfulness. Love. Courage. Steadfastness. Feminine receptivity. Presence." Then the leader asked, "In relation to the archetypal theme of death and rebirth within ourselves, what is *the place of the feminine* at the point of death and of burial?" People responded, "Stillness. Waiting. Patience. Acceptance. Being present."

As we began our work on the morning of the eighth day, the leader brought a picture of the Pieta, Mary holding the body of her son in her arms. The leader asked, "What does it add to the process that the grieving mother Mary receives the body?" I wrote, "The unity of love and grief is a circle that comes through the feminine." Then we looked at another image of the Pieta but it was a man gathering the body of Jesus into his arms. I think of him as Joseph of Arimathea, who had made his own burial site available for Jesus's body. For me in this image, he is the truly caring father. Clearly love and grief come from both masculine and feminine.

Then we saw a picture of the body of Jesus lying on a slab, and the leader asked, "What impact does seeing Jesus's dead body on this slab have on you?" I wrote dispassionately: "I've been coming to terms with mortality, finitude, with what Jesus attained his consciousness and what he sacrificed. Yet I was jolted by his dead body."

Then someone read the story of Mary Magdalene, and we mimed each part of it: as she observed the crucifixion from afar; as she followed and saw where he was laid; as she went with oil to anoint him and found the open tomb and a young man there; and then, as she turned and fled. My notes reveal a shift that took place in me: "I feel terrible tears. My beloved has died." These were not the tears of Mary Magdalene. They were, and are, *my* tears for *my* loss.

The Holy Week seminar concluded with the questions: "What is born out of this death?" "What is dead, and what is alive?" I was bereft. A lifetime friend had died. The story I had believed and hadn't even known it had changed. My childhood Jesus was no more. And what new thing came out of this realization, this death, for me? I wrote in my journal: "I have been limited by my unconscious belief in the physical resurrection. Not that I expected Jesus to save me from living my own life. What's new is that I must live my life *in this lifetime*, not in some future life."

In my last journal entry that week, I wrote, "Dear God, let me attend to the life you have given me to live not the one I might imagine or suppose." Who is this God? Is it the wholeness Jung calls the self, and I call Mystery, Great Patterning, Life, All. My prayer, I see now, is asking that Mystery, that Great Patterning, to help me be all of *my* self, now, in this lifetime. That is all I have to live.

Here I shift back from that Holy Week seminar to my first *Records* seminar and to our work with Mark's text, which says, "And they went out and fled from the tomb; for trembling and astonishment had come upon them; and they said nothing to any one, for they were afraid."[712] That is the end of Mark's Gospel.

However, Mark's Gospel ends with a footnote pointing to more, but questionable verses. Verses 9-20 do not appear in the earliest Greek manuscripts, and therefore, the RSV relegates them to a footnote. Most scholars question that these accounts were in the original Mark. My *Oxford Annotated Bible* notes: "Nothing is certainly known either about how this Gospel originally ended or about the origin of vv. 9-20, which cannot have been part of the original text of Mark."[713]

Matthew and Luke continue the story of the appearances, but not the same story. The only criterion I find to judge whether the story is authentic is consistency. Do these two accounts tell things that are consistent with what we've heard earlier?

Luke tells the familiar story in which two of the disciples meet Jesus as they walk along the road to Emmaus.[714] But only after Jesus broke bread with them did they recognize him, "and he vanished out of their sight." Luke also has a second account in which the two disciples returned to Jerusalem to tell the other disciples of Jesus's appearance. And Jesus appeared among the group, but they also did not recognize him until he made himself known to them and spoke with them. Then he "led them out as far as Bethany" and blessed them and "was carried up into heaven. And they returned to Jerusalem with great joy, and were continually in the temple blessing God."[715]

Matthew has no mention of appearances at Emmaus or Jerusalem, but says the disciples returned to Galilee, as Jesus had told them to do at the empty tomb (in Matthew's account). And there, Jesus appears and tells them to "make disciples of all the nations, baptizing them in the name of the Father and of the Son and of the Holy Spirit."[716]

The Doubting Thomas story I'm so familiar with is not in the Synoptic Gospels. It is John who tells this story,[717] and the Gospel of

John, so different in its perspective from the synoptics, is not a part of our study.

How do the words of Jesus in Matthew and Luke compare with what we've heard him say elsewhere? Matthew says that Jesus appeared to the disciples in the mountains of Galilee and said to them, "All authority in heaven and on earth has been given to me."[718] What did Jesus say about authority in earlier passages? In Luke, he says, "Why do you not judge for yourselves what is right?"[719] In Matthew, Jesus says that the disciples should baptize "in the name of the Father and of the Son and of the Holy Spirit."[720] Is this consistent with what we heard him teach earlier? Someone responded, "A Jewish person wouldn't talk about the Trinity. It's a church doctrine." Another agreed, "It's not consistent with what Jesus says earlier."

In Luke, when Jesus meets his disciples on the road to Emmaus, the narrator states, "Beginning with Moses and all the prophets, he interpreted to them in all the scriptures the things concerning himself."[721] The leader asked, "Have we seen Jesus teach in this way before?" We held our responses and moved forward. Luke describes what takes place next. The disciples rush to Jerusalem to tell their brothers what has happened, and Jesus appears among them. And he teaches them all that has been "said about me in the law of Moses," that these things are fulfilled in him. "Is this consistent with what he taught earlier?" the leader asked. "Have we seen Jesus pointing to himself in earlier teachings?" Not that I remember.

In Luke, Jesus says, "The Christ should suffer and on the third day rise from the dead."[722] The question was, "Where in the scriptures does it say that the Christ should suffer and rise?" When Peter says, "You are the Christ," Jesus speaks about the Son of man who must suffer and rise. A light bulb flashed as I saw more clearly the distinction Jesus makes between "the Christ" and "the Son of man." To my ears, they aren't the same. The quality of being human, which I believe Jesus means when he speaks of the Son of man, does suffer and die many deaths during a lifetime, and each time rises again.

End of the Story

We had come to the end of the Gospels, and the leader said, "You may close your books now." Then we turned to that hard question she had asked earlier, "What do you think happened? What in you wants this story to be literally and historically true?" Two responses put into the circle were: "The one in me who wants the Messiah to come," and "The one in me who wants eternal life, to see again those who have died."

Then she asked, "What in you wants nothing to have happened after his death?" Nothing, such as no appearances, no disciples rushing through the countryside preaching, baptizing, and dying to spread the good news, no Christianity. We wouldn't even know about Jesus's life and teachings! Would what Jesus calls the Son of man have "come alive" in me today? Would my relationship to the Mystery, the Pattern, the self, have come alive? Surely it would have, but not through this story.

Something in this inquiry about the death and resurrection is rousing great excitement in me, and I write a note to myself: "I'm 'getting' the resurrection happening *in me*! His message is coming alive in me and, I think, in each of us. I feel it blossoming in my heart!" Not just the rebirth of one person, but a psychic rebirth in each person. The leader asked, "What in us wants this to be true on a mythical or symbolic level?" "It *is* true," I thought. Myths are *true* stories about being human, about life. Life and death and rebirth happen, like it or not.

We took a break. We needed a break. When we returned, the leader asked again, "What has died; what is alive?" and I had the same response as before: *The resurrection is happening in me!* Oh my god! Thank you! My chest, heart, and solar plexus are filled with space, with *life*! This higher value this Son of man this connection with self is alive in me! I know it!" *This is an answer I've been asking for.*

In all the *Records* seminars I've attended, the leader spoke of the myths, rituals, and sacred places in the Mediterranean region that speak of dying and rising gods: Dionysus, Tammuz, Adonis, Attis,

Osiris. In the training class for leaders, the leader asked, "If one takes the Christian story of the resurrection mythologically along with these other myths, what is the Christian myth about?" Like the others, it's about life, death, and rebirth; about life as it is; about the human journey. But in the Christian story, its hero is a historical, human being. Having traveled with Jesus and his teachings, I cannot believe there was not a historical personality behind these stories. So we have a human being showing us how to carry all the burdens and gifts of all one is, to face the narrow gate, choose to do the will of God, and be willing to lose life in order to preserve it.

The leader commented, "Something happened to the disciples and they were changed. If we don't believe in the resurrection, we have to ask, what happened?" And then we proceeded through a series of questions:

1. As recorded in §149, §150, §151, the three sections which tell of the appearances, what or who is recorded as being present and alive? — Jesus appeared to the disciples in various settings and said different things to them.

2. Behind these accounts, what actually may have come alive in the disciples? What was their core experience? —This question pushes us to look behind the accounts to the archetypal patterns out of which they arose. The Son of man is in each of us. The kingdom of God is now. To experience grace, they would have to feel and know this. They knew the kingdom of God. Whatever happened to Jesus at the baptism happened to each of them aliveness. They "got" his message, as I did. This answer comes from a belief I've held since my first *Records* seminar, that there was a time, a moment, in which the disciples knew their own divinity, knew that when Jesus spoke about the Son of man, he was speaking about something in each human being. I had this image that they knew the kingdom was within each of them, that they had their own authority from which to speak and live. Jesus was not

yet the intermediary. He had not "risen" yet. And each person who had gathered around Jesus "got it."

3. What may have been the cause of their experience of this coming alive in them? —The conviction I had in 1984 that they "got" it, their own direct relationship to God, to Son of man, to self, is eroding. Why did they begin to speak about a risen Christ who became their authority to go out and baptize in the name of the Father, the Son, and the Holy Spirit? All along, it seems, the disciples thought it was Jesus who had the power and authority, which they themselves could attain through him. When Peter said to Jesus, "You are the Christ," and in the story of the storm at sea, when Jesus calmed the storm and the disciples "were filled with awe, and said to one another, 'Who then is this, that even wind and sea obey him?'"[723] They couldn't do it themselves. They woke him up, and he asked, "Why are you afraid? Have you no faith?"[724] Correct, they had no faith in their own connection to the source of authority, Son of man, self, that Jesus had found. The story has been understood for so long as a "miracle" story. I hear it as another metaphor for life as it is, storms come, and we need to have faith in our own authority.

All these years I thought the disciples had that connection, if only for a "moment," but the stories suggest this isn't so. Only when Jesus was "awake" could the storm be calmed. Call it projection, yes. They didn't claim it for themselves. It makes me sad.

Christ came alive in them! Not the Son of man, not their own relationship to their God, but Christ, their savior and mediator. They placed it all in Jesus Christ, kept none for themselves. When I still believed the disciples had their "moment" of knowing the Son of man in themselves, I wrote, "What caused the Son of man to come alive in them was a great step in the evolution of consciousness; the heavens were rent asunder, psyche as it had been was shattered and a new and terrifying insight about what humanity is came to the disciples (perhaps especially to the women)." Now I see that what came alive for them was their belief in Jesus Christ, and in him, they would find the purpose and work of the rest of their lives.

4. What may have been the outcome of this experience of a coming alive in them? —An explosion of joy, enthusiasm, and dedication that sent the disciples baptizing and preaching the Word as they understood it and dying as martyrs because of it. They came to call this creative outpouring "Christianity." Elizabeth Howes and other leaders often quote biblical scholar Julius Wellhausen: "Enthusiasm engendered Christianity, but it was the enthusiasm of the disciples, not that of Jesus."[725]

5. How long do you think it took for the experience to be formulated as we have it today? —Scholars tell us that the stories began to circulate early. Paul was perhaps the first to write of the risen Christ, some twenty years after Jesus's death. Our "official" accounts, presented in the New Testament, did not become canon for another three hundred years. But how long did it take for the disciples' experience to be told as the risen Christ? Perhaps it happened instantly, out of the depths of their terrible grief. Perhaps it took days or weeks.

I would say now that "something" had shifted in the psyches of these people even before Jesus called them to follow him. Why else would they follow after him before his fame as a healer and miracle worker had spread? Why did they stay with him? He was certainly a charismatic figure, and we know the dangers of following such figures or allowing them to be "our savior." Along with Jung and Howes, I believe that something shifted in psyche itself, a great movement in the evolution of consciousness was begun, and it's still in process—always will be—furthered by our own increasing relationship with that Son of man in each of us. Jesus's message is still being uncovered today. "It's still happening. We've been reinterpreting it for two weeks here in this room."

6. What would you say is the origin of Christianity? —Christianity arose when the disciples no longer believed that the Son of man was in themselves, but projected it onto the risen Christ. Elizabeth Boyden Howes and C.G. Jung both posited that humanity was not yet able to carry such a burden of consciousness. The Church has carried it through the story of Jesus Christ for two thousand years, and a great and necessary gift it has been. But now? Howes often spoke about something new coming forth out of Christianity, moving us beyond the Christian way of understanding the human-divine relationship. The Son of man, she mused, may well be the symbol of that new thing, that new relationship.

Jesus lived out the Son of man quality not identifying himself with the new self-aspect of God within, as the Gospel of John has him do, but using the term "Son of man" to describe the human expression of this archetype. We find in Jesus's Son of man image an inclusiveness much needed today.[726]

Has the time come for a new myth that carries us beyond Christianity? In a lengthy correspondence with Fr. Victor White, Jung writes, "Thus I am approaching the end of the Christian aeon, ... but that end is still in the future."[727] In Jung's view, "The vast majority of people are still in such an unconscious state that one should almost protect them from the full shock of the real *imitatio Christi.*"[728] In her writings and seminar teachings, Howes expressed more confidence than Jung that the individual is ready to have a direct relationship with the self and with the darkness.

7. What came alive for Jesus? What did he call it? —In 1984, I wrote, "For Jesus, what came alive was his connection to the self he called God. He knew this was available to all humans and was essential for the evolution of consciousness. He called this connection the Son of man, the kingdom of God here and now, within and about you."

8. What came alive for the disciples? What did they call it? —I had thought the Son of man had come alive in the disciples and that they

knew it. But on this day, I think that if that Son of man did come alive, they didn't understand it; instead, they called it Jesus Christ.

9. What has come alive for you? What do you call it? —The quality that the human Jesus calls the Son of man, what I call my ego's relationship with self, came alive for me. Call it, as well, the kingdom of God within.

Am I satisfied with my answers to the last three questions, what came alive? For Jesus, yes. And the disciples? Do I think Jesus Christ "alive" in them was the "cause" of their great enthusiasm, which sent them out through the lands preaching, baptizing, and dying? Yes, I think that. But I also think there's more to their experience, that behind it all "God" caused it. By "God," I mean "self." Self caused it, and I mean by that the realm of the collective conscious and unconscious, which is humanity and, for all I know, more than humanity.

This self, perhaps through the mysterious Holy Spirit, drives us by anxiety to ever new consciousness, for something in the self wants to know us and to be known. There is some great yearning for consciousness and for relationship and, as far as I know so far, only we humans can bring that about. This is what Jung means by the journey of individuation, calling humanity that "immensely weighty milligram without which God had made his world in vain."[729] Jaffé calls this the myth of meaning.[730] That's the myth I find when I see *through* Christianity to the challenge of humanity's great journey.

Chapter 17

The Journey Onward

"And to make an end is to make a beginning,
The end is where we start from."
—T. S. Eliot

End of a Seminar

It was the final morning of the final day of the *Records* seminar. The leader reminded us by saying, "Imagine you will never come to another Guild seminar again." Then she read from the brochure describing this particular seminar titled, "Paradox: Coming Home to Yourself . . . to be more at home in this world": "At the core of every wisdom tradition, the individual finds how to live in this world through relationship to the Larger Reality. In this seminar, we will explore the wisdom and the life of Jesus the Jew and how that wisdom informed his life. In that lived wisdom, we can find a mirror for our self and a way to live a meaningful life."[731]

I don't remember whether she read more, but the description continues with the kinds of questions those who attend will confront, such as "Why am I here?" "Is there a larger Reality called God?" and "What is the nature of that Other?" Yes, in these sixteen days we had met these questions in some way. But the leader didn't pause after reading the seminar description. She brought more for us to ponder, and we wrote our responses for ourselves, perhaps sharing afterward.

"What about yourself are you especially conscious of as a result of this seminar?"

I wrote, "Steadiness and vulnerability. I belong. Here and everywhere. I belong in the *all*. I *am* in the *all*."

On this final morning of the seminar, the floor in front of our chairs was an exhibition of our artwork, a profusion of shapes and colors. The leader asked us, "Looking at your drawing, what more needs to be included?" I loved the blotches, spontaneity, the lack of real pattern in my drawing, and yet, I did feel something was missing. I took a magic marker and added a magenta line weaving in and around the shapes, and I wrote on the back of the picture, "I add the *unknown* in me. First, it's a meandering path through the shapes and colors. Some are excluded from the line, and I draw another line to include *all*. *All* wants to be included."

When I speak of *all*, I am thinking of the self, which contains all things conscious and unconscious. My drawing tells me that *all* of the all, of this self, must be included and wants to be included. This is a two-way street: a relationship between my small ego self and the greater self of which I and all human beings are a part.

The leader asked another question, "What can be said about the picture? What is new?" I wrote, "Space, vitality, spontaneity a looseness, openness to the *new* to emerge. And there is a hiddenness. Sitting in my chair, the sparkles don't show much. When I sat on the floor, adding the line, facing the light, they showed up plainly. I see new things when I hold it differently. There is a lightness and dark. There is freedom and containment and inclusion. *All* is included."

Then the leader asked, "What is your central value that most governs, shapes, guides the way you live in this world?" I wrote, "Can I truly say it is to 'do the will'? To attune myself more and more to the Great Patterning in myself and in the *all*? Yes, and yet I fall so short. I suppose I must include that in my *all*. My little all of Elli striving to express the all of Eleanor, trying to harmonize with the Great Patterning."

The words *Great Patterning* had been emerging for me to describe the elusive mystery of God, or self. All my life, I've been in search of "God." On the morning before we drew our *new thing*, I rose and as I always did at Four Springs, made my individual meditative rounds greeting the directions at the central stone in the meadow near the lodge; softly ringing the three-tiered bronze temple bells hanging at the end of the grape arbor; stopping at the old baptismal font near the meditation room to make my pledge, "Let me remember to remember"; and then entering the meditation room nearby to sit for a moment in silence. Sometime in that morning ritual, these words came to me:

> Oh my Beloved Patterner *Patterning.*
> Let me hear your *Great Cry.*
> Let my *cry* meet your *cry.*

I continued onward to the art meditation room. That morning, one of the staff had placed a large painting of the empty tomb for us to contemplate. Later, I wrote, "Tears come. I come out of the building after sitting some moments before the painting and am met greeted by the oleander tree arrayed in white blossoms. An angel has appeared!"

At another seminar, working with the crucifixion and the empty tomb led to another "knowing" experience, about which I wrote later: "The tomb is empty and yet it's filled with grace." Something new is alive in me.

When the leader asked what is the most central value that guides the way we live in the world, I wrote: "To attune myself more and more to the Great Patterning in myself and in the *all*." Her next question was, "Which teaching of Jesus best supports or resonates with this primary value?" and I wrote, "These come to mind: 'Love with *all*, sell *all*,' and 'Why do you not judge for yourself what is right?'" My notes continue, "And that the kingdom is among and amid you. It is *now, here*, in this very moment, in this very gathering of people. We are in the ocean of

God-ness right now! If I remember this, perhaps all is possible, even with my failings." And I added in the margin, "The kingdom is the foundation. The others come out of this." Knowing and remembering these things will help me attune myself, do the will, listen to what the Cry requires.

The leader then asked, "What wants to be shared from this meditative writing?" I shared about the kingdom of God, calling it "the ocean of God-ness" to convey the gift of grace I've experienced with gratitude and amazement on rare occasions. Surely, that's what Jesus meant by the kingdom of God here and now, within and among us?

Someone else spoke of courage, sharing its etymological root, "act of the heart." How differently I would face challenges remembering that courage is an "act of the heart."

We had made our way through our *Records* study and had our closing banquet and ritual. On the final morning, which was a preparation for going out of this container we'd shared for sixteen days, we had a new leader who had a different approach. The leader began with this reading from Eliot's "Four Quartets":

> What we call the beginning is often the end
> And to make an end is to make a beginning,
> The end is where we start from.[732]

The leader asked, "Last night was the end of the seminar. What feelings come up for you?" and I wrote, "Amazement and gratitude; amazement at how deep the treasure is, forever to be mimed (I meant mined!). Gratitude that this is so." She brought more questions. "What do you feel as you imagine going out those gates we entered many days ago? What do you fear?" I felt challenged and I was afraid, afraid I would not persevere, would not remember to remember, or if I did remember, that I would turn away from what was needed, whatever that might be at a given time.

She reminded us of our work with the baptism and asked, "What would you say came alive for Jesus in his baptism?" I wrote, "A knowing that the kingdom was in himself and everyone, and all around," and then, "God in the human came alive." Now I'd add: "God self came alive, and Jesus *knew* it!" A holy intercourse happened, and a new relationship between human and divine was conceived.

Then we took our drawing of the new thing outside, anywhere we liked, looked at it, listened to what it had to tell us. I went to the meditation room and found two or three others there as well. This new thing and I conversed:

Me: What life, what vitality I see in you! You also look chaotic, but I'm not afraid.

New Thing: Out of chaos comes the new thing, Elli becoming Eleanor. Do you see the multitude of galaxies within me? Each harbors such creativity, such vitality and also pain, anguish, violence, and rage.

See what's in this drawing that soul drew? Galaxies and each is within you waiting to be explored.

Me: Wow! I didn't see you that way before. It's more than a lifetime's work!

New Thing: It is. You've been exploring all your life and will go on exploring.

Me: What do I need to hear, *New thing*, about the exploration?

New Thing: *Love it!* Everything you desire is in it. You love ideas, you love God now, bring more of your lightness and your *daring*! Your project *demands daring*!

Me: Whoa! Thank you!

Oh my, I'm excited to hear this. I need *daring* to bring forth what is required!

The bell sounded to call us back to the seminar room where the leader asked, referring to comments we'd made earlier, "We have called what Jesus experienced a sense of *belovedness*, kingdom within, fire and water, bubbles of champagne. When you look at your drawing what do you call it?" I wrote, "*Life Abundant!*"

Next we turned to the wilderness experience. What was it like to be in that wilderness? I knew much of wilderness, its doubts and questions, depression and despair, but also great awakenings. The seminar itself sometimes felt like a wilderness as my questions about my life and about the seminar itself surfaced. It was such a rich time. The leader asked, "What might it be like to be in that wilderness alone?" I wrote, "Alone is where the work is." Now I'd say, Lonely, challenging, stimulating, scary, filled with doubts. And yet this is where the work is.

We worked with the doubts and fears we'd face when returned to our home places where, even if we share our lives with others, we must face our wilderness alone. We took time to write our doubts and our responses to those doubts. Then the leader offered cautionary words I remember so well: "Don't try to tell what happened at the seminar, at least not too soon." "How can you convey such an experience?" I thought. "Who will understand?" Luella Sibbald had said this at my first seminar, and this young leader was giving us the same cautions many years later.

"There is danger of losing something of your experience if you share it too soon." She reminded us of our work with the nativity myth, the preciousness of the new thing born then. "Call on Joseph, the Good Father," she said, "to protect it. You'll know when and with whom to share."

After a break, a third leader took the leaders' chair. She reminded us that we would go out the gate ritually, leaving our sacred container. "How would Jesus meet the world?" "As they were going along the road," she read, "a man said to him, 'I will follow you wherever you go.'

And Jesus said to him, 'Foxes have holes, and birds of the air have nests; but the Son of man has nowhere to lay his head.'"[733]

"What is Jesus saying here?" she asked. "How do you hear Jesus speaking of the Son of man?" Someone responded, "I need a home, but Son of man will take me out of that and move me." Someone else said, "The Son of man can't be unconscious." I quoted the Gospel of Thomas, "Be ye passersby."[734] Somehow these passages are related: The Son of man has nowhere to lay his head; be ye passersby.

Then the leader asked, "What do foxes and birds operate out of?" I wrote, "Instincts. ... The Son of man is what makes us human." These dialogues helped me hone in on what I think the Son of man is. A quality in the human, but what does that mean?

To the question about foxes and birds, someone else responded, "Sense of security he carries his home within him." Was she speaking of the fox, the bird, or the Son of man? The leader picked up on it. "What do you say about the security? What is the Son of man in touch with that makes him a wanderer and yet secure?"

Another responded, "A fish in water is not thirsty." I struggled with my own ideas. "Son of man ... Is Son of man the god in the human? Or is Son of man at home in God?" The leader pushed onward. "How might the Son of man be related to doing the will?" I continued struggling to clarify my thoughts about this and I wrote: "The Son of man is in harmony with the Great Pattern. Son of man knows. Somehow it's related to yearning." After I returned home, I added, "Perhaps it is the Son of man within us who *does* the will. Who knows, discerns, chooses, and *does.*"

Another question: "How might the Son of man be related to the central value you wrote about this morning?" I responded, "The Son of man is my connection with God. Son of man is God in me. Son of man is the breath of God—a shard of God?" And after I returned home: "The Son of man is what puts me in harmony with my pattern and the Great Pattern. Or is the Son of man the pattern itself?"

I am still striving for clarity. Elizabeth Howes believes the Son of man is *an expression of* the self, not the same as the self. What do I think? I too don't think Son of man is the self. The self, I'm coming to see, is that Great Pattern which *is* the totality of the human being. My ego self is one little atom in that totality, and yet an essential one. I speak psychologically, of course; I cannot get outside psyche's box to see if there is more.

Two more questions were posed before we moved to the final passage of the morning and of the seminar. The first was, "When you go home, where will you be tempted to lay your head?" I wrote about feeling overwhelmed by work and overwhelmed by the sorrows of the world. I reminded myself that feeling overwhelmed can be immobilizing, can lead to despair and passivity.

The leader asked how we might avoid this, and my answer came readily. "Do my morning rituals and prayers; they will remind me to remember, to be conscious, to attend to the voice of the Son of man, which will guide me to do the will, whatever that 'will' is in this day."

Someone else put a thought into the circle, "Eleanor Roosevelt said to do one thing each day you are afraid to do." I wrote, "That's helpful. Do one thing I'm afraid of, or one thing that's hard for me to do. Maybe this even tells me how to approach world problems afresh."

Then the leader brought us to the second and final passage we would work with: "And when they bring you before the synagogues and the rulers and the authorities, do not be anxious how or what you are to answer or what you are to say; for the Holy Spirit will teach you in that very hour what you ought to say."[735] The leader asked us when Jesus encountered the Spirit, and we responded, "In the baptism and wilderness."

"What do you hear Jesus saying in the passage, 'the Holy Spirit will teach you at that very hour what to say'?" Someone responded, "Each moment has its own answer, and you may not like it."

"What kind of situation is he referring to?" Responses were, "Not when you're meditating or praying or reading" and "He's talking about a situation of conflict."

"What is the function of the Spirit in these situations of conflict?" I wrote, "To teach you what you ought to say."

"What might it be like to speak from an unknown, unexpected voice?" I wrote, "It's not about me. It's the *listening* in the moment that is required."

Then she asked a crucial question, "How do you know it's the Holy Spirit and not some other voice within you?" Oh, that's the hard thing, to make that discernment. I thought about our work with "doing the will." How do we choose what might be the will? It's a process of weighing the pros and cons, of choosing "the higher value," knowing I might make the wrong choice.

Although we didn't spend time on that final morning asking what the Holy Spirit is, I considered possibilities that had come to me: A creative force that "drives us by anxiety to the new thing"; the guide I hear with my inner ear, the messenger of the self, companion of the Son of man? I am, we are all, seeking words to give names to the unnamable, metaphors to describe those archetypal energies that make themselves known in our lives in stories, poetry, art, dreams, and synchronistic events. The Christian myth is rich with these patterns given the names of people and gods and messengers of God. How much we want to put them in boxes and think they will stay there.

Tearing Down the Gate

The morning was coming to a close. It was time to approach the gate and "tear it down." The container we had shared for sixteen days no longer served; it was too small. We had to return to the world. We left the seminar room and walked toward the gate together, each of us at our own pace, in our own time. I envisioned the world to which I would return. Was I ready to tear open the gate? Yes! I joined others in movement and sound as we symbolically tore open the gate. I stood for a moment, still on "this side," and then stepped forward into whatever the new thing may bring.

What I have come to understand is that when the great story told in the Synoptic Gospels is understood *psychologically* as myth, it is not about either a Jesus of history or a Christ of faith. It is about humanity's evolutionary journey out of unconscious identification with all that is to increasing consciousness of ourselves and how amazing this journey is—amazing that existence is, and that humanity is slowly becoming conscious of itself. Sheila Moon writes, "Myths are interpreters of the depths of the human, carriers of life values, dynamic movements from timelessness and spacelessness into human time and space. ... A mirror is held for the psyche of [the human] to look into and to see how it is with [him or her.]"[736] The process developed by the Guild over the past seventy-five years provides such a mirror, and a participant in a *Records* seminar begins to see in the Christian myth and in all great myths the image of herself or himself.

So, I know why I cannot call myself Christian, and why the stories of Jesus's life and teachings still enlighten me. I realize the story does not require a historical Jesus for it to continue to be compelling—I remember him well, and I wasn't even there. I know that what compels me is Jung's myth of meaning, and the Jesus story is one of the grand ways of telling it.

So what do I call myself? Not a Jungian, although his thought informs my life. In the Gospel of Thomas, Jesus says to his listeners, "Be ye passersby."[737] That's all. He doesn't explain what he means by passersby. And yet it speaks to me of being a part of this life we have been given, not standing back to observe it as we pass by, but to live it out fully, as does the Jesus we come to know in the Synoptic Gospels, the Jesus each of us remembers. Yes, that. I call myself a passerby.

Acknowledgments

Although I will acknowledge, as Hal Childs so graciously says in his foreword, that I am the heroine of the story I tell here, I have traveled many trails in company with marvelous guides and like-minded companions over a lifetime and the years of my involvement with the Guild for Psychological Studies. I have not made the journey alone by any means. I am grateful for all the companions, even ones who seemed at the time to be building walls and confusing my way. I couldn't name them all if I wanted to, but here are a few special people who have helped me along the way.

I give full credit to the Guild, whose magical, mythical, and intense seminars I attended for so many years. Those experiences have contributed to the person I am today. The three founding leaders of the Guild, Elizabeth Howes, Sheila Moon, and Luella Sibbald have been gone for many years, but I will always hold them in great respect for their vision, dedication, and love for their work. They believed in their work to the very core.

And let me credit the two leaders of my first *Records* seminar in 1984, both of them also gone now, Joan Gibbons and Clare McCaslin. With all their skill and years of experience, they opened new gateways for this questioning and sometimes rebellious seeker.

I am so grateful for the rich amalgam of seekers with whom I confronted the hurdles set before us in each seminar. We studied together, played and laughed together, and at times I suspect we grumbled, separately if not together. For the period of each seminar and often long after, we were a courageous band of Journeyers. I think now that we were what Jesus called "passersby." Faced with question after question, we rallied ourselves to the search and rarely fell into locked boxes of "right" answers.

A second major force which led to this book is the Pacifica Graduate Institute in Carpinteria, California, from which I received my PhD in Mythological Studies with an emphasis on Depth Psychology in 2008. Driven yet again by soul or self or perhaps painful dissatisfaction with the state of my life, I enrolled in this unique graduate program when I was 66 years old. I was not yet done with my questioning! What I learned there in the company of more seekers filled in many gaps in my knowledge and in my being. Among the excellent teachers at Pacifica, I will name only one, Patrick Mahaffey, PhD, who patiently served as my advisor through the seemingly endless years of completing the dissertation.

I am so grateful for the student-companions with whom I traveled in our Pacifica classes from the fall of 2000 until we received our master's degrees in 2003. Several of us continued to support one another as we pursued our doctoral degrees. Seven of us still meet regularly to share our lives. Thank you!

I cannot end these acknowledgments without expressing my gratitude to the members of the Guild Board of Directors who have supported this work with their caring as well as financial support. To Elizabeth Bremer and Jennifer Morgan, board members and longtime Guild participants and companions, I give you many, many thanks for the hours you devoted to the tedious but essential task of checking footnotes in Passersby.

Not quite finally, my thanks to Hal Childs, longtime friend, mentor and guide, external reader for the dissertation, who has dedicated his time and energy to finding the right editor to massage a scholarly dissertation into a more accessible work. He found him in Arnie Kotler, to whom I express my thanks.

More than finding an editor, even as Hal was pursuing his own scholarly work, he has himself served as editor, knowledgeable commentator, and dedicated overseer shepherding this work to publication. The dissertation would have remained hidden on its shelf without you, Hal. You know how grateful I am.

Grateful indeed for the whole journey, which is not done yet.

Permissions

Notes

[1] Marvin Meyer, ed., *Gospel of Thomas* (San Francisco: HarperOne, 1992), Saying 42.

[2] Elizabeth Boyden Howes and Sheila Moon, *The Choicemaker* (Wheaton, IL: Theosophical Publishing House, 1973), 23. For simplicity, with regret, I retain the exclusive gender language that is used in this book.

[3] Elizabeth Boyden Howes, *Jesus' Answer to God.* (San Francisco: Guild for Psychological Studies Publishing House, 1984), ii.

Introduction

[4] C. G. Jung, "Introduction to the Religious and Psychological Problems of Alchemy," *The Collected Works of C. G. Jung*, eds. H. Read, M. Fordham & G. Adler, trans. R. F. C. Hull, Vol. 12, Bollingen Series 20 (New York: Pantheon Books, 1953), ¶ 15. References to the Collected Works give volume and paragraph numbers, and when noted, page number. Hereafter, referred to in citations as CW.

[5] Lk 17:20-21; §112A. Note: In New Testament citations, Luke is abbreviated Lk, Mark Mk, and Matthew Mt. Section numbers (§) are those given in *Records of the Life of Jesus*, which presents the three Synoptic Gospel accounts in parallel form. Text used is the Revised Standard Version (RSV), which is the version followed in the current *Records* book.

[6] Jung, "Introduction to the Religious and Psychological Problems of Alchemy," CW 12:15.

[7] Jung, "Psychology and Religion," CW 11:6.

[8] Joseph Campbell, *The Hero with a Thousand Faces* (Princeton: Princeton University Press, 1972), 3.

[9] Aniela Jaffé, *The Myth of Meaning in the Work of C. G. Jung*, trans. R. F. C. Hull (Zurich: Daimon Verlag, 1983).

[10] Sheila Moon, *A Magic Dwells: A Poetic and Psychological Study of the Navaho Emergence Myth.* (Middletown, CT: Wesleyan University Press, 1970), 13. I have updated Moon's language in this book to be gender-inclusive. Emphasis added.

[11] Jung, *The Visions Seminars*, Book One (Zürich: Spring Publications, 1976), 156.

[12] Jung, "Psychology and Religion," CW 11:140.

[13] Jung, "The Function of the Unconscious," CW 7:266.

[14] James Hillman, *Re-Visioning Psychology* (New York: William Morrow, 1997), 123.

[15] Moon, *A Magic Dwells*, 10.

[16] Jaffé, *Myth of Meaning*, 136.

[17] Henry Burton Sharman, *Records of the Life of Jesus* (Palo Alto, CA: Sequoia Seminar Foundation, 1917). Reprinted in 1991 by the Guild for Psychological Studies. To order the *Records* book, visit https://guildsf.org

[18] This book derives from the author's dissertation in Mythological Studies with an emphasis in Depth Psychology awarded by the Pacifica Graduate Institute in 2008, titled "A Depth Psychological View of the Christian Myth: C. G. Jung, Elizabeth Boyden Howes, and the Guild for Psychological Studies," © Eleanor Lou Norris. https://www.proquest.com/openview/f1083f85b603014fc64efe5a3351baf3/1

Part One

Chapter 1 Jung's Vision of Christianity

[19] Jung, *Aion: Researches into the Phenomenology of the Self*, CW 9ii:69-70.

[20] Bart Ehrman, *Lost Christianities: The Battles for Scripture and the Faiths We Never Knew* (Oxford: Oxford University Press, 2003).

[21] Jaroslav Pelikan, *Jesus Through the Centuries: His Place in the History of Culture* (New Haven, CT: Yale University Press, 1985), 2.

[22] Albert Schweitzer, *The Quest of the Historical Jesus* (1913), ed. John Bowden, trans. W. Montgomery, J. R. Coates, Susan Cupitt, and John Bowden (Minneapolis: Fortress Press, 2001), 8.

[23] Marcus Borg, "Portraits of Jesus," in *The Search for Jesus: Modern Scholarship Looks at the Gospels*, ed. Hershel Shanks (Washington, DC: Biblical Archaeology Society, 1993), 84 ff.

[24] Jaffe, *Myth of Meaning*, 130.

[25] Jung, *Memories, Dreams, Reflections*, ed. Aniela Jaffé (New York: Vintage Books, 1963), 338.

[26] Jung, *The Red Book* (New York: W.W. Norton, 2012).

[27] Jung, *Memories*, 199.

[28] Jung, "Psychology and Religion," CW 11:3.

[29] Jung, *Aion*, CW 9ii, p. x.

[30] Jung, *Aion*, CW 9ii, p. x.

[31] Jung, *Aion*, CW 9ii:69-70.

[32] Jung, "Answer to Job," CW 11, pg. 357.

[33] Jung, "Answer to Job," CW 11:606.

[34] Jung, *Letters 2: 1951-1961*, sel. and ed. by Gerhard Adler with Aniela Jaffé, trans. R. F. C. Hull. Bollingen Series XCV. (Princeton: Princeton University Press, 1975), 76-77.

[35] Jung, "Answer to Job," *CW* 11:713. Emphasis added.

[36] Jung, *Aion*, CW 9ii:69-70.

[37] Jung, *Letters*, 2:260.

[38] Jung, "Religion and Psychology: A Reply to Martin Buber," CW 18: 1511.

[39] Wendy Doniger O'Flaherty, "The Uses and Mis-uses of Other People's Myths," in *The Insider/Outsider Problem in the Study of Religion: A Reader*, ed. Russel T. McCutcheon (London: Cassell, 1999), 334-335.

[40] Robert A. Johnson, *Inner Gold: Understanding Psychological Projection* (Asheville, NC: Chiron Publications/Koa Books, 2008), 16.

[41] John A. Sanford, *Dreams: God's Forgotten Language* (San Francisco: HarperOne, 1989).

[42] Jung, "Thoughts on the Interpretation of Christianity, with Reference to the Theory of Albrecht Ritschl," reprinted in *Jung on Christianity*, ed. Murray Stein (Princeton: Princeton University Press, 1999), 44.

[43] Stein, *Jung on Christianity*, 45.

[44] Stein, *Jung on Christianity*, 46.

[45] Stein, *Jung on Christianity*, 58.

[46] Stein, *Jung on Christianity*, 58.

[47] Jung, *Letters*, 2:202.

[48] Jung, *Letters*, 2:205.

[49] Jung, *Letters*, 2:205-206.

[50] Jung, *Letters*, 2:206.

[51] Jung, "Psychology and Religion," CW 11:6.

[52] Jung, *Memories*, 199.

[53] Wolfgang Giegerich, *The Soul's Logical Life: Towards a Rigorous Notion of Psychology* (Frankfurt: Peter Lang Verlag, 2001), 61.

[54] Karl Kerényi qtd. in Giegerich, 39.

[55] Jung qtd. in Giegerich, 39.

[56] Jung, "The Structure of the Psyche," CW 8:283.

[57] Jung, "Psychology and Religion," CW 11:140.

[58] Jung, "Psychology and Religion," CW 11:140.

[59] Jung, "Archetypes of the Collective Unconscious," CW 9i:7n10.

[60] Jung, "On the Relation of Analytical Psychology to Poetry," CW 15:105.

[61] Jung, *Memories*, 176.

[62] Jung, *Memories*, 183.

[63] Jung, *The Red Book: Liber Novus*, ed. Sonu Shamdasani, trans. Mark Kyburz, John Peck, and Sonu Shamdasani (New York: W.W. Norton, 2009).

[64] Jung, *Aion*, CW 9ii:12.

[65] Jung, *Aion*, CW 9ii:13.

[66] Jung, "Psychology and Religion," CW 11:88.

[67] Jung, "A Psychological Approach to the Trinity," CW 11:232.

[68] Jung, "Individual Dream Symbolism in Relation to Alchemy," CW 12:44.

[69] Roger Brooke, *Jung and Phenomenology* (London: Routledge, 1991), 98.

[70] Jung, qtd. in Brooke, 95.

[71] Jung, qtd. in Brooke, 95.

[72] Jung, *Memories*, 176, emphasis added.

[73] Jung, *Letters*, 1: 1906-1950, sel. and ed. by Gerhard Adler with Aniela Jaffé, trans. R. F. C. Hull. Bollingen Series XCV. (Princeton: Princeton University Press, 1973), 556.

[74] Brooke, *Jung and Phenomenology*, 77.

[75] Jung, "Commentary on 'The Secret of the Golden Flower,'" CW 13:75.

[76] Jung, "Individual Dream Symbolism in Relation to Alchemy," CW 12:44.

[77] Jung, *Aion*, CW 9ii:6.

[78] Brooke, *Jung and Phenomenology*, 97.

[79] Jung, "Psychology and Religion," CW 11:141, emphasis added.

[80] Jung, "The Undiscovered Self," CW 10:528.

[81] Jung, *Memories*, 254.

[82] Jung, *Memories*, 255.

[83] Jung, *Memories*, 255-256.

[84] Jung, *Memories*, 256.

[85] Jung, "The Development of Personality," CW 17:309.

[86] Jung, *Aion*, CW 9ii, p. x.

[87] Jung, *Aion*, CW 9ii, p. x.

[88] Jung, *Aion*, CW 9ii:73.

[89] Jung, *Aion*, CW 9ii:73.

[90] Jung, *Aion*, CW 9ii:69-70.

[91] Jung, "Answer to Job," CW 11:713.

[92] Jung, "The Relations Between the Ego and the Unconscious," CW 7:266.

[93] Jung, "The Psychology of the Child Archetype," CW 9i:289.

[94] Jung, *Memories*, 196-197.

[95] Jung, *Aion*, CW 9ii:44.

[96] Jung, "Individual Dream Symbolism in Relation to Alchemy," CW 12:105n34.

[97] Jung, "Transformation Symbolism in the Mass," CW 11:390.

[98] Jung, "Transformation Symbolism in the Mass," CW 11:391.

[99] Jung, "The Development of Personality," CW 17:308.

[100] Jung, *Aion*, CW 9ii:123.

[101] Jung, *Aion*, CW 9ii:126.

[102] Jung, qtd. in Jaffé, *Myth of Meaning*, 136.

[103] Jung, "The Development of Personality," CW 17:310.

[104] Jung, *Aion*, CW 9ii.

[105] Jung, *Aion*, CW 9ii:96.

[106] Jung, *Aion*, CW 9ii:79.

[107] Jung, *Aion*, CW 9ii:123.

[108] Jung, "Psychology and Religion," CW 11:146, emphasis added.

[109] Jung, *Letters*, 2:76.

[110] Jung, *Letters*, 2:76-77.

[111] Jung, "Psychology and Religion: West and East," CW 11, pp. 355-470.

[112] Jung, "Answer to Job," CW 11, p. 357.

[113] Jung, "Answer to Job," CW 11, p. 357.

[114] Jung, "Answer to Job," CW 11, p. 358.

[115] Jung, "Answer to Job," CW 11, p. 358.

[116] Jung, "Answer to Job," CW 11:560.

[117] Jung, "Answer to Job," CW 11:574.

[118] Jung, "Answer to Job," CW 11:574, emphasis added.

[119] Jung, "Answer to Job," CW 11:575.

[120] Jung, "Answer to Job," CW 11:606.

[121] Jung, "Answer to Job," CW 11:631.

[122] Jung, "Answer to Job," CW 11:631.

[123] Jung, "Answer to Job," CW 11:631, emphasis added.

[124] Jung, "Religion and Psychology: A Reply to Martin Buber," CW 18:1506.

[125] Jung, *Letters*, 2:260.

[126] Mk 1:11; §18CD.

[127] Jung, "Answer to Job," CW 11:631.

[128] Jung, "Answer to Job," CW 11:658.

[129] Jung, "Answer to Job," CW 11:757.

[130] Jung, "Answer to Job," CW 11:758.

[131] Jung, *Memories*, 338.

Chapter 2 Other Jungian Views on Christianity

[132] Robert Moore and Daniel Meckel, eds., *Jung and Christianity in Dialogue: Faith, Feminism, and Hermeneutics* (Mahwah, NJ: Paulist Press, 1990), 1.

[133] Murray Stein, "C G. Jung, Psychologist and Theologian," in Moore and Meckel, *Jung and Christianity*, 3-20.

[134] Stein, in *Jung and Christianity*, 3.

[135] Stein, in *Jung and Christianity*, 4.

[136] Stein, in *Jung and Christianity*, 4.

[137] Stein, in *Jung and Christianity*, 4.

[138] Stein, in *Jung and Christianity*, 4.

[139] Stein, in *Jung and Christianity*, 19.

[140] Stein, in *Jung and Christianity*, 19.

[141] Stein, in *Jung and Christianity* 5.

[142] Edward Edinger, *Ego and Archetype: Individuation and the Religious Function of the Psyche* (New York: Penguin, 1973), v.

[143] Edinger, *Ego and Archetype*, 131.

[144] Edinger, *Ego and Archetype*, 107

[145] Edward Edinger, *The Bible and the Psyche: Individuation Symbolism in the Old Testament* (Toronto: Inner City Books, 1986), 1.

[146] Edinger, *Bible and Psyche*, 12.

[147] Jung qtd. in Edward Edinger, *The New God-Image: A Study of Jung's Key Letters Concerning the Evolution of the Western God-Image* (Asheville, NC: Chiron Publications, 1996), xiii.

[148] Edinger, *New God-Image*, xiii, emphasis added.

[149] Edinger, *New God-Image*, xiii.

[150] Edinger, *New God-Image*, xiii.

[151] John P. Dourley, "Revisioning Incarnation: Jung on the Relativity of God," in *Shim-Song Yon-Gu: Journal of the Korean Jung Institute* 16.1 (2001), 22.

[152] John P. Dourley, *A Strategy for a Loss of Faith: Jung's Proposal* (Toronto: Inner City Books, 1992), 24.

[153] Jung, *Letters*, 2:135.

[154] Jung, *Letters*, 2:137.

[155] Jung, *Letters*, 2:135.

[156] Jung, *Letters*, 2:137.

[157] Jung, *Letters*, 2:136 n10.

[158] Dourley, *Strategy for Loss*, 136.

[159] Dourley, *Strategy for Loss*, 136.

[160] Dourley, *Strategy for Loss*, 137.

[161] Jung, *Memories*, 333.

[162] Lionel Corbett, *The Religious Function of the Psyche* (London: Routledge, 1996), 3.

[163] Corbett, *Religious Function*, 109.

[164] Edinger, *Ego and Archetype*, 131.

[165] Wayne G. Rollins, *Soul and Psyche: The Bible in Psychological Perspective* (Minneapolis: Augsburg Fortress Publishers, 1999), 77–78.

[166] Rollins, qtd. in Donald Capps, foreword to *Psychology and the Bible. A New Way to Read the Scriptures: From Freud to Kohut*, eds. J. Harold Ellens and Wayne G. Rollins, vol. 1 of 4 (Westport, CT: Praeger, 2004), x.

Chapter 3 Elizabeth Howes's Search for the Historical Jesus

[167] Howes, *Jesus' Answer*, i.

[168] I explore Howes's thinking in *Jesus' Answer to God* and in her lectures published as "Analytical Psychology and the Synoptic Gospels," "The Importance of the Study of the Records of the Life of Jesus and Its Relation to Analytical Psychology," "The Religious Function of the Ego," "The Eternal Question: What Is It? Who Asks It?" and "God, Self, Ego, and Choice." Another source is an oral history videotaped in 1986, *Conversations with the Founding Leaders*, in which Howes, Moon, and Sibbald recall the history and development of their work and of the Guild for Psychological Studies.

[169] Marcus Borg, "Portraits of Jesus," in *The Search for Jesus: Modern Scholarship Looks at the Gospels*, ed. Hershel Shanks (Washington, DC: Biblical Archaeology Society, 1993), 86.

[170] Borg, "Portraits," 86.

[171] Borg, "Portraits," 86.

[172] Howes, *Jesus' Answer*, i.

[173] Howes, *Jesus' Answer*, ii-iii.

[174] Corbett, *Religious Function*, 109.

[175] Jung, *Letters*, 2:205-206.

[176] Elizabeth Boyden Howes, "Analytical Psychology and the Synoptic Gospels," in Elizabeth Boyden Howes, *Intersection and Beyond: Twelve lectures on the commingling of religious values and the insights of analytical psychology*. Vol. I (San Francisco: Guild for Psychological Studies Publishing, 1971), 147.

[177] Howes, *Jesus' Answer*, i.

[178] Howes, "The Importance of the Study of the Records of the Life of Jesus and Its Relation to Analytical Psychology," in *Intersection: Journal of the Guild for Psychological Studies* (San Francisco: Guild for Psychological Studies Publishing, 1994). Vol I, 14.

[179] Elizabeth Boyden Howes, Sheila Moon, and Luella Sibbald, "Conversations with the Founding Leaders" DVD (San Francisco: Guild for Psychological Studies, 1986).

[180] *The Pines: Its Purpose and History*, 1942-1952 (Palo Alto, CA: National Press, 1953), 23.

[181] Elizabeth Boyden Howes, "The Eternal Question: What is it? Who Asks it?" in Howes, *Intersection and Beyond*, 18.

182 Elizabeth Boyden Howes and Sheila Moon. *The Choicemaker* (Wheaton, IL: Theosophical Publishing House, 1973), 23. For simplicity, with regret, I retain the exclusive gender language that is used in this book.

183 Hal Childs, "The Historical Jesus ... Knot!" (unpublished paper), 3.

184 Walter Wink, *The Bible in Human Transformation: Toward a New Paradigm for Biblical Study* (Philadelphia: Fortress Press, 1973), 62.

185 Wink, *Bible in Transformation*, 63.

186 Mt 3:13-17; Mk 1:9-11; Lk 3:21-22; §18.

187 Howes, *Jesus' Answer*, 12.

188 Howes, *Jesus' Answer*, 12

189 Elizabeth Boyden Howes, "Analytical Psychology and the Synoptic Gospels," in Howes, *Intersection*, 169.

190 Mk 2:27-28; §32FG.

191 Mk 2:10-11; §29G.

192 Howes, "Analytical Psychology and the Synoptic Gospels," 155.

193 Howes, "Analytical Psychology and the Synoptic Gospels," 155-156.

194 Howes, *Jesus' Answer*, iv, vi.

195 Howes, *Jesus' Answer*, 14.

196 Howes, "Religious Function of the Ego," 16.

197 Howes, "Religious Function of the Ego," 16.

198 Howes, *Jesus' Answer*, 96.

199 Howes, *Jesus' Answer*, 26.

200 Elizabeth Boyden Howes, Sheila Moon, and Luella Sibbald, "Darkness and God," in *Intersection and Beyond* Vol. II, 1986, 121.

201 Howes, Moon, and Sibbald, *Conversations*.

202 Howes, *Jesus' Answer*, 212.

203 Howes, *Jesus' Answer*, iii-iv.

204 Mk 1:11b; Luke 3:22b; §18D.

205 Mt 3:17b; §18D.

206 Howes, *Jesus' Answer*, xiii.

207 Howes, *Jesus' Answer*, ii.

208 Howes, *Jesus' Answer*, xii.

209 Howes, *Jesus' Answer*, xiii.

210 Howes, *Jesus' Answer*, xiv.

211 Howes, *Jesus' Answer*, xiv.

212 Howes, *Jesus' Answer*, xiv.

213 Howes, *Jesus' Answer*, xiv.

214 Howes, *Jesus' Answer*, xiv.

215 Howes, "Analytical Psychology and Synoptic Gospels," 147.

216 Howes, "Analytical Psychology and Synoptic Gospels," 169.

217 Howes, "Analytical Psychology and Synoptic Gospels," 169.

218 Howes, *Jesus' Answer*, i.

219 Howes, Jesus' Answer, i.

220 Howes, "Analytical Psychology and Synoptic Gospels," 147.

221 Howes, "Analytical Psychology and Synoptic Gospels," 148.

222 Walter Wink, *Transforming Bible Study: A Leader's Guide* (Nashville, TN: Abingdon Press. 1980), 101-102.

223 Howes, "Analytical Psychology and Synoptic Gospels," 150-151.

224 Mk 1:4; §17H.

225 Words in brackets are accepted alternative translations of the words in the Revised Standard Version of the New Testament used in the *Records* book. The alternatives are given at the bottom of the relevant *Records* page and called to the attention of students by leaders.

226 Mk 1:10; §18C.

227 Mk 1:11; §18CD.

228 Mk 1:12-13a; §20A.

229 Howes, "Analytical Psychology and Synoptic Gospels," 160.

230 Howes, *Jesus' Answer*, 14.

231 Howes, "Analytical Psychology and Synoptic Gospels,"160-161.

232 Howes, "Analytical Psychology and Synoptic Gospels," 161.

233 Howes, "Analytical Psychology and Synoptic Gospels," 161.

234 Howes, "Analytical Psychology and Synoptic Gospels," 161.

235 Mk 1:12-13a; §20A.

236 Mk 1:13b; §20G.

237 "Howes, "Analytical Psychology and Synoptic Gospels," 161.

238 Mt 4:1-11 and Lk 4:1-13, §20.

239 Mt 4:4; §20B.

240 Mt 4:7; §20C.

241 Mt 4:10; §20D.

242 Howes, "Analytical Psychology and Synoptic Gospels," 162.

243 Howes, "Analytical Psychology and Synoptic Gospels," 162.

244 Howes, "Analytical Psychology and Synoptic Gospels," 162.

245 Howes, "Analytical Psychology and Synoptic Gospels," 162.

246 Howes, "Analytical Psychology and Synoptic Gospels," 163.

247 Howes, *Jesus' Answer*, vi.

248 Howes, *Jesus' Answer*, vii.

249 Mk 1:13; §20AG.

250 Howes, *Jesus' Answer*, 19.

251 Howes, "Analytical Psychology and Synoptic Gospels," 163.

252 Howes, *Jesus' Answer*, 79.

253 Howes, *Jesus' Answer*, 56.

254 Howes, *Jesus' Answer*, 57.

255 Howes, *Jesus' Answer*, 57.

256 Howes, *Jesus' Answer*, 57.

257 Howes, *Jesus' Answer*, 58.

258 Howes, *Jesus' Answer*, 58.

259 Howes, *Jesus' Answer*, 59.

260 Howes, *Jesus' Answer*, 59.

261 Howes, *Jesus' Answer*, 59.

262 Howes, *Jesus' Answer*, 59.

263 Howes, *Jesus' Answer*, 60.

264 Howes, *Jesus' Answer*, 84.

265 Howes, *Jesus' Answer*, 85.

266 Howes, *Jesus' Answer*, 85.

267 Howes, *Jesus' Answer*, 85.

268 Howes, *Jesus' Answer*, 86.

269 Howes, *Jesus' Answer*, 87.

270 Howes, *Jesus' Answer*, 87.

271 Howes, *Jesus' Answer*, 87.

272 Howes, *Jesus' Answer*, 87.

273 Howes, *Jesus' Answer*, 87.

274 Howes, *Jesus' Answer*, 88.

275 Howes, *Jesus' Answer*, 88.

276 Howes, *Jesus' Answer*, 88.

277 Howes, *Jesus' Answer*, 88.

278 Mark 14:36; §140C.

279 Howes, *Jesus' Answer*, 89.

280 Howes, *Jesus' Answer*, 89.

281 Howes, *Jesus' Answer*, 89.

282 Howes, *Jesus' Answer*, 89.

283 Howes, *Jesus' Answer*, 89.

284 Lk 17:20-21; §112A.

285 Howes, *Jesus' Answer*, 168.

286 Howes, *Jesus' Answer*, 168.

287 Howes, *Jesus' Answer*, 168.

288 Howes, *Jesus' Answer*, 95.

289 Howes, *Jesus' Answer*, 97.

290 Howes, *Jesus' Answer*, 89.

291 Howes, *Jesus' Answer*, 79.

[292] Elizabeth Boyden Howes, "Son of man—Expression of the Self?" in *Intersection* 1, 174.

[293] Howes, "Son of man," 175.

[294] Walter Wink, *The Human Being: Jesus and the Enigma of the Son of the Man* (Minneapolis, MN: Fortress Press, 2002), 67.

[295] Wink, *Human Being,* 1.

[296] Wink, *Human Being,* 260.

[297] Wink, *Human Being,* xi.

[298] Howes, "Son of man," 173.

[299] Wink, *Human Being,* 17.

[300] Howes, "Son of man," 173.

[301] Although the first phrase, which contains "Son of man" is from Daniel, the rest of the passage draws from Deuteronomy, Isaiah, and Zechariah (*Records* 152n).

[302] Mk 13:26-27; Mt 24:30b-31; Lk 21:27-28; §135H.

[303] Howes, "Son of man," 172.

[304] Howes, "Son of man," 189.

[305] Howes, "Son of man," 189.

[306] Howes, "Son of man," 189.

[307] Howes, "Son of man," 190.

[308] Howes, "Son of man," 176.

[309] Howes, "Son of man," 178.

[310] Howes, "Son of man," 179.

[311] From my personal notes.

[312] Howes, *Jesus' Answer,* 41.

[313] Howes, *Jesus' Answer,* 41.

[314] Howes, *Jesus' Answer,* 41.

[315] Howes, *Jesus' Answer,* 41.

[316] Howes, "Son of man," 177.

[317] The complete verse from *Codex Bezae* is, "On the same day, seeing someone working on the sabbath, he said to him, Man, if indeed you know what you are doing, you are blessed; but if you do not know, you are cursed and a transgressor of the law." Footnote 2 in the *Records* at Luke 6:5; §32F.

[318] Howes, "Son of man," 177.

[319] Jung, "Psychology and Religion," CW 11:696.

[320] Howes, "Son of man," 180.

[321] Howes, "Son of man," 180.

[322] Howes, "Son of man," 180.

[323] Howes, *Jesus' Answer,* 73.

[324] Howes, "Son of man," 180.

325 Howes, "Son of man," 180.

326 Howes, "Son of man," 180-181.

327 Mt 11:3, Lk 7:19; §41A.

328 Mt 11:11; Lk 7:28; §41E.

329 Howes, "Son of man," 181.

330 Lk 7:22; §41C.

331 Howes, *Jesus' Answer*, 61.

332 Mt 11:19b; §41J.

333 Howes, "Son of man," 181-182.

334 Mt 11:19; Lk 7:35; §41J

335 Wink, *Human Being*, 89.

336 qtd. in Wink, *Human Being*, 89.

337 Wink, *Human Being*, 89.

338 Mt 11:19b; §41J.

339 Lk 7:35; §41J.

340 Wink, *Human Being*, 90.

341 Mk 8:27; §71B.

342 Mk 8:29; §71D.

343 Mk 8:30; §71G.

344 Howes, "Son of man," 187.

345 Howes, "Son of man," 185.

346 Howes, "Son of man," 186.

347 Howes, *Jesus' Answer*, 122.

348 Howes, *Jesus' Answer*, 122.

349 Howes, *Jesus' Answer*, 124.

350 Howes, *Jesus' Answer*, 124.

351 Howes, *Jesus' Answer*, 124.

352 Howes, *Jesus' Answer*, 124.

353 Howes, "Son of man," 188.

354 Mt 16:18; §71E.

355 Mt 18:15b-17; §78RS.

356 Howes, *Jesus' Answer*, 202.

357 Mt 27:11; Mk 15:2; Lk 23:3; §143D.

358 Howes, *Jesus' Answer*, 202.

359 Howes, *Jesus' Answer*, 202.

360 Howes, *Jesus' Answer*, 202.

361 Howes, *Jesus' Answer*, 203.

362 Howes, "Analytical Psychology and Synoptic Gospels," 164.

363 Mk 14:36, Mt 26:39, Lk 22:42; §140C.

364 Howes, *Jesus' Answer*, 197.

365 Howes, "Analytical Psychology and Synoptic Gospels," 165.
366 Howes, "Analytical Psychology and Synoptic Gospels," 165.
367 Howes, *Jesus' Answer,* 197.
368 Howes, *Jesus' Answer,* 197.
369 Howes, *Jesus' Answer,* 205.
370 Howes, "Analytical Psychology and Synoptic Gospels," 165.
371 Howes, "Analytical Psychology and Synoptic Gospels," 166.
372 Howes, "Analytical Psychology and Synoptic Gospels," 166.
373 Mk 15:34; §144G.
374 Howes, "Analytical Psychology and Synoptic Gospels," 166.
375 Howes, *Jesus' Answer,* 210.
376 Howes, *Jesus' Answer,* 213.
377 Jung, "Psychology and Religion," CW 11:758.
378 Lk 23:34; §144C.
379 Lk 23:46; §144H.
380 Howes, *Jesus' Answer,* 210.
381 Howes, *Jesus' Answer,* 210.
382 Howes, *Jesus' Answer,* 210.
383 Howes, *Jesus' Answer,* 211.
384 Howes, *Jesus' Answer,* 212.
385 Howes, *Jesus' Answer,* 212.
386 Howes, *Jesus' Answer,* 213.
387 Howes, *Jesus' Answer,* 213.
388 Howes, *Jesus' Answer,* 213.
389 Mk 16:1; §147A.
390 Howes, *Jesus' Answer,* 215.
391 Howes, *Jesus' Answer,* 215.
392 Howes, *Jesus' Answer,* 215. Emphasis added.
393 Howes, *Jesus' Answer,* 216.
394 Howes, *Jesus' Answer,* 217.
395 Howes, *Jesus' Answer,* xiii.
396 Howes, *Jesus' Answer,* xiii.
397 Howes, "Son of man," 191.
398 Howes, "Son of man," 191.
399 Howes, *Jesus' Answer,* 212.
400 Jung, *Memories,* 333.
401 Howes, *Jesus' Answer,* 223.
402 Howes, *Jesus' Answer,* 223.
403 Howes, *Jesus' Answer,* 222-223.
404 Howes, *Jesus' Answer,* 223.

405 Howes and Moon, *Choicemaker,* 23.

406 Howes, *Jesus' Answer,* ii.

407 Howes, *Jesus' Answer,* 79.

408 Howes, *Jesus' Answer,* 89.

409 Howes, "Analytical Psychology and Synoptic Gospels," 155-156.

410 Howes, "Analytical Psychology and Synoptic Gospels," 166.

411 Howes, *Jesus' Answer,* 216.

412 Jung, *Letters,* 2: 205-206.

413 Jung, *Letters,* 2: 205-206.

414 Howes, "Analytical Psychology and Synoptic Gospels," 147-148.

415 Jung, "Answer to Job," CW 11:644.

416 Jung, "Answer to Job," CW 11:645.

417 Jung, "Answer to Job," CW 11:645.

418 Howes, "Analytical Psychology and Synoptic Gospels," 148.

419 Howes, "Analytical Psychology and Synoptic Gospels," 150.

Chapter 4 Was There a Historical Jesus?

420 Albert Schweitzer, *The Quest of The Historical Jesus* (Minneapolis: Fortress Press, 1905, 1913, 2001), 478.

421 Childs, "Historical Jesus," 1. See also *The Myth of the Historical Jesus and the Evolution of Consciousness* (Atlanta: Society of Biblical Literature Dissertation Series, v. 179, 2000).

422 Childs, "Historical Jesus," 5.

423 Childs, "Historical Jesus," 10.

424 Childs, *Myth of Historical Jesus,* 223.

425 Childs, *Myth of Historical Jesus,* 224.

426 qtd. in Childs, *Myth of Historical Jesus,* 59-60.

427 Childs, *Myth of Historical Jesus,* 62.

428 Childs, *Myth of Historical Jesus,* 65.

429 qtd. in Childs, *Myth of Historical Jesus*: 65-66.

430 Childs, "Historical Jesus," 5.

431 Childs, "Historical Jesus," 5.

432 Childs, "Historical Jesus," 6.

433 Jung, "Answer to Job," CW 11:713.

434 Jung, *Letters,* 2:205.

435 Childs, *Myth of Historical Jesus,* 241.

436 Childs, *Myth of Historical Jesus,* 242.

437 Childs, *Myth of Historical Jesus,* 242-243.

438 Childs, *Myth of Historical Jesus,* 101-102.

439 Wink, *Human Being,* 8, emphasis added.

[440] Wink, *Human Being*, 7.

[441] Brian Stock qtd. in Wink, *Human Being*, 7.

[442] Wendy Doniger O'Flaherty qtd. in wink, *Human Being*, 7.

[443] Wink, *Human Being*, 7.

[444] Wink, *Human Being*, 7-8.

[445] Wink, *Human Being*, 8.

[446] Wink, *Human Being*, 8.

[447] Wink, *Human Being*, 9.

[448] Wink, *Human Being*, 9.

[449] Wink, *Human Being*, 10.

[450] Wink, *Human Being*, 10.

[451] Israel Finkelstein and Neil Silberman, *The Bible Unearthed: Archaeology's New Vision of Ancient Israel and the Origin of Its Sacred Texts* (New York: Simon and Schuster, 2002), 1.

[452] Finkelstein and Silberman, *Bible Unearthed*, 1-2.

[453] Finkelstein and Silberman, *Bible Unearthed*, 23.

[454] Finkelstein and Silberman, *Bible Unearthed*, 318.

[455] Jan Assmann, *Moses the Egyptian: The Memory of Egypt in Western Monotheism* (Cambridge, MA: Harvard University Press, 1997), 9. Italics added.

[456] Assmann, *Moses*, 2.

[457] Finkelstein and Silberman, *Bible Unearthed*, 318.

Part Two

Chapter 5 My First Seminar

[458] Hermann Hesse, *Magister Ludi*. qtd. in Moon, *A Magic Dwells: A Poetic and Psychological Study of the Navaho Emergence Myth* (Middletown, CT: Wesleyan University Press, 1970), epigraph.

[459] William Zinsser, *Inventing the Truth: The Art and Craft of Memoir* (Boston: Houghton Mifflin, 1987), 21.

[460] See James Hillman *Healing Fiction* (Woodstock, CT: Spring Publications, 1983).

[461] Assmann, *Moses*, 9.

[462] Jung, "The Phenomenology of the Spirit in Fairytales," CW 9i:400.

[463] Qtd. in Dorothy Phillips, Elizabeth Boyden Howes, and Lucille M. Nixon, eds., *The Choice Is Always Ours: The Classic Anthology on the Spiritual Way* (San Francisco: Harper & Row, Publishers, 1989), 32.

[464] Hammarskjöld, *Markings*, 169.

[465] Mk 1:12-13; §20 (This quote is more specifically from Mk 1:13; §20, but the entire paragraph includes Mk 1:12-13; §20).

Chapter 6 The Work of Discerning

[466] *This One Thing: A Tribute to Henry Burton Sharman* (Toronto: Student Christian Movement of Canada, 1959), 17.

[467] Sharman, *Records.*

[468] I draw from my notes and from Robert W. Funk and Roy W. Hoover, *The Five Gospels: The Search for the Authentic Words of Jesus* (New York: Macmillan, 1993) for this discussion.

[469] Lk 10:25-28; §83A.

Chapter 8 Into the Depths

[470] Mk 1:4; §17H.

[471] Mk 1:10-11; §18CD.

[472] Mk 1:12-13; §20A.

[473] Mk 1:11; §18D.

[474] Sheila Moon, "Prolog," from *Joseph's Son* (Francestown, NH: Golden Quill Press, 1972), 13-14.

[475] Marvin Meyer, ed. *The Gospel of Thomas: The Hidden Sayings of Jesus.* 23, (San Francisco: HarperOne, 1992), Saying 2.

[476] Mt 3:1-2; §17C.

[477] Lk 3:3; §17C.

[478] Mk 1:2; §17E.

[479] Mt 3:3; Mk 1:3; Lk 3:4; §17F.

[480] Mk 1:4; §17H.

[481] Mt 3:2; §17C.

[482] Mt 3:12; Lk 3:17; §17Q.

[483] Mk 1:7-8; §17P.

[484] Mk 1:6; §17K.

[485] Mk 1:10-11; §18CD.

[486] Mt 3:17; §18D.

[487] Mt 3:14-15; §18B.

[488] Moon, *Magic Dwells*, Epigraph.

[489] Mt 3:8-10; §17M.

[490] Mk 1:8; Mt 3:11; Lk 3:16; §17P.

[491] Mt 1:1-17; §2.

[492] Lk 3:23-38; §2.

[493] Lk 1:32-33; §4C.

[494] Mt 2:3-6; §11C.

[495] Am 9:13-15.

[496] Mk 1:13; §20A, G.
[497] Mt 4:1; §20A.
[498] Dt 8:3; qtd. in Mt 4:4; §20B.
[499] Mt 4:5-6; §20C.
[500] Mt 4:7; §20C.
[501] Mt 4:9; §20D.
[502] Mt 4:10; §20D.
[503] Mt 4:3; §20B, and 4:6; §20C.
[504] Mt 4:9-10; §20D.
[505] Mt 4:10; §20D.

Chapter 9 Ministry and Miracles

[506] Qtd. in Phillips, *Choice is Always Ours;* 32.
[507] These are Sections 21-33 in *Records,* Mk 1:14 to Mk 3:6. I indicate the actual passages when I discuss them.
[508] Mk 1:37; §26B.
[509] Mk 1:38; §26C.
[510] Lk 4:43; §26C.
[511] Mk 1:15; §21C.
[512] Lk 4:22-24; §22CDH.
[513] Lk 4:29-30; §22K.
[514] Mk 6:3; §54DF.
[515] Mk 6:5-6; §54J.
[516] Mk 1:24b; §24C.
[517] Mk 1:27-28; §24EF.
[518] Mk 3:9-10; §34D.
[519] Mk 3:11-12; §34EF.
[520] Mt 12:17-21; §34G.
[521] Mk 1:17-18; §23B.
[522] Mk 1:20; §23D.
[523] Lk 5:4; §23.
[524] Lk 5:8-11; §23 (§27).
[525] Mk 2:17; §30EG.
[526] Mk 2:24; §32B.
[527] Mk 2:27-28; §32FG.
[528] Mt 12:8; Lk 6:5; §32G.

Chapter 10 Who Forgives? What Heals?

[529] Mk 2:5; §29D.

[530] Mk 2:11; §29G.

[531] Lk 7:37; §42A.

[532] Lk 7:48, 50; §42E.

[533] Mk 2:3; §29B.

[534] Mk 2:5; §29D.

[535] Mk 2:7; §29E.

[536] Mk 2:8-9; §29F.

[537] Mk 2:10-11; §29G.

[538] Mk 2:10-11; §29G.

[539] Mk 2:27-28; §32FG.

[540] Mt 9:8; §29H.

[541] Jung, "The Structure and Dynamics of the Psyche," CW 8: 180.

[542] Lk 7:36-50; §42.

[543] Lk 7:48, 50; §42E.

[544] Lk 7:42-43; §42C.

[545] Lk 7:45; §42D.

[546] Lk 7:47-50; §42DE.

Chapter 11 Myth or History: Finding Great Truths

[547] Gen 1:1-5.

[548] Gen 1:26-27.

[549] Gen 2:4-5.

[550] Gen 2:7-9.

[551] Gen 2:17.

[552] Gen 3:4-5.

[553] Gen 3:7.

[554] Gen 3:19.

[555] Gen 3:22-24.

[556] Gen 1:1-2.

[557] Gen 1:26-27 (RSV).

[558] Gen 3:24.

[559] Herbert G. May and Bruce M. Metzger, eds., *The New Oxford Annotated Bible with the Apocrypha*, Expanded Edition. Revised Standard Version. (New York: Oxford University Press. 1973, 1977), Gen. 3:24n.

[560] Lk 6:5; §32F, fn 2 in the *Records* book.

[561] Mk 2:27-28; §32FG.

[562] John Middleton Murry, *God: Being an Introduction to the Science of Metabiology* (New York: Harper & Brothers, 1929), 181.

[563] Qtd. in Edward F. Edinger, *The Bible and the Psyche: Individuation Symbolism in the Old Testament* (Toronto: Inner City Books, 1986), 30.

[564] Lk 1:35; §4D.

Chapter 12 Choosing Life

[565] Mt 5:1; §36A.

[566] Lk 6:17; §35D.

[567] Mt 5:11; §36I.

[568] Lk 6:22; In my overview, I am referring to Mt 5:1-12; Lk 6:20-23; §36A-I.

[569] Mt 7:3-4; Lk 6:41-42; §38I.

[570] Mt 5:48; §37R.

[571] Mt 7:12; §38L.

[572] Lk 17:33; §112J.

[573] Dt 30:19.

[574] Lk 10:25-28; §83A.

[575] Mk 7:14-15; §63I.

[576] Mk 7:20-23; §63L Italics added.

[577] Mt 5:39: §37I.

[578] Mt 7:3-5; Lk 6:41-42; §38I.

[579] Mt 5:48; §37R.

[580] Mt 5:48; §37R fn 5.

[581] Mt 7:13-14; §38M.

[582] Mt 7:24-26; Lk 6:47-48; §38W.

[583] Mt 7:21; §38U.

[584] Mt 7:21; §38U.

[585] Lk 17:33; §112J.

[586] Mt 16:26; §73B.

[587] Mk 8:35; §73B.

[588] Lk 9:25; §73B.

[589] Lk 17:33; §112J.

[590] Howes, "Analytical Psychology and Synoptic Gospels," 158.

Chapter 13 The Kingdom of Heaven Is Like...

[591] Mt 13:45-46; §48O.

[592] Mt 7:21; §38U.

[593] Mt 13:9; Mk 4:9; Lk 8:8; §47F; and Mk 4:23; §47S; and Mt 13:43; §48M.

[594] Mt 13:4-8; Mk 4:3-8; Lk 8:5-8; §47B-E.

[595] Mk 4:11; Mt 13:11; Lk 8:10; §47G.

[596] Mk 3:31-35; Mt 12:46-50; Lk 8:19-21; §49A-E.

[597] Mk 4:11; §47G; emphasis added.

[598] Mk 4:14; §47M.

[599] Mt 13:19; §47M.

[600] Lk 8:12; §47M.

[601] Mk 4:26-29; §48D.

[602] Mt 13:30; §48C.

[603] Mk 4:30; §48E.

[604] Mk 4:31; §48E.

[605] Mk 4:32; §48E.

[606] Mt 13:31-32; §48E

[607] Lk 13:18-19; §99A.

[608] Mt 13:33; §48F (§99B); Lk 13:20-21; §99B (§48F).

[609] Mt 13:40-43; §48L.

[610] Mt 13:44; §48N.

[611] Mt 13:45-46; §48O.

[612] Lk 11:5-8; §85C.

[613] Mt 21:28-31; §129A.

[614] Lk 14:16-24; §103E-H.

[615] Mt 25:14-28; §136H-O.

[616] Mt 25:1-2; §136E.

[617] Mt 25:12; §136F.

[618] Lk 11:5-8; §85C.

[619] Lk 11:8; §85C.

[620] Lk 17:20-21; §112A.

[621] The *Records* includes HS references (Hebrew Scripture) and NC references (non-canonical) when Gospel verses warrant such linkage. These are found at the bottom of the *Records'* page, and the NC references are limited to the Gospel of Thomas. This reference connects Lk 17:20-21 with Gos. Thom., Sayings 3 and 113.

[622] Meyer, Gos. Thom., Saying 113.

[623] Meyer, Gos. Thom., Saying 3.

Chapter 14 Gathering Strands

[624] Mk 3:19b-21; §44.

[625] Mk 1:24; Lk 4:34; §24C.

[626] Mk 3:11; §34E.

[627] Mk 1:25; §24D and Mk 3:12; §34 F.

[628] Mk 1:7-8; §17P.

[629] Mt 4:10; §20D.

[630] Mt 11:3; Lk 7:19; §41A.

[631] Mt 11:6; Lk 7:23; §41C.

[632] Mk 8:27-30; Mt 16:13-16, 20; Lk 9:18-21; §71A-D, G.

633 Mk 6:2; Mt 13:54; §54C.

634 Mt 13:55-57; Mk 6:3; §54D-F.

635 Mk 6:5a, 6; §54J.

636 Mt 13:58; §54J.

637 Mk 8:11-13; §68ACD.

638 Mt 16:2-4; §68BC.

639 Lk 11:29; §88B.

640 Mk 8:31-33; Mt 16:21-23; §72AB.

641 Mk 2:27-28; §32FG.

642 Mk 2:10; §29G.

643 Howes, "Son of man," 171.

644 Mk 3:22; §45C.

645 Mk 3:23-24; Mt 12:25-26; Lk 11:17; §45E.

646 Mk 3:28-29; Mt 12:31; §45I.

647 Mt 12:32; §45J.

648 Lk 12:10; §91H, emphasis added.

649 Mk 1:10-11; §18CD.

650 Mk 1:12; Mt 4:1; Lk 4:1; §20A.

651 Lk 12:11-12; 91I.

652 Mt 10:20; §57C.

653 Gen. 1:2.

654 Lk 7:47; §42D.

655 Mk 3:19b-21; §44.

656 Mk 8:31-33; Mt 16:21-23; §72AB.

657 See Mk 9:31; §76B; Mt 17:9; Mk 9:9; §74I; Mk 10:33-34; Mt 20:18-19; Lk 18:32-33; §119EF.

658 See Lk 13:31-32; §101A; Lk 17:25; §112D.

659 Mk 16:5-6; §147D.

660 Mk 16:7-8; §147G.

661 See Werner H. Kelber, *Mark's Story of Jesus* (Philadelphia: Fortress Press, 1984) and Norman Perrin and Dennis C. Duling, *The New Testament: An Introduction* (New York: Harcourt Brace Jovanovich, 1982).

662 Mk 8:12; §68C.

663 Mt 16:4; §68C.

664 Lk 11:29; §88B.

665 Mk 8:32-33; Mt 16:22-23; §72AB.

666 Mt 16:17-19; §71EF.

667 Mt 18:15; §78R.

668 Mt 18:17; §78S.

Chapter 15 Jesus's Final Days

[669] Lk 9:51; §79.

[670] Lk 13:34; 101B.

[671] Mk 8:34; Mt 16:24; Lk 9:23; §73A.

[672] Lk 17:33; 112J.

[673] Mk 9:7; §74E.

[674] Mk 9:9; §74I.

[675] Lk 12:56; §96A.

[676] Lk 12:57; §96B.

[677] Lk 13:32-33; §101A.

[678] Lk 23:28; §144B.

[679] Lk 12:49-50; §95A.

[680] Lk 19:41-42; §124I.

[681] Mt 16:20; Mk 8:30; Lk 9:21; §71G.

[682] Mt 16:16; Mk 8:29; Lk 9:20; §71D.

[683] Mt 26:64; §142E.

[684] Lk 22:71; §142O.

[685] Mk 14:62; §142E.

[686] Mt 27:11; Mk 15:2; Lk 23:3; §143D.

[687] Mk 14:62; Mt 26:64; §142E, and similarly in Lk 22:69; §142N.

[688] Lk 7:20; §41B.

[689] Howes, "Analytical Psychology and Synoptic Gospels," 164.

[690] Mk 14:68; §142H.

[691] Mk 14:71; §142J.

[692] Mk 14:72; Mt 26:75; Lk 22:62; §142K.

[693] Mt 27:27-61; Mk 15:16-47; Lk 23:26-55; §143-145.

[694] Mt 27:45; Mk 15:33; Lk 23:44-45; §144F.

[695] Mt 27:46; Mk 15:34; §144G.

[696] Lk 23:46; §144H.

[697] Lk 23:45; Mt 27:51; Mk 15:38; §144H.

[698] Mt 27:55-56; Mk 15:40-41; Lk 23:49; §144L.

[699] Mt 27:46; Mk 15:34; §144G.

[700] Lk 23:46; 144H.

[701] Mk 15:37; §144H.

[702] Mk 14:25; §138J.

[703] Mt 16:24; Mk 8:34; Lk 9:23; §73A.

[704] Mk 15:43; §145B.

[705] Mk 15:46; §145D.

[706] Mk 15:47; §145F.

Chapter 16 The Empty Tomb

[707] Mk 16:2; §147B.

[708] Mt 28:1-10; Mk 16:1-8; and Lk 23:56-24:12; §147A-I.

[709] Mt 28:10; §147H.

[710] Lk 24:9; §147G and Lk 24:11; §147I.

[711] Mk 16:8: §147G.

[712] Mk 16:8; 147G.

[713] Oxford Annotated Bible; 1238n.

[714] Lk 24:13-32; §149A-F.

[715] Lk 24:33-53; §150A-F.

[716] Mt 28:16-20; §151A-C.

[717] Jn 20:24-29; §220DE.

[718] Mt 28:18; §151B.

[719] Lk 12:57; §96B.

[720] Mt 28:19; §151C.

[721] Lk 24:27; §149E.

[722] Lk 24:46; §150D.

[723] Mk 4:41; Mt 8:27; Lk 8:25; §50H.

[724] Mk 4:40; Lk 8:25; §50G; Mt 8:26; §50E.

[725] Julius Wellhausen, qtd. in Howes, *Jesus' Answer,* i.

[726] Howes, "Son of man," 191.

[727] Jung, *Letters,* 2:138.

[728] Jung, *Letters,* 2:137.

[729] Qtd. in Jaffé, *Myth of Meaning,* 144.

[730] Jaffé, *Myth of Meaning.*

Chapter 17 The Journey Onward

[731] "Paradox: Coming Home to Yourself . . . to be more at home in this world," *Invitation to Soul Work: 2004-2005.* (San Francisco: Guild for Psychological Studies, 2004), 11.

[732] T. S. Eliot, "Four Quartets," *Complete Poems and Plays: 1909-1950,* (San Diego: Harcourt Brace Jovanovich, 1952), 144.

[733] Lk 9:57-58; Mt 8:19-20; §81A.

[734] Gos. Thom., Saying 42.

[735] Lk 12:11-12; §91I; similarly, in Mt 10:19-20; §57C (91I).

[736] Moon, *A Magic Dwells,* 13.

[737] Gos. Thom., Saying 42.

Bibliography

Achtemeier, Paul J, ed. *Harper's Bible Dictionary*. San Francisco: HarperOne, 1985.

Assmann, Jan. *Moses the Egyptian: The Memory of Egypt in Western Monotheism*. Cambridge: Harvard University Press, 1997.

Borg, Marcus. *Jesus: A New Vision*. San Francisco: HarperCollins, 1987.

———. *Meeting Jesus Again for the First Time: The Historical Jesus & the Heart of Contemporary Faith*. San Francisco: HarperOne, 1995.

———. "Portraits of Jesus." In *The Search for Jesus: Modern Scholarship Looks at the Gospels,* edited by Hershel Shanks. Washington, DC: Biblical Archaeology Society, 1993.

Brooke, Roger. *Jung and Phenomenology*. London: Routledge, 1991.

Campbell, Joseph. *The Hero with a Thousand Faces*. Bollingen Series XVII. Princeton: Princeton University Press, 1972.

Capps, Donald. Foreword to *Psychology and the Bible. A New Way to Read the Scriptures: From Freud to Kohut,* edited by Harold J. Ellens and Wayne G. Rollins, vii-xiv. 4 vols. Westport, CT: Praeger Perspectives, 2004.

Childs, Hal. *The Myth of the Historical Jesus and the Evolution of Consciousness*. Dissertation Series. Vol. 179. Atlanta: Society of Biblical Literature, 2000.

———. "The Historical Jesus . . . Knot!" Unpublished paper. 2003.

Clift, Wallace B. *Jung and Christianity: The Challenge of Reconciliation.* New York: Crossroad, 1982.

Corbett, Lionel. *The Religious Function of the Psyche.* London: Routledge, 1996.

"Codex Bezae." In *Catholic Encyclopedia.* Vol. IV. 2003. Edited by John Fenton. 23 March 2008. https://www.newadvent.org/cathen/04083a.htm.

Crossan, John Dominic. *The Historical Jesus: The Life of a Mediterranean Jewish Peasant.* New York: HarperOne, 1991.

Dourley, John P. *A Strategy for a Loss of Faith: Jung's Proposal.* Toronto: Inner City Books, 1992.

———. "Revisioning Incarnation: Jung on the Relativity of God." In *Shim-Song Yon-Gu: Journal of the Korean Jung Institute* 16.1 (2001): 1-29.

Edinger, Edward F. *The Bible and the Psyche: Individuation Symbolism in the Old Testament.* Toronto: Inner City Books, 1986.

———. *Ego and Archetype: Individuation and the Religious Function of the Psyche.* New York: Penguin. 1983.

——— *The New God-Image: A Study of Jung's Key Letters Concerning the Evolution of the Western God-Image.* Edited by Diane D. and Charles Yates Dordic, M.D. Asheville, NC: Chiron. 1996.

Ehrman, Bart D. *Lost Christianities: The Battles for Scripture and the Faiths We Never Knew.* Oxford: Oxford University Press, 2003.

Eliot, T. S. "Four Quartets." In *The Complete Poems and Plays: 1909-1950.* San Diego: Harcourt Brace Jovanovich, 1952.

Ellens, J. Harold, and Wayne G. Rollins. Introduction to *Psychology and the Bible, A New Way to Read the Scriptures: From Christ to Jesus,* edited by J. Harold Ellens and Wayne G. Rollins, 1-12. 4 vols. Westport, CT: Praeger Perspectives, 2004.

Finkelstein, Israel, and Neil Asher Silberman. *The Bible Unearthed: Archaeology's New Vision of Ancient Israel and the Origin of Its Sacred Texts.* New York: Simon and Schuster, 2002.

Funk, Robert W. *Honest to Jesus: Jesus for a New Millennium.* San Francisco: HarperOne, 1996.

⸺. "Milestones in the Quest for the Historical Jesus." In *The Fourth R: An Advocate for Religious Literacy.* 14.4 (2001): 9-18.

Funk, Robert W., and The Jesus Seminar. *The Acts of Jesus: The Search for the Authentic Deeds of Jesus.* New York: HarperOne; a Polebridge Press Book, 1998.

Funk, Robert W., Roy W. Hoover, and The Jesus Seminar. *The Five Gospels: The Search for the Authentic Words of Jesus.* New York: Macmillan Publishing Company; a Polebridge Press Book, 1993.

Giegerich, Wolfgang. *The Soul's Logical Life: Towards a Rigorous Notion of Psychology.* Frankfurt: Peter Lang Verlag, 2001.

Hammarskjöld, Dag. *Markings.* Translated by Leif Sjoberg and W. H. Auden. New York: Alfred A Knopf, 1964.

Hesse, Hermann. *Magister Ludi: The Glass Bead Game.* Translated by Mervyn Savill. London & New York: Holt, 1949.

Hillman, James. *Healing Fiction.* Woodstock, CT: Spring Publications, 1983.

⸺. *Re-Visioning Psychology.* 1976. New York: HarperCollins, 1992.

Howes, Elizabeth Boyden. "Analytical Psychology and the Synoptic Gospels." In Howes, *Intersection and Beyond,* Vol 1, 47-70.

⸺. Appendix to *The Bible in Human Transformation: Toward a New Paradigm for Biblical Study,* by Walter Wink, 84-90. Philadelphia: Fortress Press, 1973.

⸺. "The Eternal Question: What is it? Who Asks it?" In Howes, *Intersection and Beyond,* Vol. 1, 17-32.

⸺. "God, Self, Ego, and Choice." In Howes, *Intersection and Beyond,* Vol. 2, 1-14.

———. "The Importance of the Study of the Records of the Life of Jesus and Its Relation to Analytical Psychology." In *Intersection: Journal of the Guild for Psychological Studies*, 13-17. Vol 1. San Francisco: Guild for Psychological Studies Publishing House, 1994.

———. *Intersection and Beyond: Twelve lectures on the commingling of religious values and the insights of analytical psychology*. Vol. 1. San Francisco: Guild for Psychological Studies Publishing House, 1971.

———. *Intersection and Beyond*. Vol. 2. San Francisco: Guild for Psychological Studies Publishing House, 1986.

———. *Jesus' Answer to God*. San Francisco: Guild for Psychological Studies Publishing House, 1984.

———. "The Religious Function of the Ego." In Howes, *Intersection and Beyond*, Vol. 1, 3-16.

———. "Son of man—Expression of the Self." In Howes, *Intersection and Beyond*, Vol. 1, 171-93.

Howes, Elizabeth Boyden, and Sheila Moon. *The Choicemaker*. Wheaton, IL: Theosophical Publishing House, 1973.

Howes, Elizabeth Boyden, Sheila Moon, and Luella Sibbald. "Conversations with the Founding Leaders," DVD. San Francisco: Guild for Psychological Studies, 1986.

———. "Darkness and God: Panel presented by Elizabeth Boyden Howes, Sheila Moon, and Luella Sibbald and introduced by John Petroni." In Howes, *Intersection and Beyond*, Vol. 2, 107-21.

Jaffé, Aniela. *The Myth of Meaning in the Work of C. G. Jung*. Translated by R. F. C. Hull. Zurich: Daimon, 1983.

Jung, C. G. *Aion: Researches into the Phenomenology of the Self*. CW 9ii. 2nd ed. 1968 of *The Collected Works of C. G. Jung* (hereafter

CW). Edited by Sir Herbert Read, Michael Fordham, & Gerhard Adler. Translated by R. F. C. Hull. 20 vols., Bollingen Series 20. Princeton: Princeton University Press, 1953-1979.

―――. "Answer to Job." In *Psychology and Religion West and East*, 355-470. CW 11. 2nd ed. 1969.

―――. "Archetypes of the Collective Unconscious," In *The Archetypes and the Collective Unconscious*, 3-41. CW 9i. 2nd ed. 1968.

―――. "Christ, A Symbol of the Self." In *Aion: Researches Into the Phenomenology of the Self*, 36-71. CW 9ii. 2nd ed. 1968.

―――. "Commentary on 'The Secret of the Golden Flower.'" In *Alchemical Studies*, 1-56. CW 13. 1967.

―――. "The Development of Personality." In *The Development of Personality*, 165-86. CW 17. 1954.

―――. "The Ego." In *Aion: Researches Into the Phenomenology of the Self*, 3-7. CW 9ii. 2nd ed. 1968.

―――. Foreword to *Aion: Researches Into the Phenomenology of the Self*, ix-xi. CW 9ii. 2nd ed. 1968.

―――. "The Function of the Unconscious." In *Two Essays on Analytical Psychology*, 173-187. CW 7. 2nd ed. 1966.

―――. "Individual Dream Symbolism in Relation to Alchemy." In *Psychology and Alchemy*, 39-223. CW 12. 2nd ed. 1968.

―――. "Introduction to the Religious and Psychological Problems of Alchemy." In *Psychology and Alchemy*, 1-37. CW 12. 2nd ed. 1968.

―――. *Letters* 1: 1906-1950. Selected and edited by Gerhard Adler with Aniela Jaffé. Translated by R. F. C. Hull. Bollingen Series XCV. Princeton: Princeton University Press, 1973.

―――. *Letters* 2: 1951-1961. Selected and edited by Gerhard Adler with Aniela Jaffé. Translated by R. F. C. Hull. Bollingen Series XCV. Princeton: Princeton University Press, 1975.

————. *Man and His Symbols*. New York: Dell Publishing Co., 1964.

————. *Memories, Dreams, Reflections*. Edited by Aniela Jaffé. Translated by Richard and Clara Winston. New York: Vintage Books, 1963.

————. "On the Relation of Analytical Psychology to Poetry." In *The Spirit in Man, Art, and Literature*, 65-83. CW 15. 1966.

————. "The Phenomenology of the Spirit in Fairytales." In *The Archetypes and the Collective Unconscious*, 207-54. CW 9i. 2nd ed. 1968.

————. "The Problem of Types in the History of Classical and Medieval Thought." In *Psychological Types*, 8-66. CW 6. 1971.

————. "Psychology and Religion." In *Psychology and Religion West and East*, 3-105. CW 11. 2nd ed. 1969.

————. "The Psychology of the Child Archetype." In *The Archetypes and the Collective Unconscious*, 151-81. CW 9i. 2nd ed. 1968.

————. "Religion and Psychology: A Reply to Martin Buber." In *The Symbolic Life*, 663-70. CW 18. 1989.

————. "Religious Ideas in Alchemy." In *Psychology and Alchemy*, 225-431. CW 12. 2nd ed. 1968.

————. "The Self." In *Aion: Researches Into the Phenomenology of the Self*, 23-35. CW 9ii. 2nd ed. 1968.

————. "Thoughts on the Interpretation of Christianity." In *The Zofingia Lectures*. CW Supplementary Vol. A, pars. 237-291 (43-60). Reprinted in *Jung on Christianity*. Edited by Murray Stein. Princeton: Princeton University Press, 1999.

————. "The Transcendent Function." In *The Structure and Dynamics of the Psyche*, 67-91. CW 8. 2nd ed. 1969.

————. "Transformation Symbolism in the Mass." In *Psychology and Religion West and East*, 203-96. CW 11. 2nd ed. 1969.

————. "The Undiscovered Self." In *Civilization in Transition*, 245-305. CW 10. 2nd ed. 1970.

————. *The Visions Seminars,* Book One. 2 vols. Zurich: Spring Publication, 1976.

Kelber, Werner H. *Mark's Story of Jesus.* 1979. Philadelphia: Fortress Press, 1984.

Meyer, Marvin, ed. *The Gospel of Thomas: The Hidden Sayings of Jesus.* San Francisco: HarperOne, 1992.

Moon, Sheila. *A Magic Dwells: A Poetic and Psychological Study of the Navaho Emergence Myth.* Middletown, CT: Wesleyan University Press, 1970.

————. *Joseph's Son.* Francestown, NH: Golden Quill Press, 1972.

Moore, Robert L., and Daniel J. Meckel, eds. *Jung and Christianity In Dialogue: Faith, Feminism, and Hermeneutics.* New York: Paulist Press, 1990.

Murray, John Courtney. *The Problem of God.* New Haven: Yale University Press, 1964.

Murry, John Middleton. *God: Being and Introduction to the Science of Metabiology.* London: Johnathan Cape, 1929.

Norris, Eleanor L. "C. G. Jung: Psychologist, Sage, Phenomenologist of the Soul." Pacifica Graduate Institute, Spring 2003.

O'Flaherty, Wendy Doniger. "The Uses and Mis-uses of Other People's Myths." In *The Insider/Outsider Problem in the Study of Religion. A Reader.* Edited by Russel T. McCutcheon. London: Cassell, 1999. 331-49.

"Paradox: Coming Home to Yourself . . . to be more at home in this world." In *Invitation to Soul Work: 2004-2005.* Guild seminars brochure. San Francisco, CA: Guild for Psychological Studies, 2004. 11.

Pelikan, Jaroslav. *Jesus Through the Centuries: His Place in the History of Culture.* New Haven: Yale University Press, 1985.

Perrin, Norman, and Dennis C. Duling. *The New Testament: An Introduction.* Edited by Robert Ferm. New York: Harcourt Brace Jovanovich, 1982.

Petroni, John. "Transformation, Truth, Transition, Training." Guild Study Center course. San Francisco, CA. November 2004-June 2005.

Petty, Elizabeth. "Drama and Religious Dialogue." In *Intersection: Journal of the Guild for Psychological Studies*, 47-58. Vol I. San Francisco: Guild for Psychological Studies Publishing House, 1994.

Phillips, Dorothy Berkeley, Elizabeth Boyden Howes, and Lucille M. Nixon, eds. *The Choice is Always Ours: The Classic Anthology on the Spiritual Way*. Revised and Abridged. San Francisco: Harper & Row, 1989.

The Pines: Its Purpose and History, 1942-1952. Palo Alto: The National Press, 1953.

Rollins, Wayne. "Jung, Analytical Psychology, and the Bible." In *Psychology and the Bible: A New Way to Read the Scriptures: From Freud to Kohut*. Edited by J. Harold Ellens and Wayne G. Rollins, 175-200. 4 vols. London: Praeger Perspectives, 2004.

Schweitzer, Albert. *The Quest of the Historical Jesus*. 1913. Edited by John Bowden. Translated by W. Montgomery, J. R. Coates, Susan Cupitt, and John Bowden. Minneapolis: Fortress Press, 2001.

Segal, Robert A., ed. *Jung on Mythology*. Princeton: Princeton University Press, 1998.

The Seminar Method Used by the Guild for Psychological Studies. San Francisco: Guild for Psychological Studies, 1976.

Sharman, Henry Burton, Ph.D. *Records of the Life of Jesus*. Palo Alto: Sequoia Seminar Foundation, 1917.

———. *Records of the Life of Jesus*. Revised Standard Version. San Francisco: Guild for Psychological Studies Publishing House, 1991.

Sibbald, Luella. *The Footprints of God. The Relationship of Astrology, C. G. Jung, and the Gospels.* Guild for Psychological Studies Publishing House, 1988.

Stein, Murray. *The Bible as Dream: A Jungian Interpretation.* Chiron Publications, 2018.

———. "C. G. Jung, Psychologist and Theologian." In *Jung and Christianity in Dialogue: Faith, Feminism, and Hermeneutics.* Edited by Robert L. Moore and Daniel J. Meckel, 3-20. New York: Paulist Press, 1990.

———. *Jung's Treatment of Christianity: The Psychotherapy of a Religious Tradition.* Wilmette IL: Chiron Publications, 1985.

This One Thing: A Tribute to Henry Burton Sharman. Toronto: Student Christian Movement of Canada, 1959.

Wink, Walter. *The Bible in Human Transformation: Toward a New Paradigm for Biblical Study.* Philadelphia: Fortress Press, 1973.

———. *The Human Being: Jesus and the Enigma of the Son of the Man.* Minneapolis: Fortress Press, 2002.

———. *Transforming Bible study: A Leader's Guide.* Nashville: Abingdon Press. 1980.

Zinsser, William, ed. *Inventing the Truth: The Art and Craft of Memoir.* Boston: Houghton Mifflin, 1987.

Index

Guild for Psychological Studies
To awaken the wisdom and passion that lives within us

The Guild for Psychological Studies envisions a world in which the significance of each person's truth, authority, and inspired purpose finds fulfillment in life and community. For over fifty years, the Guild has conducted seminars that bring together the depth psychology of Carl Jung, the *Records of the Life of Jesus* (Synoptic Gospels), the Hebrew Scriptures, and material drawn from myth, poetry, world religions, and the evolving images of modern culture and science. Using a process based on Socratic inquiry and dialogue, seminar participants carefully attend to images and feelings, discover connections between the personal and collective psyche, and often find a new commitment to the deep and unfolding truth that has been called the self or soul. To learn more about the Guild or to order copies of the *Records* book or other titles, visit https://guildsf.org

FOUR SPRINGS — GROUND TO EXPERIENCE THE SACRED

Four Springs, a retreat center eighty-five miles north of San Francisco, was acquired in 1955 by Elizabeth Boyden Howes for the work of the Guild for Psychological Studies, which she founded with colleagues Sheila Moon and Luella Sibbald. Working initially with psychologist Fritz Künkel and later with C. G. Jung, these women combined their interest in depth psychology with their individual interests in the life and teachings of Jesus, religious studies, mythology, and experiential learning.

Howes also studied with Henry Burton Sharman, a New Testament scholar who developed a method of group discussion guided by study questions designed to empower individual discovery. In place of the study of religious doctrine developed by others about Jesus, Sharman emphasized thoughtful inquiry into the Gospels to discern as far as possible what might derive from Jesus' own religious experience. Sharman's method was designed to help people engage freshly for themselves Gospel texts related to the life and teachings of Jesus. The goal of his method was individual insight, enriched by the observations of others, rather than agreement with the leader or among the group. This method was developed further over the years by Guild leaders and participants through the incorporation of myth, wisdom from other traditions, personal expression in art and movement, and the use of music and literature as well as silence and meditation.

Seminars at Four Springs have been offered on a wide range of topics, yet the seminar method remains consistent, utilizing questions and creative expression to facilitate a personal encounter with a story or a text. In addition to Guild seminars, Four Springs is available to selected educational organizations and for individual study and retreat. Visit http://www.foursprings.org

About the Author

Eleanor Norris's spiritual journey took her from childhood Congregationalism to agnosticism to Roman Catholicism to Hindu and Buddhist practice before, in 1984, it led her to the Guild for Psychological Studies' core seminar based on the text, Records of the Life of Jesus. This first immersion into the search for psychological and possible historical truths in the synoptic gospel accounts of Jesus's life and teachings (Matthew, Mark and Luke) excited her interest in the Guild's study not only of the Christian myth but other world myths, searching for the universal truths they bring. She attended Guild seminars and became a seminar leader over the course of the next twenty years. In 2001, she entered Pacifica Graduate Institute to expand the study of mythology from the perspective of C. G Jung, which led to her dissertation, "A Depth Psychological View of the Christian Myth: C.G. Jung, Elizabeth Boyden Howes, and The Guild for Psychological Studies." She was awarded her PhD in 2008. A native Californian, Elli spends her retirement years in Davis, California.

CPSIA information can be obtained
at www.ICGtesting.com
Printed in the USA
BVHW042343010622
638487BV00038B/64